About . to teach

About to teach

An introduction to method in teaching

Patrick C. Souper

School of Education
University of Southampton

Routledge & Kegan Paul
London and Boston

First published in 1976
by Routledge & Kegan Paul Ltd
Broadway House, 68–74 Carter Lane,
London EC4V 5EL and
9 Park Street,
Boston, Mass. 02108, USA
Set in IBM Press Roman by
Express Litho Service (Oxford)
and printed in Great Britain by
Redwood Burn Ltd
Trowbridge and Esher

ISBN 0 7100 8311 4 (C)
      0 7100 8315 7 (P)

Method, therefore, becomes natural to the mind which has been accustomed to contemplate not *things* only, or for their own sake alone, but likewise and chiefly the *relations* of things, either their relations to each other, or to the observer, or to the state and apprehension of the hearers. To enumerate and analyze these relations, with the conditions under which alone they are discoverable, is to teach the science of Method.

(Samuel Taylor Coleridge, *Collected Works*, 4:1, p. 451)

Contents

Preface   ix

Acknowledgments   xi

1   Introduction   1
    School experience   2

2   The background to learning   6
    The neighbourhood   6
    The school building   8
    The school   9
    The school facilities   17
    The school rules   18

3   The school and education   21
    The educational aims of the school   23
    The school and the curriculum   26
    Quality and equality   29
    The importance of examinations   32

4   The school and the individual   36
    The education of intelligence   36
    Concern for emotional maturity   41
    The development of imaginative powers   44
    Preparation for the real world   45

5   Children in school   48
    Children and school   49
    Children learning   55

6   Children with problems   63
    Fear   64
    Depression   65
    Subnormality   67

Contents

		page
	The clumsy child	68
	Economic deprivation	69
	Immigrant status	70
	Adolescence	71
	The problem of stress	73
7	*Culture conflict and the school*	*77*
	Alienation from school	77
	Youth culture	79
	Delinquency	85
8	*The teacher's art*	*92*
	Observing the teacher	92
	Focus on interaction	97
9	*The teacher in action*	*107*
	Focus on strategy	112
10	*The teacher's authority*	*125*
	The nature of the teacher's authority	125
	How the teacher exercises his authority	128
	Discipline in an educational context	129
	The exercise of discipline	131
	Authoritarianism	133
	Freedom and discipline	135
	Morale in the classroom	138
	The hard core problem	143
11	*The place of punishment*	*146*
	The dangers of punishing	149
	The act of punishing	152
	The timing of punishing	157
12	*Into teaching*	*161*
	Difficulties	170
	Bibliography	*179*
	Index	*189*

Preface

The ideas presented in this book are simple, even though they may not be simple to put into practice. They hinge on the datum that teaching is done by people, for people. Attention is drawn to much recent work in the area of education and other theory, in the expectation that interested readers will follow up references given in the text. The writer does not presume to know, or even to be able to suggest, further reading suitable to unknown persons who may happen to chance upon this essay. The reader must bear this responsibility himself, guided by his self-knowledge.

Unlike much contemporary writing on educational matters the present work shows little interest in fashionable methodologies employed in teacher training. This is because the regular habits informing and engendered by such techniques as micro-teaching, interaction analysis, and simulation exercises, though they may be of value, are at best of secondary importance in the genesis of a teacher.

Similarly, the reader will find little information about so-called teaching methods, for, as Coleridge said long ago, 'The term, Method, cannot . . . , otherwise than by abuse, be applied to a mere dead arrangement, containing in itself no principle of progression' (*Collected Works*, 4:1, p. 457). Much boredom in both classroom and lecture theatre would have been avoided if educationalists had taken Coleridge's point, that the 'principle of unity with progression' presupposed by the notion of method cannot be 'adequately supplied by a theory built on generalization' (p. 476).

The underlying theme of the following pages is that the orderly arrangement of ideas implied by such notions as teaching method and discipline is genuinely educative only if method, in the sense indicated by Coleridge, is at the heart of a teacher's teaching. 'For Method implies a *progressive transition*. . . . But as, without continuous transition, there can be no Method, so without a pre-conception there can be no transition with continuity' (p. 457). We are concerned here with the pre-conception that will lead the aspiring or inexperienced teacher into the way (i.e. method) of teaching.

Note

For the sake of clarity, the question of terminology has been resolved quite arbitrarily. All teachers are (grammatically) masculine, as are all whom they teach. Those who learn in schools are pupils, those who are preparing to teach them are students, and those who have little experience of teaching are tyro teachers — whether or not they have gained their certificates. The phraseology of the text might suggest that it is of interest only to student teachers; this is not so, being no more than a consequence of the dual need for clarity and brevity.

Acknowledgments

The author and publishers would like to thank those listed below for permission to reproduce material from the following publications: Vallentine, Mitchell & Co. Ltd for *The Diary of Anne Frank* © Dr Otto Frank, trans. B. M. Mooyaart-Doubleday; The Bodley Head for Alexander Solzhenitsyn, *Cancer Ward*, trans. Nicholas Bethell and David Burg; Faber & Faber Ltd for John Macmurray, *Reason and Emotion*; George Allen & Unwin Ltd for Willi Schohaus, *The Dark Places of Education*, and Bertrand Russell, *Principles of Social Reconstruction*; Pergamon Press Ltd for C. M. Stroh, *Vigilance: The Problem of Sustained Attention*; McGraw-Hill Book Company for Philip H. Phenix, *Realms of Meaning*, © (1964) P. H. Phenix; Methuen & Co. Ltd for Neil Bolton, *The Psychology of Thinking*; Penguin Books Ltd for Albert Hunt, 'The Tyranny of Subjects' in D. Rubinstein and C. Stoneman (eds), *Education for Democracy*, © (1970) David Rubinstein, Colin Stoneman and contributors; John Wilson, Norman Williams, Barry Sugarman, *Introduction to Moral Education*, © (1967) The Farmington Trust Ltd, Oxford; L. C. Taylor, *Resources for Learning*, © (1971) L. C. Taylor; Derek Wright, *The Psychology of Moral Behaviour*, © (1971) D. Wright; E. B. Castle, *A Parents' Guide to Education*, © (1968) E. B. Castle; Alec Clegg and Barbara Megson, *Children in Distress*, © (1968, 1973) A. Clegg and B. Megson; Society for Research into Higher Education Ltd for Mrs M. L. J. Abercrombie, *Aims and Techniques of Group Teaching*; Guardian Newspapers Ltd for extracts from interview with A.-M. Roosenburg by Jonathan Steele published in the *Guardian*, 7 April 1971; John Wiley & Sons for Ira J. Gordon, *Studying the Child in School*; Methuen & Co. Ltd for H. R. Kohl, *The Open Classroom*; W. B. Saunders Co. for D. O. Hebb, *A Textbook of Psychology* (2nd edition, © 1966); Hodder & Stoughton Educational for G. Trasler's 'Delinquency' in H. J. Butcher and H. B. Pont (eds), *Educational Research in Britain* 2; Allyn & Bacon, Inc. for Marc Belth, *Education as a Discipline* (1965); *New Society* for articles by C. Cannon, 'Tostig', R. D. Martin, Mary Warnock, P. Overy, J. P. Martin, G. R. Goodlet, P. Sadler; Granada Publishing Ltd for Ruth Mock, *Education and the Imagination*.

1 Introduction

Since teaching is not a mechanical activity, but grows out of the whole experience and understanding of an individual teacher, it cannot be taught. Teacher education can only mean helping each student to discover and consolidate those ways in which he is best able to teach. The student's tutor plays a secondary role in the training process; essentially that of critic, adviser and encourager or facilitator. He may say that the processes of education and teaching are to be understood within the context of cultural and social activity, but his student can discover what this means only through his own efforts.

Two skills, as essential to teaching as other professional activities concerned with people, are needed for this: accurate perception and the truthful interpretation of what is perceived. These are not natural skills. They have to be learnt and constantly refined. Although the individual's orientation to the world outside his own skin is a biological process, this guarantees neither the accuracy of his perceptions nor the veracity of his interpretations. Arne Trankell (1972, p. 20), who has made a special study of truthfulness in courts of law, draws attention to three conditions that commonly cause distortions:

1. The selective character of perception, which limits the interpretations of the external signals to that which has foundation in the individual's earlier experience.

2. The logical completion mechanism, which often results in a false picture of the series of events.

3. Attitudes, personal wishes and preference, which prejudice our interpretation of sense data. [Italicized in source.]

This book attempts to meet the student's (and teacher's) need for an aid to assist him to avoid traps in perception and interpretation. Such traps are essentially individual and personal so it is not a text book. It contains ideas and information intended to stimulate readers to action; in particular, to the basic teacher activities of observing and thinking. It focuses attention upon becoming the teacher each person has it in him to be, rather than upon prescriptions holding out dubious promise of 'success' in the classroom. Each teacher is unique and there is no guarantee that what 'works' for one will work for another. Furthermore, since teaching, unlike ushering, depends upon understanding the

1

realities in a particular situation, tips for teachers cannot provide a satisfactory programme for action.

School experience

In contrast to the generalized abstractions of theory, the undeniable relevance of teaching practice tends to be overwhelming; it pertains to a real job done in the real world. Armed with comparatively recent experience of being successful pupils, students sally forth eager to find an answer to the momentous question 'Can I teach?' Normally they return with the answer 'Yes'; if only after a fashion. All too often, however, this means no more than that they have demonstrated to themselves that they can survive in the classroom situation; tired maybe, but still in one piece. The importance of this discovery should not be decried.

Inevitably a student's first concern is with himself; with his self-protection and self-adequacy, his effectiveness in class control, his efficiency in handling teacher—pupil and pupil—pupil interaction; with the adequacy of his mastery of subject matter, with being able to find a place which supports rather than deflates him in relation to the power structure of the school, and with the problems of understanding the expectations of supervisors and, when necessary, of reconciling these with the expectations of the headteacher and the supervising teacher appointed by the school.

The fact of the matter is that, to nearly all students, teaching practice appears to be a time when they are thrown in at the deep end and told to get on and teach, as though it were expected that they should go ahead and gain some experience, having first picked up some useful tips through watching a class teacher for a few lessons.

A student with this impression will be on the look-out for basic tricks of the trade that might enable him to succeed as the teacher he watches is seen to succeed. Because of his own pressing need he is likely to forget that, in all probability, the foundations of such a teacher's success are not any 'wrinkles', schemes and so forth to which he himself may attribute it, but some quality of personality or leadership of which he may be quite unaware.

The student, on the other hand, is unlikely to experience the same degree of success should he attempt to imitate such a model. Rather than criticize the 'obviously' successful programme he has adopted, he is likely to attribute his failure to weaknesses in himself, or failure to apply the programme properly. A less critical student may simply settle for the 'fact' that he is an inferior teacher who has found the best and therefore the right way for him to teach. In either case, teaching practice is unlikely to be of any lasting value. Either the student will have become set in his ways even before starting his career or he will have had his confidence shaken to no purpose. He will have done little towards discovering the practical methods of teaching best suited to himself.

Should the day come in which a young teacher can start his career under ideal conditions, the situation will be little improved unless two prior conditions are first met. This need wait upon nothing but each student's exercise of his own initiative. First, before he enters a classroom on teaching practice he must be at ease with children, especially those from social strata different from his own. Familiarity is not enough. He needs the ease that stems from a deep knowledge and understanding of children as individuals, their interests, needs, anxieties and so forth, but in particular of how they relate to adults. Only a few years previously he himself was a child and much of his effort in the preceding years will have been devoted to leaving childhood behind. But now, if he is to be a good teacher he must retrace his footsteps in imagination and understanding, but not of course in his approach to life. If he leaves this re-encounter with childhood until he is facing children across the classroom floor, he is unlikely to complete the journey satisfactorily, since he will be in an artificial situation in which the children will regard him with some suspicion. He will also be there with a job to do which, in its essence, is very different from that of getting to know what children are like. He will be there primarily as teacher and not as learner.

To learn about children in such a way that theoretical studies can take on substance means meeting them in situations in which they are free to be natural. The occasional afternoon with young nieces and nephews is not enough. Some attempts have been made to provide suitable encounters for students (see e.g. Hannam *et al.*, 1971), but the numbers involved mean that no more than a small fraction of teachers in training can be provided for in such ways. Rather, students themselves can make the best provision by arranging to help in play centres, adventure playgrounds, youth clubs, orphanages and the like, where their relationship is one of being with rather than of being in charge. The uniformed organizations might provide some opportunities, though the quasi-formal adult—child relationship in these is not so helpful. Better still, they could organize their own holiday and free-time activities with and for children, particularly those from the more deprived sections of the community, since these are the children with whom they are likely to have least in common. A students' union, with help from churches, local authorities and the college, could easily arrange to run a holiday for deprived children, along the lines of a *colonie de vacances* for example. Less formal associations with children, particularly with teenagers, are also easy to engineer, just by being where they tend to congregate; though, of course, the chances of rejection by them are much higher, which is in itself an educative experience. Some schools in poor environments attempt to make provision for their pupils in holiday periods and doubtless more would if offers of help came from student teachers. A well thought out scheme offered by students who were prepared, if necessary, to camp out in the school building in order both to help pupils as well as to learn as much as possible about children, would be welcomed by many headteachers.

Since an essential attribute of a good teacher is that he is a perceptive observer, it is essential that his powers of observation should be well developed before he begins teaching. Most training institutions provide opportunities for observing in schools and some students make their own opportunities. Yet, when questioned, many admit that they find it a boring and not very fruitful occupation. They feel that they would get a better return on the time spent if it were spent on teaching. This suggests one of two things: either they believe that they have little or nothing to learn from that which is divorced from their own successes or mistakes, which is unlikely; or they do not really know what to look for when they are observing. In all probability, most of the time they spend observing is passed in reflecting upon the teacher's attempts to get over a particular piece of information, and in considering how they would fare if they were attempting to do the same thing. If observing consisted of nothing more than this, then a little would go a long way.

Much of what follows has been written in the conviction that, rather than being a waste of time, observing is among the most important elements in a teacher's preparation, and that it is through observing in a systematic manner that a student is most likely to come to understand the significance of most of his studies of education theory. After he has learnt as much as he is able from observing, then is the time to try his wings as a teacher, certainly not before. Although it may need to be taken with a pinch of salt, the advice of Kostoglotov, the central character in Alexander Solzhenitsyn's *Cancer Ward*, to the young student Dyoma, contains more than a grain of truth for the student teacher:

'But remember, education doesn't make you smarter' . . .
'So what does make you smarter?'
'Life, that's what' . . . 'In our unit there was a commissar, Pashkin. He used to say, "Education doesn't make you smarter. Nor does rank. They give you another star on your shoulder and you think you're smarter. Well, you're not." '

'So, what do you mean? There's no need to study? I don't agree.'
'Of course you should study. Study! Only remember for your own sake, it's not the same as intelligence.'
'What is intelligence, then?'
'Intelligence? Trusting your eyes but not your ears.'

2 The background to learning

Observing does not begin in the classroom. If the behaviour of children in school is to be understood, it is important to know something of their home background. As is well known, each community has its own way of life, customs and standards, constituting a subtle complex of assumptions, ideas, tastes and norms, which members share and which govern the particularities of its life. It cannot be assumed that teachers will understand, or even have sympathy with, this way of life if they do not share it, yet a system of public education which does not take into account the needs felt and conditions experienced by the people it serves is a false and dangerous one. Observing therefore is not simply a classroom activity.

The neighbourhood

Second-hand information about a school and its locality, though useful, is not an adequate preparation for entering the school as an observer, even when this is supported by a thorough grounding in social studies.

This can provide no more than generalized, though none the less useful, background information. Assumptions based on these generalizations may be likely to be the case, but an observer cannot be sure unless he makes his own investigations and observations. What is needed is the practice of constant observation, selective alertness, both before and throughout a period of school experience, so as to build up a sound knowledge of the children's background. For example, a high standard of material well-being does not necessarily imply a good environment for the bringing up of children, and the values motivating wealthy parents may well present a teacher with difficult problems. Residents of such neighbourhoods tend to lead private lives and an observer's task is not easy. By visiting public meeting places such as parks and shopping centres, however, he can learn something about the quality of parent—child relationships, noting the recreational facilities provided and the extent to which the children play outside their family groups. Similarly, visits to toy- and bookshops would suggest the provision made by parents for their children's intellectual and cultural development.

Evening or weekend walks would give some indication of the degree of paternal participation in family life. Time permitting, visits to the local clergy could well be profitable, since they are likely to know the quality of life of the neighbourhood, as well as a cross-section of the children.

But the majority of school children do not come from such districts. A quick look around may show an observer that most of the children in his school come from a comparatively poor physical and cultural environment and he may conclude, as a generalization, for example, that parental encouragement and exercise in speech, observational and play skills are below average. But it is not easy to draw general conclusions which fit the conditions in all such neighbourhoods. It does not follow that a house with a shabby exterior is equally impoverished inside, and even a poor interior is not conclusive proof that the quality of life in the home is poor, or detrimental to the children's schooling. Nor is it safe to assume, as a superficial study of sociological writings might seem to suggest, that all children from poorer areas are more accustomed to violence and alcoholism than the better off, or that they will have acquired less skill in language use, that they will have a smaller vocabulary and so an impoverished capacity for understanding and communication and thus be comparatively unable to convey their intentions, motives or feelings to their teachers. The blanket descriptions of sociological generalizations may be true of the mythical man on the Clapham omnibus and certainly help in the formulation of general theories, but an observer is concerned with particular children; and what may have been found to be true in one area is by no means necessarily true of other areas of similar appearance.

An observer's theoretical studies need to be supplemented by a thorough, if admittedly impressionistic and piecemeal, survey of the neighbourhood. Unlike the social arithmetician he will seek out open places available to children to see whether there are enough of them, whether they are suited to children of different ages and are readily accessible; whether water, other than that in gutters and puddles, is available for play purposes and for breeding tadpoles and minnows. If the houses do not have gardens suitable for children's games he will look for official play streets without traffic. If there are large blocks of flats he will look for danger-free play areas and see whether they are used by mothers with small children, and if they are not, and the streets have too much traffic to permit play in them, whether they are socially deprived and have to play in isolation on balconies or indoors. If he cannot hear them playing together he can be fairly safe in assuming this. Time permitting, visits to nursery schools and play groups for the very young, to clubs, adventure playgrounds and the like for older children, and if he is observing in a secondary school, to such places as snack bars where the young teenagers congregate, would be instructive: as would visits to any available natural open spaces where children can run wild without doing any damage, and where they can pick flowers without breaking the law. Through selective observation in this manner it is possible to build up a trustworthy picture of the culture within which the children in the school are growing up; to estimate, e.g., the extent to which mothers go out to work; to overhear the sort of conversation that forms the background to the children's lives, to hear how mothers talk about their children and in the evenings and at weekends how fathers relate to their children.

These are no more than a few of the aspects of life in the locality with which an observer could concern himself, and the list could be extended almost indefinitely. One more, however, should be mentioned, since it is a peculiarly contemporary phenomenon, more prevalent in some areas than others, and it also raises particular problems for the teacher: namely mobility, moving from one locality to another. According to J.W.B. Douglas (1967) over 7 per cent of children of primary school age move each year, a rate which, if this continues, adds up over the five years of secondary education to one child in three being affected. If there is much moving into and out of the locality many of the children will lack local roots, and will be unlikely to have kin, or other stable adult key figures in the community with whom they identify. Since it is from such figures and their example that children learn how to play adult roles, particularly in mid-adolescence, these children will depend far more upon their teachers for this example than they would in a more stable community. If the teachers have no understanding of, or no sympathy for, the children's background culture, such identification is unlikely to be possible without producing considerable tension in the children's allegiance. Armed with such background knowledge an observer will be well placed to evaluate how well prepared and equipped the school is to meet the real needs of its pupils, and if needs be, to suggest to himself possible improvements in planning and practice.

The school building

Although 'functional buildings are the tools of modern schooling; no more than that' (Castle, 1968, p. 221), a study of the school building can yield an observer useful information. On the one hand, the design will place limitations on the kinds of activity that can take place within the school. Yet on the other, by defining space, it will facilitate a large number of activities; and, by becoming familiar with it and by working out in his own mind the uses to which it could be put, an observer will acquire some measure of the degree of imaginativeness demonstrated by the school authorities, when he comes to observe the activities actually engaged in by the school. One headmaster, describing his own school, has said (Baines, 1971, p. 36), 'we try to turn the activities into experiences and work to make the building inspiring, stimulating, practical and satisfying'; and his adjectives provide a useful guide to an observer as he looks round the building. Irrespective of the age of the school, which is of less importance to children than it is to adults (unless it is semi-derelict), an observer should look for indications of the quality of life in the school; for even the most splendid building cannot conceal such tell-tale marks.

A school that aims to raise the vision of its pupils, particularly if they come from deprived homes, is likely to have an attractive garden, or at least colourful window boxes; and the decoration and furniture will be in good order, even if old and bearing the marks of time. Signs of vandalism always suggest that an observer should look out for its causes when he comes to view the life of the school. Attractive pictures and decorations on display in such a way that pupils can see and touch them are a sure indication to them that they are regarded as being trustworthy. During his stay in the school, an observer should look to see if they are changed frequently. Notice boards will be tidy and up to date. There will be an absence of litter, both inside and outside of the building. Pupils' work will be well displayed, and once again, frequently changed. There are likely to be fresh flowers, particularly in the more public parts of the building. Two parts of the building are particularly revealing: the staff room, which will speak volumes about staff values, and the pupils' toilets, which, if they are operational, fully furnished, clean and devoid of graffiti, will indicate that 'school morale is high. Although accidents in school are rare, the fact that in 1965 an estimated 35,000 children in maintained schools in England and Wales sustained injuries sufficient to involve absence from school for half a day or longer (DES, 1969, pp. 108–13), suggests that an observer should begin to train himself, in the school where he is a guest, to look out for possible dangers, such as concealed steps, or a window opening onto the playground at head height, so that he will grow accustomed to doing the same when he is a teacher himself.

The school

A thoughtful observer will not confuse the school building with the school, for as Arthur Razzell has said (1968, p. 13),

the age and design of the school give little help in assessing the value of what goes on inside. . . . The first two basic questions that need to be asked by a shrewd observer are 'What kind of school does this set out to be?' and then, 'Is it good of its kind?'

As a first step an observer will seek answers to a number of elementary questions, such as the total numbers of pupils and teaching staff, the size and relative importance of the various departments, regulations regarding dress and the reasons for these, the adequacy of allowances for parents who cannot afford uniform, whether pupils can infringe such regulations for religious or other reasons, the number and quality of publications produced by the pupils and the extent of censorship, the code of approved sanctions, the comparative size of classes, and whether there is any discrimination, the extent to which the timetable facilitates curriculum choice by pupils and to which unsupervised working is encouraged. He will also pay some attention to the way in which the school describes itself. For example, if it is called a grammar school, is this synonymous with crammer? If it is called comprehensive, what does this mean? Does it mean that divisions previously identifiable by separate buildings still flourish under one roof in the form of separate streams? Is it a euphemism for creamed secondary modern? Or does it mean a school in which 'Opportunities to contribute to a many-faceted and heterogeneous society are available for all in some form or another' (ILEA, 1967, p. 56)?

No two schools are alike. They differ in organization, methods of teaching, out-of-school activities and the games played; they differ also in their attitude to parents, punishments, rewards, academic successes, the standards of cleanliness, tidiness, and order, regarded as acceptable, and the attempt made to make the school an attractive place. Most importantly they differ in the quality of relationships they foster between pupil and pupil, pupil and teacher, teacher and teacher, teacher and home, and pupil and home. This being so, rather than entering a school with some fixed idea of an 'ideal' school, an observer should go with the intention of discovering in which ways it is good; recognizing that

Our lack of sure knowledge is a strong argument for a variety of different schools and methods, so that the merits of different approaches can be compared. One of the great problems in educational psychology is that the evidence favouring different views is so difficult to weigh and evaluate. . . . [Hence,] As in courts of law, so in many of the problems of educational psychology, the student should first consider the evidence carefully but will often have to make his or her own judgement about where the truth lies (Lynn, 1971, p. 108).

Despite the variety, however, an observer will expect to find that the school is person-centred, in that it demonstrates a mutuality of relations, in which both pupil and teacher find fulfilment and personal development in a spirit of give and take. He will expect it to be a courteous and naturally friendly place, in which relations between the head and his staff are characterized by mutual trust and respect and where the head is accessible, available, and actively interested in what his staff is doing, being ready to help with more than verbal encouragement when necessary. He will expect it to be a place where the children like to be, from which they do not rush to escape as soon as school is over, a place where every attempt is made to reward effort, to find opportunities for every child to overcome his weaknesses and excel, and where care is taken to avoid causing any child to be embarrassed by things beyond his control, such as the poverty which entitles him to free meals and tiredness due to cramped home conditions; that is, a place where responsibility is allocated in such a way that older and stronger pupils regard it as quite natural for them to help the younger and weaker and where compassion is not regarded as a weakness.

However, an observer may encounter a very different state of affairs. Alec Clegg and Barbara Megson (1968, p. 50) describe an insensitive school as, amongst other things, 'one in which those who are undistinguished intellectually count for little, those who are weak are not helped over their weaknesses, and those who make trouble are kept down by superior force and little is done to find out the root cause of their troublesomeness'.

Typical marks of such a school are that smart brains are rewarded rather than effort, those who fail examinations are resented, difficult children are regarded as a burden rather than a challenge to the power of the school for good, and little attempt is made to save the poor child from the embarrassment of having his poverty made public. Points to look for are whether pupils treat visitors respectfully when no teacher is present, whether they are free to enter and use the school out of school hours, and are free to move about in an unregimented manner, and whether they are encouraged to do what they ought because it is their responsibility, rather than made to. The yardstick above all others is the quality of relationships demonstrated; whether the pupils are relaxed and considerate to each other, the staff and visitors, both in school and in free time, whether the school is dominated by petty rules and restrictions with a prevailing authoritarian atmosphere, hectoring teachers, harsh punishments, an inaccessible head, a carefully observed pecking order in the staff room, a fear of the head among the pupils and junior members of staff, with prefects performing police duties and no pupils involved in discharging responsibilities of any other kind in the school. Casual observing might give the impression of a 'calm businesslike atmosphere', an 'atmosphere of hard work', or some other cliché-ridden assessment. A more penetrating look will disclose two separate worlds, with little love lost between them, under one roof.

An observer must remember, however, that he is not in the school to pass judgment but to learn from his experience, and should therefore go on to ask himself why the school is as it is, the difficulties it has to contend with, and how it could be improved. He will also avoid being taken in by surface appearances, for the way a thing is done often reveals more of the school's attitudes than does the mere doing of it. There may, for example, be far more creditable reasons than the observer suspects for any apparent lack of sensitivity or flexibility or of opportunities for exploration or for openness to experience. Rather than condemn he should try to understand sympathetically, and though he should try to explain failings and see how they might be overcome, it would be going beyond his brief to offer unsolicited advice. A possible reason could be something as simple as a rapid turnover of teaching staff; and the reasons for this might be equally honourable, such as the strain of rush-hour travel, a lack of suitable housing in the vicinity, or of facilities suited to the pupils, or even a local sub-culture of excessive toughness which few teachers are equipped to face.

As an aid to determining whether the school is achieving its objectives, an observer should try to obtain a clear statement of what the school hopes to do and how it hopes to do it. Many headteachers prepare a document outlining school policy for new members of staff. Even if no written statement is available most headteachers are pleased to describe and explain what they are trying to achieve, and when they accept student teachers into the school most regard it as part of their responsibility to discuss such things with them. This is not the time for the observer to air his own views, even if he should be in violent disagreement. If he is to learn from the experience, he should try to understand the headteacher's point of view. Should he fail to understand something, he should (within the limits of courtesy) ask for further explanation or information. He may still leave the school believing that the headteacher's plan is wrong or unsound; but he may well find that he has a need to rethink his own attitudes in the light of what he has learnt and witnessed.

Nevertheless, a plan in itself is nothing; to be effective it needs the understanding and willing co-operation of the teaching staff. So, through conversation with teachers and witnessing the school in action, an observer should investigate to see whether staff members are both fully aware of the plan and support it. He should also try to discover whether the plan is the product of agreement or dictation and whether it is subject to constant review. Should he observe discrepancies between the official plan and the manner of working and results produced by the school, he should try to work out why these discrepancies exist. Some light may be thrown upon the problem if he is given the privilege of attending staff meetings. If at these meetings only the trivia of school life are discussed, or discussion of matters of policy is desultory and has no influence upon the eventual outcome, this may indicate that policy is dictated and lacks the support of a convinced staff — though, of course, conclusions based on such evidence are untrustworthy. Similarly, much, possibly heated, discussion with few decisions made may indicate a lack of leadership in the school. In making such observations, however, he must remember that he is present, not to judge, but to learn and, in imagination, to consider how improvements might be made.

The school council, should there be one, will also provide useful information. An observer should notice its composition; the proportion of pupils, whether they come from all age levels and, in a streamed school, from all ability ranges. This, together with the degree of responsibility delegated to the council, will indicate clearly the extent to which the school is person-centred. To be something more than a meaningless concession to the principle of democracy, its standing orders should give a clear indication of its powers and responsibilities. More importantly, the council's decisions must be respected by those in authority, for if it has no real competence to effect decisions, or to affect decisions made elsewhere, pupils are likely to be apathetic, even cynical about it, and it will probably alienate them from the school and its purposes even more than would an honestly straightforward paternalistic regime. A council with real though circumscribed powers and responsibility for such matters as school rules, feeding arrangements, social activities, control of common rooms and clubs, is likely to have a profoundly positive influence on school morale.

Indicators of morale in a school without a council, such as a primary school, include the kind of work pupils are expected to do — which will give some idea of the scope and richness of the experiences to which they are exposed; the varieties of materials available for their work and its quality and quantity; the nature of the written work in pupils' books — which will show whether it is teacher-directed or the fruit of the pupils' spontaneous choice; the frequency with which pupils have a chance to work outside of the school on excursions and visits, the quality of the material they bring back with them — in terms both of objects and of the thoughts reflected in their future work; and whether a good supply of reference books and reading matter related to an excursion is available both before and after it takes place.

Classrooms themselves are highly informative, for, although a happy school is not necessarily an efficient school, it is important that they should be happy places, for children spend about a quarter of their wakeful hours a year in them. Furthermore, 'the classroom presents to the pupil a body of information regarding expectations for learning and behaviour. These are communicated to him not only through the physical arrangement of space but also through the nature and types of displays on bulletin boards in the room' (Gordon, 1966, p. 90). As the headmaster of a junior school reminds new members of his staff (cited, Howson, 1969, p. 146),

> A good classroom is a base for all types of work. It is art gallery, museum, workshop, display centre, exhibition area and sales window for education. An alive classroom produces an alive class. . . . Look round your classroom . . . and ask yourself 'Is it really attractive?', 'Will the displays trigger off the children's imagination?', 'Are we making the most of the space available?' Remember that display and presentation are so very important to the children in your care, who spend a great deal of time in the school, and try to make the surroundings beautiful, imaginative, stimulating, exciting and enjoyable.

If the room is used by small children, it is important to see it from the child's height, for what may seem very attractive and encouraging from a height of six feet may seem very odd from half way up. Again, a liking for tidiness and orderliness should not colour impressions. A chaotic room does not necessarily mean chaotic lessons or lack of purpose; what might be regarded as filthiness and sloppiness could be a messiness consequent upon many things happening in one room at the same time which, being unfinished, have to be left around for completion. Rather than looking for neatness, an observer should look out for that creative disorder which indicates an atmosphere of purposiveness. Young children, when they are absorbed by their work, do not rate tidiness highly! For them the important thing is availability. Hence, placement of furniture and other objects in the room is significant. As Herbert Kohl remarks (1970, p. 35), 'a teacher's room tells us something about who he is and a great deal about what he is doing'. The placement of the teacher's desk, for example, indicates whether he sees himself as the focus of the room, whether he has an eye for possible visitors who might catch him off guard, whether it constitutes a retreat or a base for small-group work, and so on. The organization of the space within the room dictates to a considerable degree the quality of the life lived within it.

Among other features of school life likely to throw light upon the human quality of the school are the houses, or other sub-units, into which the school is divided. When considering these an observer should ask himself whether they are effective in encouraging social mixing and the development of tolerance and what the apparent functions of the housemaster are — is he just an administrator and terrier for chasing academic improvement? Or is he more of a guide, philosopher and friend to the members of his house? According to Young and Armstrong (1965, p. 4), 'children in the top streams mix mainly with other similar children, even in sports, and the houses are not much more than a place to hang your coat'. If this seems to be the case the observer should see whether there are other more effective sub-units in the school, for example, a tutorial system. Where this works well nearly every teacher will have a small number of pupils of all ages, abilities and, where relevant, specialisms, whom he meets at least weekly at a regular time in order to keep informed about their progress, interests, problems and difficulties. He will also know the parents well, so that, when home and school interests clash, or one needs the support of the other, he can take realistic and constructive steps to help his pupils, just as he acts as a buffer between his pupils and his colleagues in the school. Questions to which answers should be sought relate to the effects of belonging to a particular house or tutorial group, how these can be accounted for, the opportunities available to pupils for the exercise of individual responsibility and, if the school is large, whether Taylor (1971, p. 48) is correct in claiming that 'a large school of, say 1500, does not usually generate three times as many teams, plays, magazines, as a school of 500. . . . In consequence a large majority of sixth formers now leave school without active experience of responsibility.' If he is, what steps could be taken to counteract this tendency?

A further good indicator is the attitude of the school to parents. Despite the provision in Section 76 of the 1944 Education Act, that 'pupils are to be educated in accordance with the wishes of their parents so far as is compatible with the provision of efficient instruction and training and the avoidance of unreasonable public expenditure', parents have few rights in the matter. The fact of selection, overcrowding, single-sex or denominational schools, and local authority boundaries, effectively exclude much in the way of genuine choice. Furthermore, it is the school rather than the parents that decides the subjects children will pursue and whether they will take public examinations in them. For a child with ambitious parents this is no bad thing, so long as the school exercises responsible choice. Parents have no right to forbid the use of any punishment of which they disapprove; should the school decide a pupil must repeat a year, the parents have no redress, they even have no legal rights to speak to their child's teachers about his education if the headteacher should forbid this — not even outside of school bounds and school time. In many schools they have no right to choose their child's school clothes. If the school sends their child to an educational psychologist, they have no right to see his report, and in consequence have no right to see that his recommendations are followed up by the school. Their sole inalienable right is that of demanding a school dinner for their child — so long as the cost to them is less than it costs the local authority. They also have the right to expect that, if necessary, their child will be allocated a place in a special school (e.g. for the deaf), but this does not mean that the child will go to one, for the number of places in such schools is much smaller than the number of pupils allocated. In this situation it is most important that the schools should take parents, their views and wishes, very seriously, even though, in the end, the school makes the decisions.

In attempting to evaluate the attitude of the school to parents, an observer should notice whether they are encouraged, as some might say, to interfere, to share in their children's education and to make such contributions towards the life of the school as they are able. PTA general meetings should be attended (by permission of its officers) and note taken of its involvement in the real life of the school, for often such associations are restricted to little more than raising money to provide extras for the school. Attempts made to keep parents informed about their children's performance, and likewise attempts made to learn about the children's interests and behaviour at home, about domestic events or affairs which may upset a child's performance in school should be noted; in particular, problems caused by homework, such as its taking the child so long that he has no time for other proper interests, or has to work late at night or, perhaps it is insufficient to satisfy his thirst for learning — this could indicate parental failure as much as failure on the school's part. The regularity of opportunity for parents to discuss their children with their teachers is an important clue, as are the teachers' attitudes towards these discussions, and such documents as end-of-term reports, whether they convey genuine information, requests for parental help and the like, or whether they are formal statements conveying nothing of any real substance.

A further good indicator of a concerned school is the closeness of its liaison with other agencies concerned with children's welfare, such as health visitors, social workers, probation officers, children's departments, child guidance clinics, the practitioners of the School Health Service and, in secondary schools, Youth Employment officers. Since most pupils go to their first job direct from school, careers guidance should be taken very seriously. Not only should the officers of the Youth Employment Service make regular visits to the school, but arrangements should also be made for pupils to visit (for several days if visits are to be of much use) various places of employment in order to learn what different jobs really entail (as distinct from what the glossy brochures say), and to get the feel of the work place and discover something of the reality of the job opportunities open to them. A secondary school should have at least one careers teacher, who, if he is to carry out his duties in a realistic manner, requires more time for the job than he needs for interviewing pupils; for he must be up to the minute with details of professional and industrial requirements, and also of job opportunities available at any given time. But, as Sir Ronald Gould says (1965, p. 1),

> far too many careers teachers are having to do their work without the necessary facilities. Proper equipment and accommodation are lacking. . . . It says much for their devotion to their pupils that many of the careers teachers (in fact about half in the survey) do their careers work wholly in their spare time.

He could have added that, according to the survey carried out by the NUT in 1964, few teachers had their teaching load reduced by more than four periods a week!

An observer should, therefore, be interested in the provision made for careers guidance: as to whether a special room is set aside for the purpose and a good information service is provided, whether the careers teacher is well informed both about job opportunities and the abilities and interests of the pupils and is able to match the two. The attitude of pupils to guidance offered is a good indicator of the effectiveness of the service, as is the extent to which an attempt is made to involve parents in the selection of their children's first jobs, so that the pupils are not confused by conflicting advice from home and school. Parents often hinder children in their choice, either by limiting their view too greatly or by inflating their children's ambition beyond reasonable limits, both in terms of the children's abilities and of realistic opportunities, but they can be of considerable help, particularly in encouraging and assisting their children to pursue courses of further education and training once they start work.

The school facilities

The building which houses the school and the open space provided set limits upon what can be done to make it a good school. Observing involves evaluating whether the best possible use is being made of what is available to provide facilities for both recreation and privacy, particularly for older pupils. Are they likely to regard the school as a place where they like to be, where they have opportunity to lead their own lives in their free time without unnecessary pressures? Or is the provision such that they are forced to feel uncomfortable, both physically and personally? If shortage of space precludes the allocation of rooms for use as common rooms, can pupils regard certain parts of the school as their own territory out of lesson time, where they can pursue their own interests without intrusion from authority in the form of an uninvited teacher? The same applies to sports and games facilities; though a qualified specialist should be present in such places as the gymnasium and swimming bath, if there is one.

No school can function properly without adequate equipment, so observing involves discovering how available funds are spent, and the extent to which equipment is actually used and not simply there to flatter the ego of the teacher who receives a large allocation. The provision of text books, their quality and quantity, is an obvious starting point, for books are the life-blood of the typical school. The knowledge explosion of recent years and the changes being advocated by many educationalists suggest that an observer should find a high priority put on the provision of an adequate supply of up-to-date texts and other books and a large allocation of funds to the library; yet J. Vaizey and J. Sheehen, for example, in a study of schools in West Sussex in 1967, say 'the important thing is that the one markedly scarce resource in the schools was library books' (cited, Taylor, 1971, p. 251).

Similarly, in the present age he should expect to find that a reasonable sum of money is allocated to audio-visual soft-ware and personal a/v aids, though one of the few surveys conducted, that by the University of Sussex (see MacKenzie et al., 1969) of schools in the surrounding area, disclosed that four-fifths of the schools surveyed spent less than £10 a year per school on such items. Is there much expensive equipment locked away in rooms occupied by prestige subjects to be brought out a few times a year, when other educationally-important subjects are inadequately provided for? A school that makes little realistic provision for such subjects as art, crafts and music, is not really interested in the emotional development of its pupils, neither is a school that, irrespective of the quality of the food, ignores the potential educational, social and cultural value of school lunch and permits it to degenerate into just one more experience of low standard canteen eating. In a school that recognizes its civilizing function, school lunch is a pleasant social occasion, marked by considerateness and courtesy; for communal eating has been one of the most potent civilizing agencies throughout history.

The school rules

Schools, like all other human institutions, have rules which cannot be broken with impunity; some written, some unwritten. Foolish rules tend to have an explosive effect, particularly in secondary schools, and pupils will ignore those that are senseless; furthermore, if the rule of law is brought into disrepect in this way, there is a real risk that pupils will ignore the sensible rules as well. The manner in which the law is invoked is also important, for 'rules do not necessarily induce good manners and the breaking of them can become a sportive exercise among lively children confined within a system where the only sin is to be found out', as E. B. Castle wisely says (1968, p. 224). Since children of different ages view rules in differing ways, an observer should also bear in mind Kohlberg's view that, although there is a difference between cultures in the content of moral beliefs, the development of their form is a cultural invariant and that, in the early years, children start by seeing rules as dependent upon power and external compulsion, with which they are in basic agreement; then, as they develop, they see them as instrumental to rewards and to the satisfaction of their needs; later, they see them as ways of obtaining social approval and esteem; and, later still, as upholding some ideal order; and, finally, as articulations of social principles, necessary for living together with others (see Kohlberg, 1964, 1968a, 1968b).

When considering the school rules, an observer should ask himself whether they represent a clear and coherent policy; whether the individual rules are clear, self-explanatory and for the obvious good of the community; whether children are likely to see them in the same light as rules that any reasonable pupil could accept without argument. If they are incoherent, the school authorities are likely to be genuinely uncertain and muddled about what the rules ought to be, or if they are certain about the rules they ought to have, they are uncertain of their ability to justify them to their pupils and the outside world; it could even be that, although being certain about both the rules and their justification, they do not wish to spell them out in case this should get them into trouble with their pupils or with public opinion. There is, of course, a fourth possible reason, as disreputable as it is relatively common: authority's desire to manipulate the rules to its own advantage. The absence of a coherent set of rules is a barrier to communication, breeding anxiety and hostility amongst pupils and a general atmosphere of distrust and uncertainty. It also generates confusion within the teaching staff. When rules are obscure or incoherent, as John Wilson has said (1967b, p. 434),

It might be more useful for authorities to examine their own motivation in these cases, rather than engage in lengthy but unreal disputes about the alleged justification, and, of course, to help their pupils to examine the pupils' motivation for wanting to break the rules or

rebel against them. At least we could be told what sort of reason it is
— if the authorities know.

An observer should make himself familiar with all the conventions,
protocol, traditions, unwritten rules and stereotyped procedures of the
school and ask himself to whom and how far they are useful; whether
they generate problems, inhibit flexible communication, clarify the
situation for all concerned, are at best dead wood and at worst a
nuisance, or whether they provide a kind of ritual which is enjoyable
for its own sake. Some will be the product of fears or desires that ought
rather to be faced honestly, others may have resolved real problems in
the past but will now be used by certain members of the community to
create new problems, operating them unfairly to their own advantage.
In the final analysis, school rules can only be justified if they help to
make life as enjoyable and profitable as possible for all the members of
the school community.

3 The school and education

An experienced observer will readily agree with Wiseman and Pidgeon (1970, p. 22) that, 'Significant differences exist among teachers and educationalists about priorities in educational aims. Some regard schools as primarily concerned with cognitive development. Others think of them as serving certain vocational and social ends. Some argue that they are institutions for the total education of children.' His experience may even suggest that some schools primarily attend to their custodial function (for in some areas delinquency rates are highest when schools are closed) and that others are really concerned with no more than preparing children for public examinations. William Taylor rightly suggests (1969, p. 22) the probability that

> the views we hold regarding the nature of human ability and the limits of individual educability are very much influenced by the particular type of demand that the occupational and social structure is seen as making upon the schools, and these views will clearly have a great deal to do with the way in which we organize our educational system and the pattern of teaching within individual schools.

Charity James (n.d., p. 5) suggests that these views are often jaundiced, for 'when one comes to list the provender that the young need for [their] vitally important journey [through adolescence] one comes to realize the meagreness of what some receive, and is sad for them − and sad for ourselves too that we can't be prouder of the adult society we are asking them to join'.

Whatever else may be expected of schools, their primary function must be to educate, and, although there may be disagreement as to how this is to be done, there can be little disagreement that

> the educated man is one whose mind has been opened to the surprising richness and significance of phenomena; who understands adequately the human society in which he lives, is prepared to make a critical evaluation of that society and is committed, where necessary, to changing it; who has acquired skills of learning and acting;

and who gives service to his fellow men and accepts it from them
with grace (Methodist Conference, 1970, para. 8).

Of course schools are not the only agencies responsible for educating,
but their role is crucial. Most children start school anxious to learn,
though they may differ in what they wish to learn; yet before long
many dismiss schooling as a sacrifice of time better devoted to games
and holidays. They sense that the free conditions experienced out of
school are more conducive to meaningful learning. Teachers are servants
of school authorities, and in many schools 'much of the curriculum is a
result of the inertia of tradition and a curious academic myth about
"scholarship" and "mental discipline" ' (Wilson, 1967b, p. 415). Yet

> teachers are still paid to teach it. The GCE and other examinations
> are still there; parents, headmasters and educational authorities still
> have certain expectations; the teachers have to work the system
> however much they disapprove of it . . . the gulfs between ordinary
> teachers, headmasters, local authorities, parents, government depart-
> ments, departments of education and training colleges has produced
> a situation where the average teacher cannot be expected to do
> much more than cope adequately with his job, survive, and if pos-
> sible make a bit more money (pp. 415–16).

As early as 1929 the *British Association Report on Formal Training*
stated the conviction that:

> We can no longer retain any school subject solely on the ground that
> it provides 'Mental discipline', nor should we speak of the 'educative
> value' *of a subject*. Educative value exists not in the subject *per se*
> but in the way in which it is studied. It consists in 'learning how to
> think', in forming interests, or sentiments about a subject, and in
> building up such habits as perseverance, independent attack of prob-
> lems, application of previous knowledge. Any teaching which fails to
> foster such mental processes is uneducative, however much informa-
> tion it may succeed in driving in (cited, Gurrey, 1963, p. 40).

From the pupils' perspective, compulsory schooling ought to
promise that teachers will ensure that all pupils are successfully
educated to the limits that personality and abilities will allow. The
curriculum may have faults, but this does not explain why so many
pupils freeze up and lose interest in organized learning. An observer
should notice how little most pupils actually learn in the time available
and try to account for this. For example, four years of secondary
school mathematics represents about 500 hours of class work, resulting,

22

for most pupils, in minimal comprehension of mathematical thinking and scant knowledge of a few mathematical processes.

The educational aims of the school

The true aims of any school are not those enunciated by the headteacher or his staff, but the aims disclosed through the practices of the school. These cannot be evaluated against a rigid concept of education. For as Martin Buber says (1961, pp. 129–30),

> There is not and never has been a norm and fixed maxim of education. What is called so was always only the norm of a culture, of a society, a church, an epoch, to which education too, like all stirring and action of the spirit, was submissive, and which education translated into its language.

The disintegration of traditional bonds precludes the possibility of an agreed norm in the present age. This in itself casts serious doubt upon Richard Peters's (1965) notion of education as initiation into a culture. Peters's conception reflects the grammar school's academic tradition of making pupils learned. As he says (1967, p. 20), 'educational processes are those by means of which public modes of thought and awareness, which are mainly enshrined in language, take root in the consciousness of the individual and provide avenues of access to a public world', and 'what is essential is the grasp of a conceptual scheme for ordering facts' (ibid.). Although Peters claims that his interest in conceptual analysis is distinct from any practical concern, his position is generally understood as though it were identical with that of R. M. Hutchins (1970, pp. 9–10), who takes education 'to be the deliberate, organized attempt to help people to become intelligent. . . . In this view, education leads to understanding; it has no more "practical" aim', and claims (p. 10) that an educational institution 'is interested in the development of human beings through the development of their minds. Its aim is not man power, but manhood'; but manhood narrowly conceived.

This conception of education hardly satisfies the injunction of the 1944 Education Act that local authorities should provide for the 'spiritual, moral, mental and physical development' of children. ' "Training the mind" ', as the British Association Report, 1929, states, 'is an abstraction, and . . . only when some person with all his qualities of personality, abilities, gifts and weaknesses, and all his physical nature, is using his mind – to control, improve, apply or to further some actual process or experience is there a realistic situation' (cited, Gurrey, 1963, p. 19). On this view the duty of the schools, especially, is to stimulate their pupils' desire for learning, rather than to make them learned, to encourage them to achieve mastery of skill and the wish to attain to excellence in expression, in reasoning, in all their mental and in their physical activities that are constructive and worth while (Gurrey, 1963, p. 26).

As A. N. Whitehead puts it (1950, p. 47), 'The only avenue towards knowledge is by discipline in the acquisition of ordered fact', but this should not be confused with education, which is the acquisition of the art of the utilization of knowledge, of 'relating it to that stream compounded of sense perceptions, feelings, hopes, desires and of mental activities adjusting thought to thought, which forms our life' (p. 4); the business of education being 'the evocation of curiosity, of judgement, of the power of mastering a complicated tangle of circumstances, [and] the use of theory in giving foresight in special cases' (p. 8). As D. H. Lawrence asked (1933, p. 86), 'why should we cram the mind of a child with facts that have nothing to do with his own experience?'

An observer is likely to find that in practice many teachers do not agree with Hirst and Peters (1970, p. 88) that 'education is not just a matter of the meeting of minds; it is a process of *personal encounter*' (italics added), though they accept that education 'is to be understood in terms of a family of processes through which people become committed to what is valuable in a way that is illuminated by some breadth and depth of understanding' (p. 109). But again there is little agreement about what is valuable in the so-called 'public modes of experience' that make up a curriculum. As a successful product of traditional schooling an observer may have some difficulty in seeing, with Anthony Arblaster (1970, p. 54), that many teachers of differing opinions agree only 'in seeing education as a process of imprinting certain ideas and values upon the impressionable minds and characters of the young'.

Yet his observing is likely to show that there are few who accept that education is, or ought to be, 'an essentially critical activity. Its function [being] to encourage people to think independently, to doubt, to question, to investigate, to be sceptical and inquisitive ... towards the most important and the most relevant issues in the society' (ibid.), and not to reflect some current consensus or 'conventional wisdom'. Michael Oakeshott likewise (1967, pp. 161–2) maintains that

the business of the teacher (indeed, this may be said to be his peculiar quality as an agent of civilisation) is to release his pupils from servitude to the current dominant feelings, emotions, images, ideas, beliefs and even skills, not by inventing alternatives to them which seem to him more desirable, but by making available to him something which approximates more closely to the whole of his inheritance;

an inheritance that comprises the spiritual world of human achievements; beliefs, values and meanings and not abstractions nor things (p. 158), for 'Teaching is not taming or ruling or restoring to health, or conditioning, or commanding, because none of these activities is possible in relation to a pupil' (pp. 157–8). However valid in the nineteenth century, the belief that educating refers to handing on accumulated wisdom and experience to a specially selected 'academic élite', and to instilling literacy and numeracy into 'inferior pupils' to fit them for their place in 'the scheme of things' is irrelevant today.

Whatever views on education an observer may hold, they should be put to the test by noting the effect that the education he observes pupils actually receive has on them. From his theoretical studies he will have learnt that, among other things, the study of education is the study of the way in which models of inquiry are constructed, used, altered and reconstructed, and he is likely to have investigated some of the particular models employed, making judgments about the character of the elements found in a given view of the education process and the way in which these elements are weighted and emphasized in relation to each other. The importance of this theoretical study is to be found in evaluation of the claims made by each model user about his concept of the education process. This can be attempted in the abstract, but, for most students, it only takes on reality when they are in a position to witness and form empirical judgments about the consequences of such concepts. Marc Belth sees the practice of propounding theories as lying at the heart of education.

When man experiences an event and finds that it extends beyond his powers of explanation . . . he propounds a theory, and from it makes a model by which the event is explainable. Unconsciously or consciously, he establishes a comparative relationship between something he has just undergone and what he already knows well. In that relationship, he ascribes the properties of what he knows to the events he is trying to explain (1965, p. 60).

Writing about the importance of the evaluation of theories Belth adds (p. 104),

in spite of the fury generated by opposing groups, it is quite possible that the cumulative knowledge of how the consequences of educational procedures depend upon the models employed will foster a rising sense of agreement about the kind of models which ought to prevail if the educational processes are to be deliberately nurtured.

But, as W. R. Bion has observed (1970, p. 55), 'Controversy is the growing-point from which development springs but it must be a genuine confrontation and not an impotent beating of the air by opponents whose differences of view never meet.' This is good advice to an observer discussing with others what he has observed.

The school and the curriculum

Observing provides an excellent opportunity for examining the difficulties involved in planning curricula so that, despite the limitations imposed by the public examination system, they provide a sound general education for pupils. In his philosophy of curriculum planning, Philip Phenix maintains (1964, p. 5) that, 'human beings are essentially creatures who have the power to experience *meanings*. Distinctively human existence consists in a pattern of meanings. Furthermore, *general education is the process of engendering essential meanings.*' Although, 'in practice, meanings seldom appear in simple form; they are almost always compounded of several of the elemental types' (p. 8), he maintains that for the purpose of curriculum analysis and construction it is useful to distinguish the basic ingredients in all meaning, and to order the learning process for general education in the light of these elements. Despite Paul Hirst's doubts regarding the validity of Phenix's theory (Hirst, 1974, pp. 54—68) it provides a useful frame of reference for observation, being more fully worked out than Hirst's, which is itself of doubtful validity (Woods and Barrow, 1975, pp. 31—4).

In Phenix's view there are six fundamental patterns of meaning, and each realm of meaning can be described by reference to its typical methods, leading ideas, and characteristic structures. In general terms these are: (a) *symbolics*, comprising ordinary language, mathematics, and various types of non-discursive symbolic forms; (b) *empirics,* which includes the physical and life sciences; (c) *aesthetics,* which contains the various arts; (d) *synnoetics*, which embraces philosophy, psychology, literature, religion, in their existential aspects; (e) *ethics*, which 'includes moral meanings that express obligations rather than fact, perceptual form, or awareness of relation'; and (f) *synoptics*, which 'refers to meanings that are comprehensively integrative. It includes history, religion and philosophy. These disciplines combine empirical, aesthetic and synnoetic meanings into coherent wholes' (p. 7).

Since these fundamental types of human understanding are interdependent, it follows that a curriculum should provide for learning in all six realms. For if any one is missing, a basic ingredient in experience is missing. Because *'the basic realms are such that all of them are required if a person is to achieve the highest excellence in anything at all.* . . . It follows that learning in the six realms is necessary even when the goal of specialized mastery guides the construction of the curriculum' (p. 271). Furthermore, because people differ, no one curriculum suffices for everybody, and to foster most effective learning, 'curricula need to be designed as far as practicable to take account of each person's particular aptitudes and enthusiasms' (p. 275).

Given the enormous stock of human knowledge available to be learnt, an observer should investigate the principles underlying the selection and organization of the content of any curriculum he encounters. Again, taking Phenix as his guide, he should expect it to respect four main principles: (a) the content should be drawn entirely from fields of *disciplined inquiry*, that is to say materials produced in disciplined communities of inquiry by acknowledged authorities; (b) the items chosen should be particularly *representative* of the field as a whole; (c) the content chosen should exemplify the *methods of inquiry* and the modes of understanding in the disciplines studied; (d) the materials chosen should be such as to arouse *imagination* (pp. 10–12, also pp. 302–10). The last of these is essential to education, for the ability to draw reasoned conclusions requires the ability to enter imaginatively into the minds of others, to feel the force of their prejudices, and so forth. To encourage pupils to accept the conclusions of others uncritically and unimaginatively is to indoctrinate not educate, and to reinforce the pervasive, if unconscious, indoctrination in the so-called free world; 'a world where power and success express themselves so much in stentorian lying, hypnotized leadership, and panic-stricken suppression of freedom and criticism' (Frye, 1967, p. 123).

A further important aspect of a curriculum is its direction, whether or not it is directed primarily towards future employment. Such direction, excepting cases of severe mental subnormality perhaps, is unsatisfactory for, as Northrop Frye (1967, p. 88) and others have shown, 'leisure is growing so rapidly, both in the amount of time and the number of people it affects, as to be a social complex equal in importance to employment itself' (see also e.g. Martin and Norman, 1970, pp. 452–3). This means that leisure can no longer be equated with idleness or distraction, which, as Frye says (p. 89), are not leisure but 'a running away from leisure, a refusal to face the test of one's inner resources that spare time poses'. Like employment, leisure demands discipline and responsibility. In employment man is essentially functional, replaceable; in his leisure activities he is essentially himself, a performer who is judged not by his role but by his skill in performance. Leisure skills have to be acquired, and the acquiring and practice of the basic skills is a proper charge on education.

The social and economic conditions under which many children are brought up ensure that when adequate provision is not made they are given a narrow expectation of opportunities for living and are led to believe that their significance lies only in their work, and this in a world with diminishing work opportunities and in which much of the work available is alienating. Such an education is a preparation for a life of dissatisfaction. At best its victims are being prepared to participate in life as spectators; gazers at the popular press, the television screen, the football field and the like; even passive spectators of their own situations or predicaments, unable to take any creative action to affect either their domestic or their civic environments, excepting perhaps through outbursts of violence originating in their inner frustrations (Freire, 1972).

An observer is likely to encounter a number of experimental curricula, developed both nationally and locally. Should he do so, he should attempt to discover the steps taken, either by the school or by individual teachers, to evaluate them; for a new curriculum does not automatically match up to its creator's intentions. He may discover that no form of assessment is attempted, for, as Wiseman and Pidgeon comment (1970, p. 78), 'resistance to the formulation of behavioural aims is only to be expected in a profession which, by tradition and by training, has long become used to working to implicit rather than explicit goals'. On the other hand, a school that gives high priority to assessment may have been seduced, by a predilection for figures over one for the informed opinions of skilled observers, into giving disproportionate weight and status in the final assessment to that which is easily measurable. Such an assessment is no less dangerously selective and partial than an assessment based entirely upon untested opinion.

The ease with which public examinations have attained the status of the only acceptable criteria of success in many schools suggests that there is a danger, if emphasis is placed upon predeterminable changes anticipated in pupils' behaviour, that results in human terms will be ignored in favour of those that can be simply totted up and precisely figured. It is comparatively easy to test knowledge retention and retrieval, but by no means easy to obtain objective evaluation of 'behavioural' changes under such headings as ability, understanding, or attitude. Even Wiseman and Pidgeon, who argue strongly for systematic evaluation, admit that no teacher can 'afford to eschew measurement techniques of a more subjective nature, accepting some loss of precision in the interests of cogency, thus incorporating observation, judgment

28

and personal assessment as valid measures of pupil behaviour and reaction' (1970, p. 83).

Whatever an observer may feel about so-called objective testing of a curriculum, his periods of observing are likely to provide his only opportunity to consider the pros and cons, without being under any obligation to decide whether or not to employ such methods in his own work. He might find it a useful exercise to consider any so-called objectively validated syllabus in the light of Phenix's observation (1964, p. 321) that 'no definitive guidance can be offered for organizing the subject matter for instruction. No one plan is best for every teacher and for all students in all situations', and to attempt to work out how he would need to modify the syllabus if he were to use it himself.

Quality and equality

A fundamental fallacy incorporated into the 1944 Education Act was the belief that the provision of free and compulsory education for all would provide an equal opportunity for all children. As the perceptive Italian boys at the 'School of Barbiana' have written (Barbiana, 1970, p. 86),

> the English don't fail students in their schools. They divert them towards schools of lower quality. In school, then, the poor perfect the art of speaking badly, while the rich keep polishing their language. They can tell from the way a man speaks whether he is rich and what kind of work his father does.

They rightly regard this as being a deprivation for all children. As they say (pp. 27–8), 'To be a happy student . . . you have to be a social climber at the age of twelve. But few are climbers at twelve. It follows that most of your young people hate school. Your cheap invitation to them deserves no other reaction.' And (p. 88), 'A school that is as selective as the kind we have described destroys culture. It deprives the poor of the means of expressing themselves. It deprives the rich of the knowledge of things as they are.'

When observing with the focus on the provision of an equal opportunity for all pupils, an observer should look to see how the particular needs of individuals are met, for 'Equality of provision is not identity of provision' (Tawney, 1931, p. 51). If equality of opportunity is to mean anything real in the school situation it must be interpreted in terms of equality of consideration; which implies that, once common human needs have been met, there will be considerable differentiation in the treatment meted out to individuals. Some (e.g. Birley and

The school and education

Dufton, 1971) suggest that equality of resources with equality of concern would provide a more suitable guide to action, though appropriateness of resources would seem to be more important. The basis upon which resources are apportioned and the degree to which concern is shown on behalf of all are clearly as important as awareness of differences in individual ability. Unfortunately an observer may find that a school fails to distinguish between recognizing specific differences and passing general judgments of superiority or inferiority upon pupils; favouring the former and neglecting the latter.

It is of course absurd, even degrading, to regard superior ability as a ground for bestowing honour, or as a basis for recognizing worth. Every ability is basically a given personal datum, and not in any way merited or meritorious. An observer's best measure for estimating the extent to which equality is acknowledged in a school is the degree to which the uniqueness of each pupil is not only recognized, but dominant in decision making at all levels; for 'Just as each individual knows himself to be unique, so he sees that his neighbour is also unique. Human equality is an equality in uniqueness' (Jenkins, 1961, p. 21). Tawney (1931, p. 187) reminds us that 'inequality is a matter, not merely of quantities of income, but of quality of life'. School can do little about the former, but it can do much to ensure that each individual is prepared to experience the highest quality of life of which he is capable. The evidence needed for estimating the quality of the effort made is to be found in the attitude both of the staff towards pupils and of pupils towards staff, for, as Daniel Jenkins puts it (1961, p. 113),

if we are to have an educational system which has a considerable measure of equality of opportunity, as justice and enlightened self-interest both demand, we must also have one where the fundamental equality of all men is asserted in such a way as to give people humility, patience and courage to face and make the best of the inequalities which will then emerge.

It is tempting to think that streaming in a school is clear evidence of inequality of treatment. This need not be the case. As a recent UNESCO survey (Yates, 1966) makes clear, research over the last forty years is inconclusive. Pupils have to be gathered into groups for the purpose of instruction and, as yet, it is by no means clear what principle should underlie such groupings, although it is evident that 'the over-all aim must be to achieve that method of grouping which provides the environment best suited to stimulating the cognitive and affective development of all the children' (Simon, 1970, p. 152). A danger implicit in streaming is that where children are streamed teachers are streamed as well; that is to say, the most effective teachers teach the most quick-witted children, and the least experienced and poorest teachers teach the weakest. Another is that the equipment is also streamed, the best available being allocated in sufficient supply to top streams, whilst the remaining streams make do with whatever is left, which is often insufficient for their needs, out of date, or in poor condition. In some schools even the rooms are streamed on the same principle. In such schools it is rare to find classes in the top streams in ill-lit, uncomfortable or inconvenient rooms whilst the lower streams are housed in comparative splendour.

Similarly, the absence of streaming does not, however, ensure the absence of inequality in treatment. Many teachers operate a system of streaming within the classroom, both with streamed and non-streamed classes. According to the Plowden Report (DES, 1967, para. 806) this

can be more damaging to children than streaming within a school. Even from the infant schools there still come too many stories of children streamed by the tables they sit at, of 'top tables' and 'backward reader' tables, and newcomers to school mystified by what they conceive to be the art of 'reading backwards'.

It would seem to be the case that what is far more significant than streaming are the expectations of teachers of streamed classes. Since the common denominator normally employed when allocating children to streams is their present lack of attainment, and teachers have a pronounced tendency to accept allocation to a particular stream as a definitive indication of a child's real ability, there is some force in Hilda Himmelweit's contention (1970, p. 12), that 'we have an education system which grooms for failure more than it grooms for success; and . . . within that system streaming is an invention of the teachers to reinforce the system of grooming for failure'. Since in a streamed school friendships are generally made within streams, and in a non-streamed school with children of similar abilities, an observer should notice the attention paid to encouraging mixing across ability boundaries, and the steps taken to ensure that leading positions in school life are not the prerogative of the academically more able pupils.

Apart from the more obvious disadvantages experienced by coloured or foreign children in some British schools, there is a form of discrimination analogous in its operation to streaming. If such a school continues to operate as though it had a purely indigenous population, such children are bound to regard themselves as different, as outsiders. Should the school, with the best of intentions, make special provision for, and place stress upon, improving their linguistic attainments, whilst aiming to preserve the native ethos of the school, this too is likely to be alienating. Although no best way of approaching the problems peculiar to such schools is known, certainly the attitude of the teachers to non-native children and the attitudes of those pupils' families to the school, are of crucial importance. It is an established fact that a high proportion of immigrant children, particularly those from the West Indies, are failed by their schooling and, since only about 15 per cent of newly qualified teachers are likely to encounter immigrant children in their first posts, an observer in such a school should take advantage of his situation to discover what can be, and is being, done to prevent such children from declining into comparative educational sub-normality, or self-dislike for being coloured (see Coard, 1971; DES 1971a, 1971b; Townsend, 1970).

The importance of examinations

Despite the fact that public examinations are of no significance once a pupil has obtained his first job or a place in an institution of higher education, few schools can afford to ignore them, on account of the exam-conscious external pressures which influence them. Public examinations can have a marked, and often depressing, influence upon the quality of the education provided by a school. As Page says (1970, p. 221), 'So long as [higher education] is not available to all who want it there will be some test or other to determine who may have it, and there will be a consequent distortion in the schools.' An observer should pay careful attention, therefore, to the attitude of teaching staff towards examinations. Is it the custom to enter as many pupils as possible, for as many subjects as possible, sacrificing depth in study for breadth of 'success', even though few pupils actually need to pass O level, for example, in more than five or six subjects? Are examinable subjects the only ones afforded serious study by both staff and pupils? Does concentration upon examinations conceal the fact that school studies should be enjoyable? Do the teachers talk possessively about *their* examination successes, as if these indicate their worth as teachers? Or are they more concerned to stimulate genuine appreciation of their subject matter and to facilitate an harmonious and creative community in which individuals are respected, and their views given serious consideration?

In many schools public examinations are supplemented by a regular battery of tests and examinations, ranging from the end-of-the-school-year internal examination to the weekly subject test. Since examining in any formal sense is justified only if it serves the learning rather than the assessment process, an observer should try to determine whether the school looks upon testing as an end-in-itself, or as a means of making the processes of education more effective. For

When evaluation takes place, it must always be in terms of real purpose on the part of the learner. It is only worthwhile to the extent to which it is useful in improving learning. Insofar as education is concerned, the development of human beings is the goal. The actual extent to which a student achieves that goal cannot be measured with finality. The best that can be done is to make judgments as to what is most helpful in a particular situation (Connell, 1948, p. 127).

Despite the fact that most sensitive teachers who have developed skills in observation are capable of grading pupils, so far as this is necessary, and of identifying the help required by individuals, few seem to trust their abilities sufficiently to dare to abandon testing, despite the dangers inherent in testing. For example, the test situation encourages convergent thinking – in most tests there is normally only one 'right' answer. The divergent thinker, the one who asks awkward questions, whose mind is apt to go off at a tangent and to think creatively, is at a disadvantage. If divergent thinking is inhibited the development of creative potential may be warped; yet refusal to conform can lead to an experience of continuous lack of noteworthy success, which is more than most children under parental pressure to succeed at school can bear. There are, of course, those pupils who, for whatever reason, always do less well than most in the test situation, and who consequently suffer the repeated humiliation of being regarded as less able, even stupid, both by their teachers and their peers. Such categorization may mean no more than that a child's abilities remain undiscovered, or that his teacher has not discovered the gaps in his knowledge or experience that prevent his being able to understand, or whatever else may underlie his failure.

No child who has not been severely damaged by his schooling likes to fail or fails intentionally, for failure is painful. The hurt caused to a person through failure often removes any grounds or incentive for his continuing his studies seriously, encouraging him to drop out and to long for his first job, which he hopes will give him the status school denies him – even though recognition of this status may be restricted to himself. Failure in the end-of-year examinations may cause a pupil to be kept down in his so-called 'own best interest'. In effect this wipes out a year of his life, causing him to lose friends and breaking up his world. It is hardly surprising that a repeated year is often little more rewarding than the first time round. The bright pupil is no less vulnerable to tests and examinations, for it requires a strong character not to be affected by a constant succession of marks and praise that seem to imply that one is superior to one's peers, is more cultured than them; whereas it probably implies no more than that one's culture is different from theirs, that one's up-bringing happens to coincide with certain unacknowledged expectations of the school. It could even imply that, outside of the narrow world of school, one would be justly regarded as being a rather dull fellow. Success in artificial tests and examinations stimulates vanity and does nothing to dampen selfish ambition, nor to suggest that high rank entails an obligation to serve others, because one is able to. An observer will find that schools recognizing such an obligation are rare. Tests and examinations that are not absolutely essential for career purposes represent an incredible waste of time. Far from being able to help pupils in any sort of difficulty or trouble, the teacher is compelled to stand by, mute and ineffectual, whilst his pupils slave away to produce the mechanical results he already expects from them.

Children should be in school to develop their own powers, not to jump over hurdles, to develop imaginative thinking about realities, not to perform intellectual athletics; for life does not consist of a series of unreal tests performed against an arbitrary time limit, nor in gathering information of peculiar if incomprehensible interest to someone else. Yet many schools interpret their function as training children to perform in such ways. An observer in an exam orientated school should pay special attention therefore to pupils put into the position of repeatedly failing tests, or at least of doing poorly. He should notice how they attempt to sustain their self-esteem so as to avoid feeling diminished in their own and others' eyes, how some find protection in not trying, or by adopting the role of bold-as-brass heroes, certain to fail, thereby gaining a degree of respect from their peers on account of their bravery. He should notice also the extent to which tests or examinations expected by pupils determine their study behaviour; for example, the amount of memorizing they undertake, the extent to which they re-read previously studied texts — particularly text books containing quantities of pre-digested 'facts' assembled in the requisite order — and the effort they put into attempting to remember such facts, in contrast to endeavouring to apply stimulating ideas or methods to new and interesting situations. Further than this he should notice the effect of examinations upon teachers; the pressures upon them to prepare pupils to perform the right tricks, and the staleness that comes from teaching the same circus acts year after year. He can scarcely avoid the dictatorial influence that even internal examinations have upon the syllabus; dominating what is learnt and the manner in which it is learnt, and the dependence of teachers upon the system for knowing what to do.

Even the effect that the warning of an impending examination or test has upon pupils is instructive. The pretence that they are simply a means of testing what has been learnt, that is to say of showing that all that had to be learnt has been learnt, is a mockery of the reality; namely, that pupils cram their memories with facts to be retained just long enough to ensure a pass. If tests must be given, the only one likely to reveal what a particular pupil's knowledge and ability actually are is the unexpected one. Most pupils regard such tests as very unfair, and the results are likely to be unflattering, both to teacher and taught. Only children utterly warped by propaganda about the importance of examinations fail to look upon them as a rather unpleasant game, in which the winners are known in advance, and for which, if they are to save face, most require due warning in order to limber up and polish their tricks. Weaker candidates who have not dropped out face a special hazard, for such confidence as they may have gained between tests is often destroyed by fear and anxiety, and they rarely do themselves justice. Occasionally, of course, they do and it could possibly be argued that the chance of such a success justifies tests, for able pupils have no need of them. Nevertheless, why must a pupil be good at something that really interests him, if he is to be allowed to study it beyond a very elementary level? Why shouldn't he study it even though tests might show that he is bad at it? For his weakness surely indicates no more than that the teacher has not discovered how best to help him to be less weak.

Clearly, assessment is important, and from time to time a teacher needs some guidance, other than his own observation and intuition, as to what each of his pupils knows, understands or misunderstands, is confused about or has difficulty over, or has gained some grasp of but lacks understanding of in depth. Who is better placed to provide this necessary perspective than pupils themselves? As Dr Abercrombie says (1970, p. 12),

> in the present climate of dissatisfaction and distrust about the whole system of examinations, whether for entrance to secondary education or to a profession, it is essential that we reconsider the role of assessment in education. Given a sound educational environment in which collaboration in the learning task is based on mutual respect, and competitiveness is not destructive, red in tooth and claw, but a spice that enhances individual differences, assessment by students of their own and others' work can be well integrated into the educational process.

But it should be noted that 'self-assessment is only likely to be of value in situations where the pupils believe that the teacher is not concerned to evaluate and possibly condemn them but is only concerned with teaching them' (McIntyre, 1970, p. 169).

4 The school and the individual

The adoption of IQ testing, both for purposes of selection and record keeping, has led to the school system being more concerned with generalized models of young humanity than with individual persons.

The education of intelligence

Intelligence has little to do with an ability to perform certain specific mental gymnastics, even though tests employing them may provide psychologists with information professionally useful to them. From his research into machine intelligence, Donald Michie (1971, pp. 370–1) has determined that ' "intelligence" on any reasonable definition is related to a particular activity rather than being an absolute term'. That is to say, it is related to integrated cognition; the effective knitting together of many skills, rather than to depth in any one skill. Intelligence has little to do with success in traditional school activities, though this may indicate genuine intelligence in some instances. It is disclosed in the manner in which people respond to life; especially to new or unusual situations. It is not a matter of how much is known, but of knowing what to do with what is known – knowing how to put it to the best use; and with knowing what to do when something necessary for behaviour to be intelligent is not known.

Intelligence is the quality by which man controls and exploits his material environment advantageously. It is essential for ordering human society, but the term should not be restricted to purely intellectual intelligence. 'Human life, like all life, only completes itself in the connexion of immediate apprehension with action which expressed what it has become aware of', as John Macmurray says (1935, p. 72).

It is in this immediacy of response in action to conscious perception that all the activities of thought inevitably fail. Intellectual intelligence can never be a substitute, therefore, for the immediacy of perceptual activity. It may enrich it by raising it to a higher level, or it may impoverish it by negation and repression.

36

The intelligent person may possess perceptual abilities, but not because he is clever. Yet our education system almost exclusively rewards the clever person, that is, the one whose mind works more quickly than others'. The world is laid at his feet and comparatively little effort is made on behalf of the rest, who are expected to achieve happiness, success or satisfaction entirely under their own steam. Because, on the whole, teachers are drawn from the ranks of the comparatively quick-witted it is not surprising that attempts to improve the system make only slow progress, and this chiefly in the area of increasing manifest cleverness, rarely by fostering the qualities intelligence should subserve.

Despite the continuing controversy over the determinants of intelligence no compelling evidence has been produced to overthrow Donald Hebb's mediating contention (1966, p. 155), that

heredity by itself, can produce no behavior whatever; the fertilized ovum must have a nutritive, supporting environment for its growth, before behavior is possible. Similarly, learning can produce no behavior by itself, without the heredity and the prenatal environment that produce the structures in which learning can occur. The two collaborate. Further, it seems highly probable that heredity makes some kinds of learning easy or inevitable, others hard, and thus guides learning.

He concludes: 'Theoretically, therefore, we may consider that the function of early experience in the mammal is to build up the mediating processes which, once they are established, make possible the very rapid learning of which the mature animal is capable.'

Similarly, claims to be able to assess a child's promise for the future are unhelpful, for available prognostic schemes fail to explain the 'over-achievers', who are as numerous as 'under-achievers'. Since intelligence is not fixed but modifiable, it cannot be implied that any understanding or concept a child holds is simply a function of his ability. 'His concepts', as Ira Gordon stresses (1966, p. 13), 'are heavily influenced by the culture to which he has been exposed.' Furthermore, since the ability to think is not an independent faculty or transferable skill of the mind, being related to events, subjects, or problems in specific areas of experience, it follows that simple generalized measures of 'intelligence' are at best likely to be misleading; for failure to learn may as readily indicate a failure in teaching, or some other lack, as a lack of ability, and it is clearly nonsense to regard over-achievers as doing more than they are potentially capable of doing.

Since intelligence is not some mysterious power or faculty of the mind, possessed in quantifiable amounts and determining potentiality for achievement, the results of tests, even those ostensibly designed to eliminate cultural handicap, should not be regarded as a true measure of a child's potential, for 'there is no such thing as a culture-fair test, and never can be' (Vernon, 1968, p. 213). The truism that the intellectual capacity of every individual is limited by his heredity is of less importance to a teacher than the fact that, through intellectual stimulation and learning, the intellectual capacity of a large proportion of children can be substantially increased, irrespective of any scores they may achieve in psychological tests (see Vernon, 1969). The fiction that intelligence is a measurable human attribute stems from a metaphor linking mental ability and athletics, which derives from Francis Galton, the founding father of IQ testing, who believed fallaciously that lively minds are like lively bodies (see Galton, 1892, p. 12). As athletic ability is not manifested in one generalized form of athletic prowess permitting a meaningful comparison between, for example, a tennis player and a boxer, so too the manifold ways in which intelligence may show itself cannot be compared meaningfully (see Hudson, 1972). A more realistic approach to the concept of intelligence is to regard it as 'a fluid collection of skills whose development is demonstrably affected by early experience and subsequently by the quality and duration of formal education' (Yates, 1966, p. 86). If intelligence is thought of as a substantial number of personal intellectual abilities, which collectively can be regarded as that person's intelligence (see e.g. Guilford, 1967), it is to be expected that the vast majority of children will be above average in some of these abilities. This means that a teacher's primary responsibility is to discover the particular abilities of each pupil and to foster his development of these, not only to enable him to experience genuine success and reinforce a positive self-image, but also to build a firm basis for future development in wider fields. Crude universal intelligence tests applied generally provide little more than a pseudo-scientific excuse for ignoring pupils as individuals, despite the passionate discussion that may accompany subsequent pigeon-holing.

An observer in a school in which due regard is paid to the uniqueness of each pupil should note whether the teachers concentrate only upon known abilities in pupils, for this too is a disservice. The development of some skill in such essential fields as literacy and numeracy, which do not come easily to all, is, for example, an important stimulus to the development of every form of intelligence. Despite the claims made on behalf of particular systems and methods of instruction the obstinate fact remains that the most profound school influences upon pupils' abilities and attainments are their teachers' attitudes and expectations. Because intelligence is not something quantitative but rather a quality of behaviour, intelligent behaviour is possible only for a person with opportunity for appropriate experience, whose past experience is available to him when needed, without distortion or denial, and who is open to new experience or information and knows how to gain it.

An observer will see that the approach of a true teacher to his pupils is governed by the key questions 'can this child bring all relevant aspects of his experience to the job in hand, sense the requirements of the problem and actively seek any new experience needed to resolve the problem either by using past solutions or generating an original solution?' If the pupil at that particular moment is doing so he is being intelligent, whatever his speed of working may be. From this perspective teaching means endeavouring to remove any restrictions upon and limitations to a pupil's behaving intelligently, and in particular the pupil's inner limitations. For, as Robert Bills says (1969, p. 82),

> a person who sees himself as inadequate or unacceptable will not rely on his own experience to the extent he should in reaching adequate solutions to his problems. If a person distrusts himself sufficiently, he will avoid situations which require him to develop intelligence, fearing that he will fail if he attempts to solve certain problems or involve himself in certain tasks.

Such teaching involves concern for the quality of relationships within the classroom, for 'if a person believes that other people are unimportant, he cannot use their experience in solving problems' (p. 82). But this concern is shown through example rather than by exhortation or instruction, for 'it is not necessary to teach children to develop respect for other people; respect appears to be a natural outcome of relationships in which children are loved and cherished' (p. 85).

When intelligence is considered outside the context of IQ tests, interest focuses upon social and cultural processes in terms of which particular ways of life are defined; for it is these that shape thought and give it meaning. The objective measurement of intelligence in this context is inconceivable. In this sense, at least, the teacher has nothing but himself to offer as a criterion to his pupils.

It does not follow, however, that IQ and other tests, though dangerous, are valueless. They can help a teacher to perceive something of how or why a pupil is not being stimulated by his interaction with his environment, though in order to use test results in this way he needs to know what experience and interests do stimulate him, and be at least as interested in the pupil's actual performance during the test as he is in his final mark. But such diagnostic assistance is unlikely to be needed, except in those rare cases when personal knowledge of a child provides no clue to what the teacher ought to do. Yet as Lian Hudson has said (BBC Radio 3, 2 March 1971),

> the IQ is not a measurement that is achieved by magic. It requires one to sit down dutifully and take seriously a set of tasks that, to a very large number of people, lack any obvious point. Such willingness is a matter of attitude, and even the most willing may approach such a situation feeling inadequate, if they have previously been persuaded that they are not among nature's elect. The measurement of intelligence, in other words, is a social event, and the social psychology of the testing situation is something about which at present we know almost nothing.

In other words, although a teacher may learn something of real value from testing, it will be mainly from what might be described as its spin-off, not its 'objective' results.

The artificial nature of the IQ concept is further illustrated by the fact that 'the ability to be productive with computers is not the same as IQ' (Martin and Norman, 1970, p. 391). Some children with high IQ ratings have been found to be highly incompetent when dealing with a computer terminal, whereas others with comparatively low IQs have been found to be far better able to cope with the new situation. Intelligence testers do not pretend to test anything but intelligence defined as the all-round ability or mental efficiency children display in everyday life, a loose mixture of all sorts of overlapping abilities, partly acquired, but limited by some quality of the central nervous system which can be neither observed nor measured; in other words, an intelligence that is a hypothetical potentiality, strongly influenced by stimuli in a child's environment from birth onwards. Hence, every intelligence test always tests both more and less than innate ability, and the tester can have no idea how much more or how much less. To dismiss slower children as hopeless cases on such evidence, or to lower one's expectations of them, is irresponsible. Few people ever work even near to the full extent of their intellectual ability and all but the very slowest have much in hand, so long as they are not psychologically or culturally crippled. They may require more patient explanation and encouragement than academically more nimble children do, but, unless the potential of Soviet children is better than that of British and American children, there is no other explanation for the unintelligent behaviour of many children in British schools (see Bronfenbrenner, 1970). The solution to present problems seems to lie in abandoning the off-the-peg marketing attitudes which dominate British education, encouraging, even compelling, teachers to accept ready-made products as best-buys for the expenditure of their time and energy.

Closely related to intelligence are special interests and aptitudes and it is as these grow that intellectual power begins to develop, within the limits of innate intelligence. An observer should notice, therefore, the extent to which teachers use and encourage such features as they come to their notice; even though this may conflict with a prepared programme of work. They may cover the whole spectrum of human activity, within the limits of what is available to children, in terms both of inner resources and the environment, and are most likely to come to the fore during adolescence, as the capacity for intelligence approaches its effective peak. When a developing aptitude coincides with a particular field of school studies there is a danger that teachers may pounce upon it and develop it exclusively. A pupil, being unaware of other abilities he may have because they are over-shadowed by this success, may well find that it is not an ability to which he would really have wished to devote so much time and attention. The dangers in pushing a pupil where he does not really want to go are easily ignored; but the cost is high both to the pupil, who may well resent the wasted years and opportunities, and to those whose supporting sacrifices are eventually rewarded with apparent ingratitude.

Concern for emotional maturity

An education that concentrates solely upon the acquisition of facts and the development of depersonalized reasoning cannot be regarded as a good education. The development of rationality is right and proper, but objective rationality is a chimera and cannot be an ideal for living life. 'Reason is emotion's slave and exists to rationalize emotional experience', as Bion says (1970, p. 1). Schooling is concerned with preparing children to live, and they have to learn to live with the whole of their bodies, and not just with their heads. Intellectually controlled action is only possible through a process of inhibition. Though training in this is an important element of education, equally important is the enabling of children to act with their whole being, their actions being spontaneous, emotional, non-mechanical and, humanly speaking, free. 'The intellect itself cannot be a source of action', as John Macmurray reminds us (1935, p. 45). For

> All motives of action are necessarily emotional, but the intellect can use the emotion of fear to paralyze the positive emotions, leaving only that one free to determine action which corresponds to the planned purpose. Such action can never be creative, because creativeness is a characteristic which belongs to personality in its wholeness, acting as a whole, and not to any of its parts acting separately.

As Macmurray insists, 'all *real* action is creative, and it is only possible in relation to direct sensuous awareness' (p. 45), being the product of discipline, 'the integration of a multitude of simple capacities which are trained to act together harmoniously to a single end' (p. 84) not only within the individual, but also inter-personally so as to create a community of free co-operation. This conception of discipline

> demands, in the first place, the integration, throughout all life, of theory and practice. Activity, which is the expression of skill, is primary. Theory is for the sake of action. Knowledge is a means to life, not an end in itself. . . . The integration of theory and practice is impossible unless we recognize that. . . . Our bodies are not merely instruments for the mind to use. . . . If we treat the body as an instrument, its skill in action becomes utilitarian. . . . It is the mind that is instrumental. Hence it follows that true discipline must begin with the education of sensibility (pp. 86–7).

This being so, it follows that the education of sensibility is the basis of all true education and discipline. This basis is not irrational, for every essential expression of human nature must be an expression of reason. A conception of reason applicable only to the abstractions of impersonal science is either false or, at least, inadequate. Since conceptual thinking is not the only characteristically human mental activity it follows that reason must be capable of emotional as well as intellectual expression. Hence Macmurray defines reason (p. 19) as 'the capacity to behave consciously in terms of the nature of what is not ourselves . . . our capacity for objectivity'. Reason, therefore, 'is the capacity to behave, not in terms of our own nature, but in terms of our knowledge of the nature of the world outside' (p. 20), and 'The development of *human* nature in its concrete livingness is, in fact, the development of emotional reason' (p. 50).

The construction of the future cannot be left to some form of blind social evolution, for that which is human is created, and created by persons. An observer will notice that a school concerned for the creation of the future will pay particular attention to the emotional development of its pupils; teaching them how to attend to and respond spontaneously to all that is around them; seeking to initiate them into a genuine appreciation of the vision of artists in whatever medium they may work, including the sciences, and helping them to develop a lively awareness of true art as an expression of the personal, a vision of what might be real, a possible blueprint for the future, and so forth. Scientific expertness and intellectual dexterity are essential tools for the creation of the future but, without the vision that comes only with the development of 'emotional reason', they are blind guides, more than likely to lead to dehumanization. Science is concerned with impersonal facts, with information. Information is always *about* something, not knowledge *of* it. The scientist is rightly concerned with depersonalized information that can be shared by everybody everywhere; for the personal is always unique. Information only becomes knowledge as the individual responds to it emotionally, and makes it part of his real world, but in so far as it is knowledge personalized it is not truly scientific, though not necessarily less true.

The greatest difficulty facing teachers today, no matter what they may teach, is that of teaching children how to be true to the scientific without being untrue to the reality of their emotional nature and afraid of spontaneity, for

> Primarily each of us is afraid of himself; because of this we are afraid of others; and these secret fears in the mass are the root of the injustice and squalor of our civilization. The supreme condemnation of a civilization is that it is inartistic, that is to say, impersonal, inhuman, unreal. . . . A civilization that has lost the capacity of the artist is a prey to spiritual paralysis, to an inner rotting of its human powers. . . . If we are to make peace in the world, we must make peace with our own souls (Macmurray, 1935, pp. 158–9).

Failure to educate the emotional life is failure in the primary business of education. Emotional life is the essence of human life; the intellect is rooted in it, and being essentially instrumental is the subordinate partner in human activity. At best the intellect can enable us to live better but, when dominant, it can become a substitute for living, for thinking is not living. Living is an end in itself; thinking can only be a means to that end. True education, education in living, requires the development of the instrumental intellect in subservience to life itself. This entails sensitizing pupils to the world they inhabit, in all its aspects and for its own sake; encouraging a fineness in expressive activity, encouraging an honesty of response to phenomena and situations with no hiding of true feelings behind a screen of fraudulent decorum. Regrettably, an observer is likely to find that sensitiveness is habitually suppressed or sentimentalized in most schools, for sensitivity often hurts. Yet the capacity to perceive beauty requires the capacity to face ugliness, just as the capacity to experience joy involves vulnerability to sorrow and pain. But just as indoctrination into ready-made and officially approved reactions to stimuli, whether social situations, paintings or whatever else, has no place in education of the emotions, neither has an uncritical indulgence in emotion and the expression of feelings. Such education demands emotional honesty refined by honest thinking, paying due regard to honesty of feeling about the conclusions arrived at. Education is thus a dialectical and not just a dialogical process.

The development of imaginative powers

Closely linked to education of the emotions is the development of pupils' powers of imagination. Few would disagree with Ruth Mock (1970, p. 14) that

> to a great extent our lives are dominated by able and quick-witted individuals whose imagination, often through no fault of their own, has since infancy been discouraged or suppressed, and who in consequence, and in spite of their often impressive intellectualism as well as of their declared intent, have little human sympathy or perceptive understanding.

No amount of factual knowledge can replace the need for imaginative comprehension if a person is to be sensitively aware of the reality of the human world around him. Without imaginative understanding, any knowledge or study, however intellectually advanced it may be, can result only in limited comprehension with the associated dangers of opinionated intolerance and uncalculated cruelties. Imagination should not be confused with irrational day-dreaming. Like the intellect and the emotions the imagination needs discipline, to be firmly rooted in the real world no matter how far flights of fancy may legitimately extend, for as Coleridge said, it is 'the unifying power of the mind which brings together what will aid its purpose and rejects all that is impertinent and unessential' (cited, Keatinge, 1916, p. 164), and

> in the imagination of man exist the seeds of all moral and scientific improvements; chemistry was first alchemy, and out of astrology sprang astronomy. In the childhood of those sciences the imagination opened a way, and furnished materials, on which the ratiocinative of a maturer stage operated with success. The imagination is the distinguishing characteristic of man as a progressive being; and I repeat that it ought to be carefully guided and strengthened as the indispensable means and instrument of continued amelioration and refinement (cited, Walsh, 1970, p. 9).

The imagination thrives on stillness and quiet, but is dulled and eventually destroyed by any compulsion to self-assertion. In many schools the provision of opportunities for quiet and solitude is difficult to make, particularly in economically deprived areas. Yet, under even the most cramped conditions some provision can be made. The need for training in stillness, and for opportunities in which it is possible to be creatively still, is emphasized by the fact of contemporary intolerance of quietness and aloneness. Since few children have the opportunity to learn how to be still, particularly since the experience of the stillness of genuine religious devotion is no longer a commonplace, the provision of suitable opportunities and locations for education in stillness should be a priority in every school. Although an observer is unlikely to find much evidence of this provision, it would be a useful exercise to see how it could be made in any school in which he is observing.

Preparation for the real world

A disturbing aspect of contemporary schooling is that it is preparing children for a world that may not exist by the time they achieve full adulthood. For the quick-witted minority this may not be serious. For most, however, this is a disastrous state of affairs. James Martin and Adrian Norman (1970), on the basis of many years spent on the design and implementation of advanced computer systems, are convinced that, within a decade, computerization and cybernation will be so cheap and advanced that they will have a greater influence upon life than is generally imagined. Without sharing the expectations of the Doomwatch popularizers they are concerned that uncontrolled industrial expansion and technological development are likely to lead to irreversible degradation of the quality of life for most, if not all, people. Furthermore, job opportunities, other than unskilled labour, will depend largely upon a person's ability to cope with machines, and in particular with computer terminals, for 'even the best system of engineering and foresighted planning will not change the natural talents of men and women, and thus make everyone's skill valuable to computerized society' (p. 450).

The quality of life in the near future will depend ultimately upon the nature and quality of the political decisions taken in the interim. Until these decisions are known teachers will be at a considerable disadvantage whilst attempting to prepare pupils for the future. Some things, however, are already certain, such as the importance of being able to understand the human significance of computers and to 'communicate' with them. Hence, although only a minority will be involved in elaborate computer techniques, all should be made familiar with the basics of terminal operating. In a school with a terminal an observer should notice whether its use is reserved for the school's élite, those most likely to be able to familiarize themselves with computer communication at any time, or whether particular attention is paid to those least likely to have such opportunities after leaving school.

The importance of education for leisure is obvious. If leisure time is not to be destructive of personality it must be spent actively, employing publicly acceptable and identifiable skills. The nature and extent of the provision for leisure activities may depend ultimately upon the decisions of politicians, yet a major problem already confronts teachers, namely, how can a leisured class, which may well be a majority class, be created without the traditional substructure of slaves or some lower class to perform routine tasks for it?

Teachers themselves will not be unaffected by the changes about to take place. As costs decline it will become cheaper to employ computers (or other machines) than teachers as instructors. Teachers will then be freed for the more difficult tasks of teaching children to explore, to debate, to innovate, and to appreciate conflicting viewpoints. In other words, they will be more concerned with the real business of education than they have been as mere trainers of potential members of the work-force. The teacher whose culture is superficial, or who is emotionally under-developed, will be ill-suited to this task. This suggests that, both collectively and individually, teachers have a responsibility to deepen and extend their cultural lives in every possible way, not just for their own sakes, but also for that of their pupils; for there can be little place for the narrow specialist or the philistine among those providing for the general education of the young in an age of rapid cultural change.

The discoveries and developments of the recent past and near future are neither good nor evil. They present mankind with opportunities for doing either. Whether or not an individual does good rather than evil will depend more upon the values he respects than on anything else. Because of this the quality of future life will depend more upon the teachers of the present young generation than upon most other sections of the community. The real problems facing mankind in the near future will not be technological, but will concern the use to which technology will be put. If the future deciders are to make humane decisions, they must have truly human and adaptable teachers, not teachers who pretend to be able to provide the answers to, and to make the decisions about, their pupils' problems. In other words, they need teachers who can create learning environments in which young people can learn the processes involved in identifying, clarifying and developing their own values. For

It is when we deny our feelings and hide them from others, when we accept the first alternatives and don't look ahead to consequences, when we allow others to make our value choices for us, when we do not act on our beliefs and ideals, *then* we relinquish control over our futures and find ourselves floundering in a world and a body we do not understand (Kirchenbaum and Simon, 1974, p. 270).

5 Children in school

The good teacher is a person who is always learning from his pupils. To do this he must observe them carefully, for observation is a requisite of all learning. It stimulates thought and understanding, and widens the scope and intensifies the quality of knowledge. An observer must also enter the classroom with his eyes wide open and, whatever expectations he may have derived from his theoretical studies, must go in prepared to experience the situation fully and then withdraw to reflect upon that experience in order to refine his theoretical expectations. To go in prepared to teach without any first-hand study of the strange world of the classroom would suggest that the ability to teach has little to do with children, whereas it is learnt gradually from children, through mutual response in personal interaction. To become a good teacher requires direct experience of children, and to give full attention to this as an observer, bearing no other responsibility, is an important first step.

It is easy to slip into the habit of regarding children as instances of types and to expect them to conform to type; but as some Italian boys have recently reminded us, 'each boy is different, each historical moment is different and so is every moment different for each boy, each country, each environment, each family' (Barbiana, 1970, pp. 98–9). Should an observer be fully informed about the background, experience and results of all available psychological tests completed by an individual child, he would still not be in any position to know with certainty what to expect from him in a given situation.

It is probably true to say that no child is born stupid or lazy, although children certainly learn and develop at widely differing rates. A child is more than a fixed latent ability which just requires developing through good training. If he is subjected to psychological pressures analogous to those experienced by Pavlov's dogs, it is, of course, possible to condition him to produce anticipated behaviour. But, if he is not subjected to such distorting pressures his development is open-ended. 'The intellectual, biological and emotional structure he has at any given moment is both a product of the history of his transactions and the shaper of his present and future transactions' (Gordon, 1966, p. 5).

48

Children and school

Whether or not schooling assists in a child's development depends upon his teachers' skill in presenting situations that demand shifts on his part; and whatever behaviour or learning may be elicited by a particular situation depends upon all the factors in the transactional situation: the learner himself, the teacher, the material or skill to be learnt and the situation (proximate and general) within which learning takes place. Whether or not the setting is appropriate depends upon the degree to which it is consonant with the culture within which the pupil has been and is being brought up; upon whether this culture has enabled him to build the prior intellectual structure necessary for the mastery of the concept or understanding required of him. Teachers sometimes mistake failure to learn after having been taught as an indication of a pupil's lack of native ability, whereas it may well indicate something quite different.

Any development in the child, including school learning, is a development from the structure and organization he has developed previously. The manner in which a task is presented to him also affects this development. He will not be engaged by it if it is too hard for him, that is to say, too far removed from his previous experience and, in consequence, from his present stage of development; or too easy, so that it has no power to motivate him because what it demands is well within his competence. Should it be too far removed from his emotional needs, or too threatening to his self-concept, it will similarly fail to engage him. He will undertake to master a task if it is in keeping with his level of aspiration and goals; and if it matches his present structure as a person as he sees it. In its turn, success in a new task modifies this structure (the complex organization of his concepts) and also his self-esteem (his view of himself as being competent).

A difficulty faced by many children is their teacher's belief that, because his pupils do not share his own culture they have no worth-while culture. Yet, every people and social sub-group has a culture, rich to those who value it, and it is this that each child brings to school with him as a gift to his teacher, which not only provides much of the basic material the teacher needs to be successful in his work, but which also can broaden or deepen the teacher's culture. Sometimes a 'difficult' pupil is regarded as lacking in culture, whereas in truth, his teachers find him uncomfortable because he calls the school's culture into question through his refusal to conform. Such a pupil is bound to be the loser no matter what strategy he may adopt in school. Should he conform he will be made insecure in his home culture; should he refuse to conform he is likely to be in an environment that will not encourage him to learn. He is likely to feel unwelcome in school and, as a result, there is a good chance that he will drop out and will identify exclusively with those who are scornful of the values respected by the school. Such children are often regarded as anti-social, whereas they are far more likely to be products of insensitive teachers and schools.

All children, unless they have suffered some severe damage, want to learn. This does not necessarily mean that they want to be told what to do, and when and how to do it, but rather, that they want to find things out for themselves, which is essential if they are to grow in understanding. Since learning without understanding is a humanly worthless activity, they are right to follow their inclination to get as close to the raw materials of learning as they feel they need, and not to accept learning meekly at second hand according to some pre-ordained and, to them, meaningless programme. They rightly want to discover how to be responsible for themselves and their own ideas; that is, to be involved in the learning process with heart and imagination as well as with their heads. They want to learn how to organize themselves, just as they want to learn how to get on with other people — to learn how to share, to help, to enjoy other people, to be stimulated by them and to be satisfied both by their company and by what they are doing when they have learnt how to organize themselves in a way which includes following the inclinations of others as well as their own inclinations. That is to say, they want to learn how to develop as human beings in order to be able to respect themselves on account of their personal achievements.

Pupils need their teachers to help them by ensuring that they discover the important aspects of life, and also by showing that they understand their pupils' real difficulties. These last may have little to do with the ability to master tasks set before them, being located more in the realm of understanding why it is worth striving after mastery of such tasks. What they never want are teachers who look down upon them as being somehow sub-human because they are undeveloped adults. Their chief interest is in the human element in life, and they often feel a need to be able to discuss with their teachers the most intimate elements of being human, and to do this as equals; even though they realize that their teachers have far wider experience of life than they do. They start on a quest for truth, beauty and integrity. Whether or not they persist depends in no small part upon their experience at school.

From a child's point of view it is his teacher's job to make learning exciting and to interest him in the surprises concealed in each topic. If the topic is worth studying he expects the teacher to reveal his own enthusiasm for it, to disclose his certainties about it, together with what he accepts as being the proofs which justify them, and also his opinions

— with due acknowledgment that they are no more than opinions. What he finds intolerable in teachers is remoteness and lack of sympathy, whether for himself or for the content of lessons. Similarly, he has little sympathy for teacherly concern over trivialities at the expense of what is really interesting (a ploy often used by teachers to bolster up flagging authority), for unwillingness to admit to ignorance or uncertainty, and above all for unwillingness to form a genuine relationship with pupils. Confronted by such teacher behaviour it is not surprising that many pupils look upon teachers as sub-human, beyond understanding or, as Anne Frank put it in her Diary, 'freakish'. A girl of 16 puts it thus (Blishen, 1969, p. 20), 'There is no substitute for the infectious human element, the teacher deeply in love with his subject. He alone will set fire to my soul . . . [T]each me not to be apathetic, share your wisdom, listen to my ideals.' It is noteworthy that she wrote 'share your *wisdom*' and not 'your information and knowledge'. It is a sad fact that the human element is just as infectious when it manifests hatred, boredom and indifference.

It is wrong to think that pupils' opinions do not matter and that those of teachers, the experts, are of greater importance. As Miriam Goldberg and her associates discovered, in accounting for differences between pupils in their academic attainment the differences between teachers counted for more even than the differences in pupils' IQ (see Goldberg *et al.*, 1966, especially pp. 61–2, 105 and 162). No-one who has made any study of social interaction can doubt that the social interaction of teacher and pupil is bound to be affected by the attitudes and expectations which each of them holds with respect to the other. D. F. Swift (1965) goes so far as to suggest that children differ not only in how favourably they look upon teachers, but also in the conditions upon which they are prepared to adopt a favourable attitude towards them. He suggests that it could be that both middle- and working-class pupils have an equally favourable attitude towards a teacher whom they think to be competent and conscientious, but that working-class pupils are more likely to withdraw their favour if they think that he is not.

This being so, an observer should give priority to developing sensitivity regarding observing and interpreting pupils' actions and reactions, rather than to watching the teacher's performance. As a guide to his observing he should keep in mind what the school expects its pupils to learn in the way of knowledge, skills and values, and regardless of whether he agrees with these priorities, how they are taught — including the emotional climate in the classroom, the materials and facilities employed, the methods of teaching and evaluation used, and the general requirements and routines of the school. He should note the teacher's reactions to pupils. Similarly, he should note the structure of the pupils' peer society, the membership of peer groupings, the status arrangements between and within groups, and the roles played within the class by groups and individuals. The characteristic activities, language and the 'rituals' of groups or individuals towards adults and one another in general should not be overlooked.

When studying a particular pupil an observer should take into account his level of physical development in relation to his age and the development of other members of the class (see Tanner, 1961), his apparent health and supply of energy, and his ability to co-ordinate his activities. Any defence mechanisms he employs against particular experiences or persons should be noted and an attempt made to account for them, as should willingness to seek out experience or to participate, his work output, its quantity and quality, the material he both likes and dislikes using, and his skill in using them. Also worth noting are the pupil's willingness to obey rules and regulations, the values to which his activities and demeanour pay testimony, and any remarks he may make about his own ability; also his reaction to a teacher's expressed approval or disapproval; whether or not he initiates contact with his teacher or attempts to avoid him. Any remarks he may make about the teacher will be informative about himself, as will his reactions to the activities of his peers, particularly his willingness to participate or not in activities with them. Finally, he should look for any indications of self-consciousness in the pupil. When observing adolescents he should pay particular attention to any self-consciousness that seems to have its roots in a child's physical appearance.

Armed with such information an observer will be well equipped to estimate the part played by the teacher in the lessons observed. However, he should hesitate before blaming the teacher for any apparent failure of a lesson, quite apart from it not being his business to apportion blame. He should remember, for example, that whereas controlling one's attention is difficult for adults, it is more so for children. One of the most important things a child has to try to learn whilst at school is to be aware of his own state of mind. Without this self-awareness he often will be unaware that his mind has wandered off the subject, that he is day-dreaming. As a result he will not know whether he has understood something until he puts his understanding to some kind of test. He can be certain that he really has understood something only when he has acquired the habit of concentrating, and of constantly checking with himself that he does in fact understand the matter in hand. This is closely related to the development of willingness to accept the deferment of satisfaction; and acceptance of the fact that satisfaction in many matters depends ultimately upon the prior mastery of certain skills, knowledge, etc. It is noticeable how often a day-dreaming pupil starts when a teacher calls him back to 'reality'. He does not do this because he has been found out so much as because he has failed to notice that he has stopped attending.

When observing pupils doing written work, it should be noticed how many of them appear to be doing little or nothing. If they don't seem to be worried about it the observer should consider whether this could be because they prefer doing nothing, despite the known penalties for such behaviour, to the discomfort of trying to do something without the relevant understanding needed for success; thereby at least avoiding the disappointment of getting it wrong, or, in some classes, of being held up to ridicule for stupidity, a more painful experience than being called lazy, for a pupil can claim at least some credit for having shown initiative or courage in putting a teacher in his place by disobeying him. He should notice also how the teacher reacts to this inactivity, and whether inactive pupils are willing to make an effort when help is at hand.

A further pupil stratagem to be looked for is that of doing the work set without ever checking it for correctness. He should try to establish whether this is because the pupils in question customarily succeed in getting their work right or because they are afraid, being certain that they will have made many mistakes, to dare to look out for them. If their basic, fatalistic, idea is that of getting the peril and agony out of the way as quickly as possible, and the teacher is not satisfied with passing a simple judgment of right or wrong upon his pupils' efforts, he should look to see what steps he takes to help them overcome it. During question and answer sessions he should notice whether the pupils tend to watch the teacher very closely before answering. This is normally a sign that the teacher gives clues to the right answer by his facial expressions or bodily movements. Such sessions have little or nothing to do with testing children's knowledge but are exercises in 'mind reading' that are of no use to pupils; all they can learn from them is that, with a bit of bluff and attention to irrelevant clues, you can often get away with something. An observer may learn what not to do however.

Such general observation of children in the classroom will soon give the observer a clear picture of the pupils' attitude towards schooling, whether they regard the chief business of school as learning, as getting done, getting out of the way, or evading with a minimum of effort and unpleasantness, the tasks imposed by authority. It will show him whether their motivation stems from the pleasure of learning, or the knowledge that if the task is not done 'they' will make life unpleasant, as may be expected if the job is not done 'right'. In the latter case few pupils will leave school with a strong motivation to continue learning, either formally or informally, throughout their lives. It will also show him whether they conceive of schooling in terms of unrelated tasks imposed upon them, each one an end in itself and each to be got out of the way as quickly as possible; or as a continuing exploration and means of extending experience in a variety of ultimately related fields.

Unfortunately, he is likely to find that there is more than a grain of truth in Albert Hunt's contention (1970, p. 46) that pupils do not learn much about subjects at school, but that,

> from a very early age the child becomes part of a pattern he never fully understands and is powerless to change. It is a pattern that is made up of rituals . . . that follow each other in quick succession for no apparent reason. . . . His life is part of a scheme that has been devised by people he does not know, and into which he is expected to fit without question.
>
> And it is here that we come to the real content of our education structure. At school, the child is taught by experience that it is normal for other people to organize his life. . . . [Consequently] he will *know* as an experienced fact that he must expect to be governed by other people who know better than he does.
>
> Eventually he learns that . . . it is his job to fit into the situation *as it exists* – and never to imagine that he might be capable of changing anything.

If this really is how school appears to many children, L. C. Taylor cannot be far wrong when he says (1971, p. 239) that 'many adolescents at their studies must feel as we would if forced to attend numerous lectures on the Sumerian tablets'. Yet, for most children, the awareness that school exists for their sake and the feeling that they matter as persons, not simply as potential credits to their teachers, are essential if they are to be the beneficiaries of schooling. Unless they are very secure at home, or are particularly well motivated to learn for some other reason, they are unlikely to learn well unless they are conscious of an underlying love within the classroom. Before they can begin to learn more than conformity they need to be able to relax and not be unnecessarily anxious.

This is particularly true of children who come from a background marked by poor economic, moral and cultural conditions. It is not easy, however, for a teacher to ensure that his kindness and gentleness are not mistaken by such children for weakness. They can be ruthless towards a weak and ineffective teacher, that is to say, one who really knows neither what he is doing nor why. They present a challenge to any teacher since they are likely to be unobservant, having little or nothing to observe at home, excepting potential danger, whatever form that may take. Since learning depends upon the ability to observe, a teacher needs to provide much opportunity for them to talk with him, to plan work with him, and so forth. He should give them continuous encouragement to examine closely the things that are happening about them; he should also bring many interesting things, and things uncommon to the neighbourhood, with him to school, so as to introduce the children to them and to let them handle them – in contrast to just seeing them, for example, on the TV screen.

Because of the difficulties involved in effecting creative relationships with their pupils, many teachers succumb to the temptation to conceal their genuine concern behind an all too effective screen of efficiency, which makes them appear to be cold and unloving. The question of the proper relationship between a teacher and his pupils is always difficult for, if effective learning is to take place and the pupil is to be prepared for life in the community – which is inevitably less intimate than life at home – the pupil–teacher relationship must to some extent be progressively less generally intimate as the pupil advances in his school career. The solution for a teacher lies in knowing the individual needs of each pupil regarding supportive tenderness. In the light of this he can work out when and by how much he should withdraw, and how he can do this in such a way that the pupil does not suspect a deep-level coldness towards him on the teacher's part. Many children first starting school are scared of the teacher and try to treat him in much the same way as they treat their mothers, a demand which, of course, cannot be met in full. As they grow in experience and confidence a teacher progressively distances himself from any intrusive interest in the details of their lives, endeavouring to stimulate increasing concern for matters of learning as closely related to their out-of-school world and interests as he can make them. By the time a pupil reaches secondary school he ought to have been prepared to expect and accept relatively limited, and sometimes impersonal, relationships with most of his teachers. But he has the right to expect to be able to form a close relationship with at least some of them. Unlike his earlier school experience perhaps these should generally receive their expression outside the context of formal schooling. All too frequently however they are totally lacking, or are particularized in the form of favouritism bestowed.

Children learning

It has long been known that feelings and emotion play a critical role in blocking or enhancing learning, and that they are a major determinant of what will be learnt in any situation (see Prescott, 1938). The self-concept, or organization of images which each person has about himself-in-the-world, develops over a period of time from the reflected appraisals of others. As a child is reacted to, these reactions are built into his self-image. This perceived self-in-the-world is the only reality he can know, and his behaviour is, of necessity, consistent with these perceptions. As Ira Gordon puts it (1966, p. 52),

The child's personality organization can be seen as not only a motivating, but also a selecting factor in how he behaves toward school. From the point of view of Rogers, Combs, and the perceptual, humanistic psychologists, the major motivating force for the child is the maintenance and enhancement of his already developed personality organization, or self.

There is however a further element in his self-concept, that of adequacy: the way in which he perceives what he should be, if he is really going to be adequate and effective as a member of the community. He derives this from the expectations his models have of him; those who seem to him to be much more effective than he is, among the more important of whom are his parents and teachers. The perceived self and the concept of adequacy together make up his self-concept. The degree to which there is a discrepancy between them is the source of his primary motivation. He is constantly striving to become more like his picture of himself as adequate. Awareness of discrepancies leads to the formulation of, and the attempted realization of, goals which will decrease these discrepancies. These actions are responded to by others and, in its turn, this response leads to a continuous re-evaluation by the child in the constantly changing situation, which he initiates. 'Consistent responses indicating that he is becoming more adequate stabilize the new behavior and lead to a change in the perceived self. He becomes more like his concept of adequacy, and this change is called learning' (Beatty, 1969, p. 87). A change which is found to work is used more and more, and the self-perceived self changes into that of the new person, which has previously been experimented with successfully.

As W. H. Beatty explains (1969, p. 88), 'The concept of self theory in this form helps to clarify the source of motivation in behavior and makes clear that learning must involve a change in self if it is to persist. However, this may not be too helpful to a teacher working with a particular child, until the teacher gets to know him very well.' This indicates the importance of the observer spending as much time as possible with the same limited number of children if he is to gain much from observing them. As will be seen later, extensive observation of a teacher in operation is not necessary for the observer to learn what he has to offer him; and no amount of observing of teachers can make up for a lack of observing their pupils. An observer need know nothing of the subject the children are studying, and need have no special interest in the appropriate techniques for teaching it, to benefit from studying the children.

When a teacher ignores a child's feelings he is likely to stultify the child's capacity for learning, for the child is not aware of making comparisons between his perceived self and his concept of adequacy; he is aware only of his feelings. But these feelings are his sole measure of the satisfying quality of the incoming data with which to compare his self-concept as-it-is-now. Inevitably they are of varying degrees of pleasantness or unpleasantness. Since children experience much unpleasantness regarding the adequacy of their self-concept, it follows that, if they were encouraged to share their feelings about things which happen in the classroom, the teacher would be better placed to determine whether or not learning was taking place. He would also be in a better position for discovering why certain children find learning unpleasant and in consequence difficult. A child's feelings provide the clearest evidence of the effectiveness of the teacher's teaching. Unfortunately, children receive many suggestions, both from parents and teachers, which suggest to them that their feelings are wrong. They are told, for instance, that cabbage is good for them and that they ought to like it; that doing arithmetic is fun, so they ought to enjoy it; that having an injection doesn't really hurt, even though it feels to the child as though it does! If the child is a 'good' boy, who accepts what he is told by his elders and betters, he is being taught to distrust his feelings, and, in consequence, to reject his most important valuing process.

The incorporation by an individual of the values by which he lives is effected by the ways of behaving which make him feel more adequate; in other words, those which bring him pleasant feelings. When the incoming data of others' perceptions of him are widely discrepant from what he perceives himself to be, and the feelings raised in him are highly unpleasant, his ability to learn is likely to be paralysed, at least in part. Emotion generates energy, so if a discrepancy between the child's self-concept and the incoming data is to be dissipated so as to lead to a positive and creative change in the self, the resulting emotion needs to be expressed and faced directly by all the parties involved in the situation. If instead of disapproving of a display of strong emotion in the classroom the teacher were simply to listen sympathetically to his pupils' verbal expression of emotion – whether it be anger, grief, love or whatever it may be – in most instances the need for further action would disappear. When more than this is called for such sympathetic listening could create a climate in which sufficient understanding and trust would be generated to enable the teacher to propose effective ways in which the energy could be utilized creatively.

If education is understood to be more than merely training the intellect, the importance of the acceptance of feelings and emotion in the classroom can be seen as being more than therapeutic. For:

having one's emotional reactions appraised as unacceptable while one is growing up leads to a concept of self which is stunted and immature in relationship to the ability to express one's self. The child perceives himself as an emotional person, but the models from which he gains his concept of adequacy build a picture which seems to value emotional control as the ideal. . . . The damage that some people do when they act on emotion is in large measure due to their inability to express themselves appropriately. A picture of adequacy stressing only control tends to suppress emotion, until it becomes so strong that it breaks through the carefully constructed dam . . . [and] produces disorganized behavior (Beatty, 1969, p. 90).

The development of the intellect helps the child to estimate his value to society, but it is his feelings that help him form his estimate of his value as a person, and the latter, being the primary source of all perceived values, is the more important of the two.

Since climate in the classroom — a subject about which much remains to be learnt — is at base the feelings generated in the children by the teacher, it is of great importance that these feelings should be given expression. Similarly, feelings generated in the teacher by his pupils, though they are likely to be more mature and, bearing in mind the nature of his responsibility, more restrained, should also receive appropriate expression. Many teachers make the mistake of confusing maturity with giving the appearance of being as lacking in personal feelings as a tailor's dummy. If his pupils are to learn how it is possible to express one's self when one feels emotion, whether pleasant or unpleasant, and how to do it in such a way that neither one's self nor others are hurt, a teacher, being the most mature person in his classroom, must accept their expressions of emotion as both normal and natural. Should he regard such expression as acceptable, he will not be tempted to give even indirect indications — such as the appearance of being shocked, even though the expression may sometimes be uncontrolled and excessive — that the expression of feeling is unacceptable to him as a person. As a teacher his responsibility is not that of a judge of feelings, but of one who helps the young to discover how to express the energy generated by emotion in mature and creative ways. He will do this best by presenting them with a good example of one who feels deeply, but who does not permit his feelings to hurt or damage either himself or others. In living, the intellect can be only a means to an end; and if its development is made the sole end of education, that which is purely instrumental usurps the place of life itself.

Young people, particularly during the years of infancy and child-hood, are extremely vulnerable to adult influence, but overt verbal emphasis upon standards, whether of behaviour or work, is unlikely to have much positive effect upon them. High standards of behaviour are most commonly a reflection of personal example. A good teacher sets the standard by his own performance. Yet even such a teacher cannot stimulate genuine interest in a planned programme of work, if his pupils have no particular interest in what he feels they ought to be learning. To do this he must somehow build upon their natural interest in new things, and is most likely to succeed if he can successfully associate the job in hand with the children's concept of play. The world of the young child is essentially one of play and, since a school is an abnormal society far removed from the main business of ordinary living in the world, it remains throughout most, if not all, of a child's schooling a place in which one plays. As the work of Iona and Peter Opie (1959, 1969) has shown, when children are left alone they produce complex associations and temporary social orders. Through their spontaneously produced games and adaptations of songs and stories to fit their own personalities they demonstrate their capacity for role playing as serious and noteworthy actors. For the child, this play, unlike play in the adult sense of escape, is work. It involves the developing of languages for communication, the presenting and defending of social selves in difficult situations, the defining and processing of deviants, the constructing of rules of entry into emergent social groups and rules of exit from them, and so forth. In their group play children are facing up to the problems involved in taking account of one another; they are creating situations in which they have to learn how to learn. Similarly in individual play the child is creating learning situations for himself.

Clearly an important part of schooling is that of enabling a child to make the transition from the important work of children's play to the equally important business of ordinary living-in-the-world after having left school. Part of the teacher's function is so to influence his pupils' playing that it approximates more and more to the latter. R. F. Dearden claims (1967, pp. 80–1) that 'a child's socialization largely consists in his being taught to recognize, respect and by degrees to involve himself in these seriously purposeful activities which make up the main business of ordinary living'. His definition of play as 'a non-serious and self-contained activity which we engage in just for the satisfaction involved in it' (p. 84) may be an adequate definition of adult play and of some aspects of children's play, but it ignores the large element of self-teaching in socialization. So far as socialization is concerned, therefore, he is wrong in regarding spin-off from play – such as increased awareness of aspects of the self, of others, and of the world, and familiarization with phenomena, situations, and so forth – as having nothing to do with education. Formal education is generally conducted in an unreal and abstracted situation, and, as Dearden says of play, 'is neither the pursuit of purposes dictated by common prudence, nor is it the fulfilling of an obligation to anybody' (p. 81), other than to the player himself who 'takes it seriously' because he regards it as an activity which is 'worthwhile in itself'. It might be more accurate to say that all non-technical education is a play activity. That children tend to regard school work in terms of play is suggested by their frequent refusal to take it seriously; for as Dearden says of play as a serious business, 'the point to be noticed here is that this "taking it seriously" is itself part of the game, while the game as a whole, considered not from the inside but in its relation to ordinary life, remains non-serious' (p. 82). Since 'we may place ourselves under the spell of the serious as part of the game, but we remain free to break it without neglect either to our interests or to our obligations' (p. 82), when children regard a particular 'game' in their schooling as being not worthwhile in itself, they simply contract out of playing it.

The importance of group play cannot be over-emphasized, for it is in such group play that children learn how to communicate and this is, or should be, the most important thing that any child learns and should be central to all education. Because children are aware of their need to learn this they are frequently more upset than is realized when a teacher fails to pay serious attention to their attempts to express their own ideas. As a 17-year-old boy pointedly remarks (Blishen, 1969, p. 63), 'What use are qualifications if one can't communicate with others?' The 'School of Barbiana' is equally insistent on this point and suggests that schoolchildren should be taught 'many languages, even if not so well, rather than one to perfection. So I could communicate with all kinds of people . . .' (Barbiana, 1970, p. 26), for what is needed in inter-personal communication is not a profound academic knowledge of grammar but the ability to speak, having something of value to say to and share with others, and above all, being listened to attentively.

Although the factors commonly associated with inferior reading ability are poor teaching, inappropriate methods, overcrowded classes, frequent changes of school, frequent illness or absence due to other causes, social factors, subnormal intelligence, poor vision, impaired hearing and emotional maladjustment, it is not unlikely that those which are within the teacher's control can be comprehended under the heading of the teacher's failure to grasp the conversations of his pupils and to enter into their language communities. The consequence of this is that he is unable to correlate their reading materials with their actual language. For a young child language is not an abstract entity with associated meanings but is intimately related to his relationships with other persons, the situations in which he uses language, and the activity in which he is engaged at the time when he is using language. In other words, language is living, particular, and to a certain extent unique, and rather than using just one general all-purpose language the child uses several. The problem of inferior reading ability is not of course confined to the early years of some children's schooling.

In school many children call upon no more than a small part of the capacity for learning, understanding, and creating, with which they were born. Much of this failure can be put down to poor climate in the classroom, and the observer should attempt to evaluate this in any classroom he visits. Careful observation should show him whether the pupils are failing because they are afraid of failing, in terms of disappointing or displeasing the teacher; or because the teacher is anxious on their behalf. It could show that they are failing because they are confused, because so much of the teacher's verbalizing makes little or no sense to them; either because it is formulated in accordance with adult logic, the teacher's language rather than their own, because it is in strong contradiction with what they have heard elsewhere from what they regard as a reliable source, or even because it bears no relation to what they really know from their own experience — the rough model of reality which they carry around in their memories.

In a classroom in which morale is high the observer will find that the pupils exude confidence, that they willingly exercise their reasoning powers, that they work in a spirit of co-operation and sympathy, and generally achieve good academic standards. He will find that they are alert and generally have a zest for learning; that they are prepared to use their initiative and are not always asking for permission before performing any petty yet necessary task, like sharpening a pencil or fetching a book. He will also find evidence that their knowledge is active rather than passive, that they can use knowledge learnt in one context in another not obviously related context. Furthermore, he will find that they will not be distressed if they make a mistake, but will try to learn from it without any prompting from the teacher, that they are self-disciplined, can be trusted and can trust themselves to work without constant supervision and without being under any sort of a threat.

The manner in which the teacher supervises what is happening in his classroom is clearly important for morale. This is given detailed consideration elsewhere; however, as a rough measure five general classifications might usefully be taken into account when an observer is considering children and their learning as a main focus of his attention. (1) Morale will be low in a class in which the pupils fear the teacher who 'rules with a rod of iron'; the classroom will be exceptionally quiet, pupils will hardly dare to move and the atmosphere will be tense — any learning that takes place, and there may be much, will be motivated by fear not love of learning. (2) Morale will also be low in a class which is restless, in which there is much evidence of inattention and in which the pupils' behaviour is noisy; for this indicates a lack of respect for the teacher and, unless the teacher is disinterested, he will appear to be nervous and even distraught. (3) Morale will be higher if the room is fairly quiet, with some whispering and inattention, and if the teacher restores order with an occasional reprimand or warning look: in such classes the teacher is normally sensitive to minor lapses in conduct. (4) It will be higher still in classrooms in which the teacher is not normally on the look-out for misconduct; in such classes pupils are normally attentive to the job in hand and work proceeds with little or no interruption. (5) Classes in which morale is highest are those in which pupils are obviously actively interested and busy with their school work; there may be a general buzz of conversation, but this will be related to the work; the atmosphere will be free and natural, and usually there will be no question of misconduct (making allowances for youthful high spirits), even when the teacher is out of the room. The pupils will be seen to be able to govern themselves and will clearly wish to do so. Should a pupil create a disturbance, his peers will effectively cope with the situation and restore good working conditions.

The teacher's attitude towards his pupils will also give the observer some useful clues. If he is critical, fault-finding, harsh and definitely unfriendly, morale will be low. If he is aloof and talks down to his pupils, is impatient with interruptions and digressions, it will not be much higher. It will be higher if the teacher is serious, reserved and sets exacting standards; but it will not be particularly high, for such teachers customarily stir up competitive effort which boosts the few at the expense of the many. Morale will normally be highest when the teacher is friendly towards his pupils, but not over-familiar with them, and is ready to enter into conversation with them and, without rebuke, is prepared to accept any opening gambit from a pupil in order to direct the ensuing conversation along worth-while channels. He normally gives evidence of a ready, but not hearty, sense of humour and he usually seems to be able to satisfy his pupils that he has a good understanding of their points of view.

6 Children with problems

It is an abuse of language to speak of problem children. There are children with problems, and they sometimes cause their teacher problems, but the child himself is not the teacher's problem. If he is a problem to anyone he is a problem to himself. To call a child a problem child is to succumb to the temptation of categorizing pupils; of depersonalizing them. One stereotyped problem child is the stupid child: the child who seems to be lacking in intelligence and creativity and unable to understand the instructions and explanations he receives in class. In many cases such children appear far less dull outside classrooms and quite able to pick things up quickly – some, for example, can perform prodigious feats of memory regarding league football results and matches long past – and to develop self-initiated play in a creative fashion. In other words, outside the classroom they are doing what satisfies their interests, plans, dreams, worries and so forth, and they probably appear to go stupid in class because they are keeping their time, energy and thought for what they feel to be important; that is to say, their own lives as they are able to live them.

Such a child may well feel unable to afford much of himself in order to please his teacher, so he adopts the stratagem of stupidity as a means of escape. The underlying reason for his classroom behaviour may be fear, an inability to see any good reason for being in school, or a mixture of both. The result is always the same, boredom and resistance to schooling. Very young children, excepting the most obviously defective, or those like Pattie O'Driscoll in Iris Murdoch's novel *The Time of the Angels* who had been 'brutalized by unhappiness into a condition which resembled mental deficiency', are not stupid; though some are slower at learning than others. They have positive attitudes and, unless they have suffered severe frustration at home or have been actively dissuaded from doing so, plunge into life, for they are naturally curious about their world and its limits. Yet after a few years at school many are apathetic, bored, and listless, their curiosity in the school-room has been deadened, they are stupid.

This is unlikely to be a natural development; it doesn't happen to all pupils. The reason must lie in the tasks children are given to do, or in the attitude of their teachers to them. Their capacity for concentrating on school work either never develops or it atrophies, because experience has taught them that school work is not interesting, or the effort to please demands a higher price than they are able to pay. As a consequence, their attention shifts to what does interest them, and they pay no more attention to school work than is needed to get by, or to get away with being stupid. An observer should notice how children, if they are presented with situations, materials, and problems, that are interesting and exciting to them, even though their natural rate of working is slow, not only manifest a high degree of attention, interest, concentration and involvement, but also develop the habit of wanting to act intelligently in most if not all situations. To notice this development, however, he would need to observe the same children at intervals over an extended period of time. Habits, both good and bad, are easy to acquire, but difficult to break. The observer will find that whereas pupils who have developed the habit of acting intelligently find it comparatively hard not to learn something in any situation, those with a well established habit of acting stupidly find it comparatively hard to learn anything, even when they wish to do so. They will have convinced themselves that, so far as school is concerned, they are 'thick' and not worth bothering about. They will have stopped thinking in school, and the only hope for them is a teacher who, with much love and patience, may be able to start them thinking again, by finding materials for study which really interest them.

Fear

Fear, which destroys intelligence, is a common element in stupidity. Signs of fear in pupils' faces, voices, gestures, movements and ways of working, are not normally pronounced, for children try to conceal their fear in school, whether it is a fear of trouble, embarrassment, punishment, disapproval, loss of status, or whatever it may be. In written work, for example, indications may be of a pupil's anxiety about being right, or of his lack of conviction, which leads him to form letters indistinctly when he is uncertain of a spelling. A pupil who looks upon school work as essentially keeping teacher happy is unlikely to think adventurously and will stick closely to answers known to be approved of by the teacher. If he is aware that his rate of working is slower than that of the majority, fear of ridicule or shame may make him withdraw, distrust his own answers, and in time even suspect that the world is a fundamentally unreasonable place, events being the outcome of fate. If work is going to be correct it will be correct, and vice versa. Such a child is likely to make a stab at getting a quick answer before he has even considered what he is trying to do, and to be unable to concentrate upon or attend to the task. To do a piece of work means to strike out into the dangerous unknown with no clear reason for doing so other than teacher's orders.

The pupil who has not learnt to think cannot stand uncertainty. Because having no answer to a set task or problem imposes great strain he is likely to regard any answer as better than none, for it relieves the pressure. Yet, without thinking intelligence cannot develop. An observer will expect to see a teacher with such a pupil concentrating upon the child's capacity for thinking, and not just upon getting answers from him. Children crave security. Only as they gain confidence in the stability of the world around them can they learn to tolerate the strain of unanswered questions and unresolved problems and learn to think about things without panicking. It is true that some children are slower than others at apprehending the world as it is, in learning how to think clearly, or in accepting the dependability of the world as assured. All this means is that they require more time. A child's behaviour is related to his intellectual and emotional development, rather than to his calendar age. When a teacher demands behaviour believed to be appropriate to the calendar age of such a child he may be asking more than can be given. If the child has been brought up to be well behaved he may well concentrate upon keeping his teacher happy, at the expense of learning. A child who is mentally and emotionally 8 years old cannot naturally play the role of a 12-year-old. He would have to concentrate his attention upon the negative objective of not doing what is natural to an 8-year-old.

Depression

For healthy learning to take place, emotion must be directed toward the situation or person which arouses the individual to action. A child inexperienced in inter-personal relationships is often unable to know himself as a person; and consequently adopts an objective stance *vis-à-vis* himself, envisaging his self as an object and, acting as though it were another person, directing the emotion at himself. Such emotion is often experienced as depression; in simple terms, the inability of the self to act when action seems called for. Although little is known about depression in children, the possibility of there being a connection between it and such inflexible behaviour in children as breakdown in motivation, opting out, inability to listen and remember, slowness in the completion of tasks, appears to be strong. Such behaviour is often put down to laziness or stupidity, and an observer should take advantage of being able to study children displaying it without having responsibility for teaching them. Of course it cannot be taken as positive evidence of psychiatric disorder. However, if a pupil manifests other symptoms associated with depressive illness, his teacher should be careful not to make too great demands upon him. Symptoms indicating possible depression include persistent headaches, fits of dizziness, feelings of emotional suffocation, food fads, abdominal pains or constipation, disturbance of the menstrual rhythm; in young children, severe rages beyond the child's control; in adolescents, lack of interest in members of the opposite sex. Knowledge of the child's home, his performance in other lessons and out of class, his attitude towards food and so on, can help both teacher and observer in such cases.

Since being depressed means, among other things, having a low estimate of one's self – a very poor self-image – carelessness on a teacher's part can easily reinforce or intensify this estimate of worthlessness. On the other hand a child who feels deep down that he has real value in his teacher's estimation may be helped to overcome his depression, hence to improve his performance, and so to avoid the condition becoming chronic and developing to the point at which psychiatric help becomes essential. Young people are extremely vulnerable to adult influence. As Erwin Stengel comments (1969, pp. 55–6),

> The lack of a secure relationship to a parent figure in childhood
> [0–15 years] may have lasting consequences for a person's ability to
> establish relationships with other people. Such individuals are likely
> to find themselves socially isolated in adult life, and social isolation
> is one of the most important factors in the causation of suicidal acts.
> Fortunately, the 'broken home' . . . has no permanent ill effects, if,
> as often happens, parent substitutes are found who compensate for
> the lack or loss of the primary love object.

But children who move frequently, for example, are unlikely to establish firm relationships with adults outside the home other than with their teachers. J. W. B. Douglas in his longitudinal study (1967, p. 57) claims that 32 per cent of his sample moved to a new area in their primary school years alone. Suicide attempts by children under 15 are rare of course; but, for example, Professor I. H. Mills has reported (*Guardian*, 6 September 1971) nearly 15 per cent of all medical admissions to hospital in Cambridge in 1970 were attempted suicides and 50 per cent of all new patients admitted to psychiatric units were aged between 15 and 20. As Stengel says (1969, p. 55), as a general rule, 'traumatic childhood experiences tend to make the individual unstable and liable to break down under emotional stress'. Schools that fail to provide for emotional education, and teachers who are unwilling to establish firm and warm relationships with pupils, must bear some responsibility for this situation.

Subnormality

The general level of intellectual development in some children, whatever their individual gifts may be, is so much lower than that of the average that they would be better suited to a special school. However, the paucity of such schools means that an observer is likely to encounter some of them in the classes he observes. A study of 11,000 children, conducted by K. Pringle *et al.* (1966), suggests that not less than 13 per cent of those children were already in difficulties by the age of 7, that two-thirds of these were not receiving any special help, and one-third had not even been referred for investigation of their problems to either the school health or the school psychological services.

It is no more possible to generalize about educationally subnormal children — however that phrase may be interpreted — than it is about normal children. The intellectual strengths and weaknesses of each child must be known, so that, so far as possible, a specific programme of learning can be devised for him. A 'subnormal' child usually has a level of language development below that of his over-all mental development. To be able to help him his teacher first needs to know whether his difficulty is one of speaking or one of understanding language; it could be either. Furthermore, since a child's initial performance on a task bears little relation to the level finally achieved, he needs to determine the child's relative assets and deficits, and to build upon the former. In presenting work to the pupil he needs to divide the task into finely graded steps, to employ carefully worked out incentives, to devise a greater number of approaches to a problem or task than a more able pupil would need and probably to provide more time for learning to take place — though this may not always be necessary.

To plan an appropriate learning programme properly necessitates making a far more thorough and continuous assessment of the whole range of the pupil's development than is needed for a less unusual child, including perhaps his progress in specific processes within a particular sphere of ability. It should be remembered that learning disabilities need not necessarily affect all aspects of the child's intellectual functioning to an equal extent, though such children often have difficulty in concentrating their attention, and in the early years may well have to learn how to. Because they are likely to be bewildered by the world at large consistency between school activities and home culture is particularly important, as is co-operation with the family and perhaps even parental involvement in the school, if this is at all possible. Since care of such children in a normal class is time consuming and makes such great demands upon the teacher, an observer may well be of considerable assistance if he pays particular attention to them and, under guidance from the teacher, helps them with their learning. He would learn much to help him in his future career.

The clumsy child

In his report for 1966—8 the Chief Medical Officer of the Department of Education and Science drew attention to a generally unrecognized problem:

> Rebuke is one of the occupational hazards of a school child and whilst this is sometimes warranted there are occasions when a child is unpopular and gets into trouble for reasons outside his own control of which the teacher or parent is unaware. Defective hearing and petit mal are classical examples and to these may be added specific clumsiness (DES, 1969, p. 90).

Such children are so clumsy in gait and manipulation and prone to articulation defects and visuo-motor disability that it interferes with their schooling. Although the available evidence suggests they are of normal or above average intelligence few make satisfactory progress in school. One report indicates that spelling and arithmetic presented the greatest problem to them. Brenner *et al.* comment (1967, p. 259),

> we can also confirm . . . that when these disorders are present without obvious neurological signs the children affected seldom receive the understanding and sympathy which might be thought their due . . . such children are often accused of laziness or misbehaviour, or suspected of being mentally dull. In spite of mounting problems at school, none had been referred to the educational psychologist or the child guidance clinic.

In fact, in the period under review only one child was referred for specialist help, and this was to a child psychiatric clinic because of emotional disturbance rather than difficulty in learning. Should referral be made as soon as such children come to notice, either as backward or naughty children, 'parental anxiety may be allayed and the children may less often be unfairly rebuked; in either case, psychiatric disorder in the child becomes less likely' (DES, 1969, p. 91). The extent of the problem does not appear to be fully known, but it is likely that in unstreamed primary schools each class would contain such a child, if they were evenly spread over the country. In secondary schools they are likely to be in remedial units, or to have been designated mentally retarded.

Economic deprivation

The cycle of deprivation experienced by many children naturally affects the teacher. The sleepy, hungry or frustrated child is constantly irritable and merely keeping a class in order can become an endless struggle. However, children who arrive at school ill-shod, ill-fed, over-tired, or in need of medical attention, are not necessarily the victims of parental laziness. According to Frank Field, Director of the Child Poverty Action Group, 'poor families can't win in this business. If the mother doesn't go to work, income is too low to provide properly for the family. If she does she is accused of neglecting her children' (*Guardian*, 4 March 1971). Sheer physical pressures operate against deprived children. As Don Brazier, a primary school head in Birmingham, wrote (*Guardian*, 4 March 1971), 'Take a West Indian child, for instance. They are extroverts to the nth degree. They need room to let off steam. But they live in overcrowded homes, they come to overcrowded schools, there is just nowhere for them to play and release all their exuberance.'

In the face of such pressures it is not surprising there are so many 'maladjusted' children in our schools. According to the Chief Medical Officer of the Department of Education and Science, between 1957 and 1967 the number of children treated at child guidance clinics increased from 32,011 in 229 clinics to 61,358 in 367 clinics. 'On average, one school child in 124 (1/124 in England, 1/129 in Wales) attended a child guidance clinic in 1967' (DES, 1969, p. 14). Ratios varied and were as high as 1/26 in Grimsby. The increase in children under treatment was due, in the main, to an increase in psychiatrists employed, yet there is still 'a widespread shortage of medical and educational provision for severely disturbed adolescent boys and girls' (p. 17); quite apart from those who are less disturbed, but are still in need of specialist help (see Clegg and Megson, 1968, *passim*). Similarly, it is not surprising that there are so many children with speech disorders. 'The number of school children treated for defective speech increased from 49,187 in 1957 to 67,894 in 1,420 clinics in 1967. This increase was not due to more children having defective speech but to more treatment facilities for them' (p. 17). 'On average, one school child in 112 (112 in England, 105 in Wales) was treated by speech therapists in 1967' (p. 18), the ratio in Northamptonshire being as high as 1 in 34. In his report he states that,

> Every child who has difficulty in school requires physical (including neurological) and psychological examination to discover defects of vision, hearing, movement or speech, or disturbance in emotional or intellectual development that may be a primary or contributory

cause of his difficulties. The influence of social factors also needs to be considered. Frequently, a number of disorders contribute to his poor performance in school (p. 84).

They may *require* such examination, but many are not examined because facilities for examination and treatment are insufficient to meet the demand. An observer should, nevertheless, discover what facilities are available, how they are brought in on a particular case and also the attitude of the school towards their being called in, just as he should when he begins his teaching career; for no teacher can teach efficiently if a proportion of his pupils are not fit for learning.

Immigrant status

To be an immigrant pupil is to have a potential problem. Unless the family has been established in the United Kingdom for longer than the ten years customarily assigned to immigrant status, an immigrant child is almost certain to experience a conflict of cultures. To be successful in school he needs to feel at ease there. Whether or not he does so depends largely upon the attitudes of teachers and the non-teaching members of staff with whom he may come into contact. It depends also upon the establishing of a good relationship of mutual confidence and understanding between the school staff and the child's parents. If such confidence and understanding are to be established something needs to be known of the social and religious customs of the child's country of origin, and of his personal religious tradition; particularly in the case of a girl, for many come from countries in which women are scarcely emancipated. In a school geared mainly to the needs of British children, such a child may have problems regarding clothing, changing for PE, diet and such like; quite apart from more serious cultural problems. Even when every effort is made to help him feel at home in the school, he is likely to need an extended period of time before adjusting fully to the social circumstances and customs of his new environment, if only because the members of staff, being British, cannot help creating an essentially British environment.

Many immigrant children have little knowledge of English on arrival in this country. The parents of those born here are likely to have spoken only their own language within the home, which is probably the only environment known by a child before entering school. Even if it should be English, it is likely to be very different from the vernacular of the locality, which again may be different from the English of the school's teaching staff. In consequence, immigrant children are likely to be slower than average both in learning to speak English and in learning to express themselves clearly and fluently. Lack of fluency impedes not only subject learning but also adjustment to school life; and 'As with all children, native or immigrant, behaviour problems will follow if difficulty with language is not promptly recognized and dealt with' (DES, 1969, p. 20). Even a firm grasp of vernacular English does not obviate all problems; for example, the real educational challenge of West Indian children is equipping them to profit from a verbalized school system, since their culture is not so verbal as ours. As the editorial of *New Society* (18 March 1971) commented,

> whilst it may be true that the presence of immigrants in Britain only highlights the deficiencies already built into the social fabric, it is also true that the problems the immigrant faces are worse than anyone else's. And of all the injustices, stunting of intellect is the most explosive.

The chief cause of such maiming is insensitive school provision.

Adolescence

But problems are not just the consequence of abnormalities. The problems of adolescents, for example, are experienced in varying degrees by all children and are often penalized unjustly, thus adding to pupils' difficulties. It might be thought that a student-teacher, as a recent graduate from adolescence, would be very conscious of these. But, since his memories are likely to be painful and disturbing, he is apt to push them out of his conscious mind as he endeavours to adapt to adult status as a teacher and, when problems manifest themselves, he may tend to suppress them with undue haste because they disturb his own security.

Although the problems of adolescence mostly concern secondary school teachers, the development of middle schools has introduced them into their top forms, particularly in the case of girls. The adolescent's approach to life is different from that of the child, and an adolescent in a community of children tends to feel out of place. It should be remembered that 1·4 per cent of all girls are sexually mature by the age of 11, and that girls from one-child families tend to reach puberty early — 53 per cent starting their periods before 12 years 10 months, the figure for all girls at the same age being 39 per cent. From the point of view of the teacher, it is a regrettable fact that early maturity makes adolescents restive sooner, and prolonged schooling makes them restive longer. Underlying this restiveness is the adolescent's experience of considerable uncertainty and insecurity, for adolescence is rather like a second period of infancy.

The adolescent tends to worry about his competencies, his normality — both in view of the changes taking place in himself, and also in view of the fact that they do not take place at the same time as they appear to in some or many of his peers — also about his capacity for self-control and about his status *vis-à-vis* adults. Common consequences of his problems are moodiness, inconsistency of behaviour and resentment of demands for regularity — for he almost always identifies this with childhood. This resentment presents the adolescent with a particular problem since, on the one hand, he is likely to regard such demands as unreasonable, yet, on the other, he is likely to be aware that such regularity is necessary for him, since it provides the security within which his 'new self' can be tried out in public. The intensity of adolescent feelings is illustrated by Anne Frank (1954, pp. 63—4) who wrote when she was thirteen,

> I'm boiling with rage . . . because of the horrible words, mocking looks and accusations which are levelled at me repeatedly every day, and find their marks. . . . I can't let them see the wounds which they have caused, I couldn't bear their sympathy and their kind-hearted jokes, it would only make me want to scream all the more. If I talk, everyone thinks I'm showing off; when I'm silent they think I'm ridiculous; rude if I answer, sly if I get a good idea, lazy if I'm tired, selfish if I eat a mouthful more than I should, stupid, cowardly, crafty, etc. etc. . . . and although I laugh about it and pretend not to take any notice, I *do* mind. . . . I do my very best to please everybody far more than they'd ever guess.

An observer is likely to see conflicting desires in older pupils, who sometimes expect to be treated as adults, yet at other times wish to be more childishly dependent. This is confusing both to pupils and teachers. Some will be in love with the idea of romantic love and may attempt to test their ability to love and their capacity to be regarded as lovable on one of their teachers. This too can present problems if the teacher is young and inexperienced. He may be flattered; he may equally well be disturbed and rebuff the pupil. Neither response is helpful to an adolescent who is in need of sympathetic but firm guidance if he is to experiment appropriately and to be supported when he is in danger of failing — a very acute fear in adolescents. The strains of adolescence generate fluctuations in interest and enthusiasm and at times perseverance is difficult if not impossible; a temporary break-down in relations at home for instance may so disturb an adolescent's security that, quite properly, he will regard the resolution of the problem as the most important work to hand. Hence the importance of encouraging a breadth of interest in adolescent pupils, and of making every effort to ensure that some genuine insight of value results from even the most transitory burst of enthusiasm for a subject, topic or idea. The importance of a teacher being genuinely approachable should not be underestimated for during adolescence a child is faced with the problem of establishing a new kind of relationship with his parents. Since many parents resist this change a teacher may well be the only adult to whom many pupils can turn for help, reassurance and guidance.

The problem of stress

It is clear that many of the problems of school children are the product of stress that originates in modern living conditions. In the medical world the term stress is usually taken to refer to the physical and psychological effects of over-exertion, particularly of mental over-exertion. As R. D. Martin puts it (1970, p. 1087),

> It is possible for human beings to exhibit symptoms of stress almost entirely as a result of intellectual pressure. . . . It is an important point that one can include man's intellectual functions within the concept of human social stress and that one is not forced to specu-late about divisions between innate, conditioned and insight-controlled behaviour patterns. The vital thing about stress is that the responses involved are generally of a universal kind, though the causes may vary widely. The phenomenon of stress is so all-embracing that Selye [1957] suggested that there is some source of 'adaptation energy' to cope with any stressful experience. He regar-ded the production of such adaptation energy as essentially limited; when it runs out the organism dies. One can even regard old age as a condition where the source of adaptation energy is drying up. This fits in with the various indications that continued stress leads to premature 'ageing' and eventual death.

Although most research into the effects of various degrees of social stress has been conducted with animals, and the results of such work cannot be extended uncritically to human society, it is reasonable for Martin to suggest (ibid.), as a working hypothesis, that 'as a general principle, it may be that, in all mammals, stressful experience, either from the general environment or specifically from members of the same species, produce changes in the body chemistry, and that these changes give rise to certain pathological alterations (say, in behaviour) if stress is continuous'. For example, tree-shrews which grow up in a stressed population never achieve normal body weight, even if stressful

73

experiences are later eliminated; also, when tree-shrews are moved to a new cage they often produce those gastric symptoms commonly associated in humans with travel, particularly to foreign countries; symptoms due, not as is commonly supposed to a change of diet, but that are a stress response to a novel situation; social factors naturally playing a large part in any such response.

The county educational psychologists of Essex report (*Guardian*, 24 April 1971) finding a much higher proportion of poor readers among pupils in Basildon new town's primary schools than in the more established schools in the surrounding area. This suggests that many of the poor readers were emotionally disturbed as a result of their having moved into a novel situation. According to Hans Selye (1957), observed changes in body chemistry are basically responses to short-term stress and their physical manifestations are by-products of the attempt to respond with top-performance under conditions requiring special effort. The problem is not this 'general adaptation syndrome', which in itself is harmless, but the continued excitation of the syndrome. Experiments with animals show that it is not overcrowding that leads to bizarre self-destructive behaviour, but the pressure of competition. The competitive pressures of the 'rat-race' also reveal symptoms of stress in man which confirm that competitive and aggressive policies are inappropriate in school. Hence, school work should be planned with human tolerances in mind, which means accepting some 'inefficiency' and reducing competition to the inescapable minimum. Stress in children can be generated by so simple a matter as having an 'odd' even though common surname, for such names have been found to be a significant factor in psychiatric disorders in children (Bagley and Evan-Wong, 1970).

Although there is no agreement among experts about the extent to which stress, as distinct from poor economic conditions, generates failure in children, the figures speak for themselves. For example, about 2 per cent of all pupils in full-time education in school are in special institutions or attending child guidance clinics and remedial centres. Five per cent of pupils in the Newsom Report survey were described as creating serious behaviour problems. D. H. Stott (1966) suggests that 8 per cent of girls and 11–15 per cent of boys show indications of behaviour disturbance. Since behaviour problems in school stem primarily from learning failure – which is a consequence of deprivation of affection and security rather than of economic distress – it comes as no surprise to learn that 'one child in five has no stable home even before he is born – his world is shaky even before he can yell at it' (Smithells, 1971, p. 313). The striking increase in sexual activity among adolescents, to which the statistics on illegitimate births and legal abortions testify, which indicates craving for affection, personal meaning and significance, as does the rapid increase in the number of attempted suicides among young people (see Stengel, 1969); the increase in the number of children taken into care and the reasons for this, as recorded in the Registrar General's statistical reviews, all tell the same story.

Clearly a teacher is severely restricted in what he can do to relieve children under stress, but he can at least be aware when a child is under stress. Knowledge of the child's background will help, though different children behave in different ways under virtually identical conditions. Since the anxious child may be undetectable except when he is under stress, a teacher should look for signs of possible stress when the child is working, such as tense facial expressions, darting looks round the room to see what other children are doing or how they are coping, a busily working tongue, intense scratching or rubbing of parts of the body or spasmodic and feverish movements of any kind. It is often difficult to distinguish signs of stress having a social origin from those due to the strains of adolescence. When help is clearly needed it is not enough for the teacher to be 'nice and kind'. If he cannot supply the need identified himself, he must approach the appropriate agency. School failure is of course often simply a way of hitting back at frustrating, domineering or possessive parents or society in some other form and, more than anything else, children who fail simply lack a sound basis for self-respect, and this lies at the root of their being stressed. What J. P. Martin has to say about criminals (1971, p. 332), many of whom, so far as their criminality is concerned, are little more than victims of stress, is just as true of school children.

> Criminals, like everyone else, need someone to care for. Criminals are often said to need help, and so they may; but even more they need to be needed by others. A capacity to give help, to be responsible for others, is a better basis for self-respect than to receive assistance, however skilfully it may be given.

Not only does adolescence cover the whole of a child's secondary schooling, it is also a period of high idealism and vulnerability, a time when serious hurt can be experienced, particularly when idealism fails or is subjected to ridicule. For most adolescents, unless they have very ambitious parents, working for examinations is a comparative irrelevancy which interferes with the real business of life at this stage of development; namely, coming to terms with one's self as self and as a member of society. Hence, whilst normal stress in adolescence may disrupt formal learning habits, it is not in itself a sign of mental trouble.

The teacher's main difficulty lies in interpreting from the indications of stress in his pupils whether it is normal or requires attention from a specialist. Yet, since normal adolescent stress problems, compounded by a degree of social stress, may well contribute towards the generating of serious problems for the child, he should be generous in providing support, encouragement and opportunity, both to exercise responsibility and to be genuinely involved with others. There is probably little he can do directly to reduce stress already generated, but, by such simple expedients as permitting mobility whilst they are working and providing opportunity for some release from the constant pressure of the proximity of other people and of demands that cannot be met, he can avoid increasing it. It should not be forgotten that the good pupil, the one who co-operates in everything at school and who stays at home out of school hours, may be suffering from stress more than many others; certainly as much as the troublesome ones. Both suffer from a lack of real friends and are unsure of their real identities.

7 Culture conflict and the school

Alienation from school

'The child from a poor family and a bad neighbourhood is confronted in school with an alien culture. Failure to adjust rapidly to this culture has meant failure in school.' These words, written of the American situation (Hutchins, 1970, p. 26), are equally true of the British scene, and of all countries which have adopted the traditional Western pattern of academic education. 'The African drop-out leaves school for the same reason as his American counterpart', as R. M. Hutchins says (pp. 52–3); 'the effort required to master the alien culture is disproportionate to the benefit he thinks he will receive from it'. The beginnings of the process can be seen as early as the first years in the primary school (see Douglas, 1967, p. 28 *et passim*). Alienation may have many different root causes, and may also show itself in different ways. An observer should learn to recognize signs of alienation and to evaluate the efficacy of any steps taken against it that he observes. Concern about alienation is not just a piece of covert social work however – it is also essentially an educational concern. As Mary Warnock says (1971, p. 157),

> alienation – the sense that decisions are made remotely, which are irreversible, and the reasons for which are unclear – may have a widespread effect not only on people's happiness in a vague sense of the word, but more precisely on their willingness to work or to accept sacrifices. These remote and apparently whimsical decisions must not be made too often. All this is obvious though. But a way to avoid the feeling of severance from decisions which affect us is extremely hard to discover.

Alienation is a common problem in large schools. This is not so much a consequence of size as such, but of possible consequences of size, especially bureaucratization. There is generally a greater need to spell out rules and procedures and this can lead to impersonality in relationships. Whether or not someone is alienated depends, by and large, upon what he hopes to gain from his membership of the

77

institution, whether school or factory. Since acceptance as a person is a strongly felt need in most children, unless a child is exceptionally secure in his out of school life, failure to gain acceptance as a worth-while person in school is likely to lead to a degree of alienation (see Musgrove, 1971, pp. 60–4).

The sort of child likely to become alienated in a primary school is one less well socially 'trained' than his teacher might wish. An insensitive teacher will keep him on stricter rein 'for the sake of discipline' (i.e. the teacher's convenience) than more compliant pupils. Such a child is, for example, not allowed out of sight, or not usually permitted to share in potentially messy activities. In extreme cases he may even be banned from a class or group outing, 'because he can't be trusted' or for some other equally rationalizing excuse. Such exclusions and the other restrictions he suffers hurt him more than most children, because he is less well drilled than they to sit still, be quiet, or suffer boredom, without rebelling. Rightly, he feels unwanted and unaccepted.

A more serious yet more common cause of alienation is repeated failure, which leads to demoralization, defeatism, and reduced effort, which in their turn lead to worse failure. When failure becomes really bad a basic personality factor generally determines whether the pupil becomes apathetic in the classroom, or an aggressive troublemaker. The latter tendency, once established, develops progressively, for an aggressive pupil attracts exemplary punishment which reinforces his hostility and generates more extreme rebellion. The possibility of constructive education ceases with teacher and pupil locked in a struggle which each feels he must win if he is to maintain his self-respect.

Alienated early leavers generally express their alienation in terms of boredom (see Schools Council, 1968, paras 104–13, 115–18 and 123–6) and appear to derive little benefit from schooling. For many the last years at school seem to be pointless and the prospect of paid work attractive. Though disappointment with work often follows few want to return, except when the employment situation is bad; even then they would prefer work to school (see SCRE, 1971). Of a substantial sample of Scottish early leavers, one year out of school, it has been said: 'Once the young people left school they seemed to have little enthusiasm for the more serious forms of literature; indeed, over one-third of them appeared to have read little of any description, serious or otherwise, since leaving school' (ibid., p. 126). The most probable explanation is that the culture and values of school struck these ex-pupils as being quite alien to the secure culture of the home environment. Daniel Jenkins (1961, p. 131) goes further. 'It has been said', he comments, that it takes about six weeks for life on the shopfloor of the average factory to remove all traces of years of schooling from many young people. Whether that is true or not, it is certainly true that among manual workers in particular, the world of school and the world of work appear to be pulling in opposite directions.

Since in a competitive world, job satisfaction is unlikely to be achieved by many who are unable to pass competitive examinations, formal education should at least fit them to discover possible satisfaction in creative and healthy recreational pursuits. Because it doesn't, many alienated pupils feel like prisoners, subject to pettiness and boredom, like the prisoner sewing mailbags, the result being a sense of frustration and uselessness. Alienation is not, however, confined to potential early leavers. Another form, just as serious and potentially more dangerous, is that manifested by those alienated from most of their fellows. Schools sometimes encourage pupils to pursue such an approach to life in terms of adding to the glory of the school. An editorial in *New Society* (31 December 1971) has described such a pupil as 'the pure technician, the classless bright young man without background, with no other original aim than to make his way in the world and no other means than his technical and managerial ability', adding from an article published in the *Observer* in 1944,

> it is the lack of psychological and spiritual ballast, and the ease with which he handles the terrifying technical and organisational machinery of our age, which makes this slight type go extremely far nowadays. . . . This is their age; the Hitlers and Himmlers we may get rid of, but the Speers, whatever happens to this particular special man will long be with us.

To concentrate attention upon the technical job, as such schools do, without giving equal consideration to the moral problems redefined by powerful techniques and technology, is to generate serious potential danger to the well-being of society. Even Albert Speer (1970, p. 524) comments on the Speer of the 1940s: 'Dazzled by the possibilities of technology, I devoted crucial years of my life to serving it. But in the end my feelings about it are highly sceptical.'

Youth culture

A further form of alienation most commonly found among more able pupils goes under the name of youth culture. It has its origin in the lack of common standards and norms in the community as a whole.

Personality is substantially affected by early social experiences, and children from a variety of different backgrounds and cultures are segregated from the bulk of the adult world and exposed for long periods to the concentrated influence of their age-equals. If they grow out of or fail to grow into sympathy with their teachers' culture, the compulsion to adopt peer dominated other-directedness (Riesman, 1950) as a satisfying substitute for involvement in the community of learning is strengthened. This is due more than anything else to the failure of schools to encourage the use of imagination and empathy by pupils. When a pupil identifies with a specific peer group, for there are many specific youth cultures having much in common rather than a single monolithic youth culture, the norms of the group acquire tremendous influence, overriding any private notions he may have about right and wrong conduct, even eliminating all thought of them.

Since schools can only be successful to the extent that their pupils are committed to what they have to offer, the teacher who simply looks upon the local manifestations of youth culture as a threat to his efforts, which to him represent standards and values that are self-evidently good, merely confirms his pupils' estimate of school as a place where teachers and others have constructed a complex set of meaningless rules and unstated expectations, supported by unjust rewards and punishments. In so far as a youth culture rejects school it rejects the deferral of gratification and the acceptance of subordinate status by pupils (in comparison with all adults but especially with teachers), and, in general terms, emphasizes spontaneous gratification of desires and repudiation of the subordination of youth to adults. In youth culture teenagers are grown up; that is to say, they are equal in status to adults though different in kind. Understandably, commitment to youth culture fosters under-achievement in traditional school work and bad conduct and attendance records. Regrettably, many teachers do not recognize the stress generated by having to choose between being pupil and teenager when a young person is trying to adjust to a new awareness of himself, to give shape to his life and to make himself into the kind of person he wishes to be (or to be seen to be by others if he feels the need to defend himself from attack).

So far as education is concerned unreflecting conformity to the norms of a youth culture is no worse than unreflecting conformity to the norms mediated by parents and teachers. Rather than engaging in unfruitful battles with his pupils a teacher should try to counter such conformism by creating conditions in which his pupils can experience personal responsibility and develop positive qualities of character; that is to say, to create conditions in which they can be true to themselves and so be true to other people. The extended period of schooling, exploitation of the teenage market and the need to be free from childish dependence upon parents, impose considerable strains upon young people today. In membership of a youth culture they find relief; it might even be called the opium of youth. On the other hand, to those who are not alienated it can provide relaxation from hard work and worry. The fact that most teachers may prefer to work in their gardens and to listen to Radio 3 is neither here nor there. On its own terms, youth culture can provide intellectual stimulus. For example, as Paul Overy puts it (1971, p. 158), not only is rock music 'central to the lives of a very broad spectrum of people of all classes aged under 25' it also

> seems to occupy the same position of 'centrality' in the alternative press that English literature had for F. R. Leavis and the *Scrutiny* critics in the 1930s and 1940s. For articulate and intelligent young people today, rock music is not *just* a cultural phenomenon, but a kind of embodiment of (to use a phrase of Leavis's) 'lived life'. An activity which combines artistic expression with moral fervour.

Without necessarily liking the public expression of youth culture genuine educators will understand its dynamics and sympathize with what is good in it; accepting that young people today, being no longer destined to follow in their parents' footsteps, are faced by a great range of possible choices both for life style and career. Since the traditional teacher—pupil relationship is an extension of a parent—child relationship originating in a society in which such hope as a child had for his future depended, by and large, upon conformity to parental wishes, and this parent—child relationship is now rejected by many adolescents, it is hardly surprising that many pupils regard teachers as unnecessary. Even those wishing to obtain crucial certificates are likely to consider teachers useful only in so far as they facilitate the obtaining of such certificates if the nature of the relationship is not changed.

A disturbing aspect of youth culture is the use made by some of drugs; not their common occasional experimental use, which it would be unnecessary and unwise to make much fuss about in a sedative-dominated culture, but their regular, even habitual, use by a small minority. A teacher should avoid officious investigation; but if he detects a sudden and marked decline in a pupil's ability to do his work, or any marked change in his behaviour pattern, a possible explanation could be drug misuse. He should not, however, jump to conclusions; such symptoms can indicate disorders other than drug taking. If, after careful and discreet investigation, regular drug misuse seems to be reasonably certain he should approach an appropriate remedial or therapeutic agency. Whether protocol demands that the approach should be made through the headteacher depends upon the head in question. Some, being more concerned for the school's image than the child, might forbid the teacher to proceed, in order to 'deal with' the situation by concealing it or through expulsion. Sound common sense must determine how he makes his approach. As in all cases where help is needed, however, he should ensure that the help needed is actually given, and given quickly; for if the pupil is using LSD, psychoactive drugs, or stimulants, delay could result in his suffering considerable physical or psychological damage. Although it is dangerous to generalize about misusers of drugs, the evidence suggests that an established drug habit is often a symptom of psychological disturbance, rather than a cause of it, and investigation will disclose a history of psychiatric treatment (see e.g. Smart and Jones, 1970).

Another form of youth culture with which many teachers find it hard to come to terms manifests itself in gang violence. Hell's Angels and Skinheads are striking recent examples of such cults. A school has a legal obligation, which devolves upon the teacher, to try to help every pupil however disagreeable he may be felt to be. Furthermore, in the light of the 1944 Education Act, this obligation is not confined to help in academic matters. If teachers reject pupils such as Skinheads, they are likely to find help from no-one else in the adult community. Two essays by 14-year-old grammar school girl members of the cult (West Riding, 1971, pp. 1–2) suggest that, in a rather different convention, the Skinhead conforms closely to the ideal recognized by many conventional teachers. A Skinhead's appearance may seem ridiculous to an unsympathetic teacher, but to his friend 'the Skinhead gear is very good and sensible', 'true Skinheads always look neat. Their clothes are smart and expensive. Their boots are always polished to perfection.' 'Always looking neat and tidy he can always get into the best places because of his appearance.' If they wore more traditional clothes they would be applauded and held up as good examples to the rest of the school. If they are not permitted to attend school in Skinhead 'gear' it is not surprising if they express their feeling of rejection by wearing scruffy clothes.

Skinheads admire toughness, but so do members of rugger clubs and the army. The difference between the rugger player, the soldier, and the Skinhead, seems to be that the former accept and presumably like the external imposition of discipline; whereas Skinheads 'resent the police and any form of discipline', yet they appear to have a strict code of their own. Rugger forwards are generally proud of their reputation for toughness, similarly, what is most important for Skinheads is that 'they have a reputation [for toughness] and to be a Skinhead means to live up to this'. A difference might be seen in the fact that Skinheads 'look for trouble, even if their numbers are opposed in a fight, they try their best to win and still hold a name'; though this sounds very like determination to score a try in a needle match. Furthermore, they are not work-shy, don't use drugs, and have a strong bond of mutual understanding in their groups. They also claim, 'we are not the ones that start the trouble, but usually provoke the opposition to starting it', and provoking the opposition is a time-honoured occupation in most communities, including that of the House of Commons!

It could be argued that the basis of such cults as the Skinheads is a quite proper need felt by its members to be accepted as individuals and to be allowed to express individuality without crippling restraint. It is easy to see the attractions of cult membership to one who lacks socially acceptable status symbols, for, 'if you are within their groups, and have been accepted as one of them, they are great to you. That is the time when you finally learn what great people they are, and what fantastic personalities they have. Belong to them and they will recognize you in the way you want to be recognized. They will go out of their way to help you as well.' Such words would describe the perfect school. Yet the cultists seem to be compelled to create communities in conflict with the basic values represented by school in order to gain such experiences; and this suggests that schools must bear at least some responsibility for the development of such violent sub-cultures. It would seem that the real objection to Skinheads and their like is that they are different; that they espouse physical rather than the psychological or commercial bludgeons that are socially more accept-able in our culture. Yet is it really worse to break a head than to break a spirit? If, like good soldiers or businessmen, they are 'ready for action and to prove to their mates they have got what it takes', and they are the victims of prejudice (as they almost certainly have been from before the time they joined the cult) it is at least possible to understand why they equip themselves with weapons, even though it may be agreed by most that they are wrong to do so.

What a teacher can do when confronted by manifestations of youth culture depends ultimately upon the person he is. From his observing an observer may learn that the only really effective weapon a teacher has is the hard discipline of accepting or loving behaviour. As the classification suggested by G. W. Allport (1954) indicates, there is nothing sloppy or sentimental in such behaviour. According to Allport the steps in *unloving* behaviour, none of which have a valid place in schooling, are

1. Antilocution: speaking out against other people or saying nega-tive things about them.
2. Avoidance: staying away from people, not having contact with or approaching them.
3. Discrimination: subjecting another person to an unpleasant or undesirable experience one is unwilling to impose upon oneself.

4. Violence: striking out against another person or physical attack.
5. Extermination: killing or destroying; the final irreversible level.

And the stages in accepting and *loving* behaviour are

1. Speaking out in favour of another person, saying good things about him which cause him to be better.
2. Deliberately seeking out, approaching and moving towards others and interacting positively with them.
3. Altruism: unselfish doing of good things, giving of self.
4. Positive loving behaviour: physically touching, caressing, embracing; showing others in physical ways that they are good and worth-while.
5. Creation of life: the ultimate intimate relation of the sexual act, in its potential for the creation of life; the epitome of loving behaviour.

In the twentieth century there has been a superabundance of evidence that rationality and verbal intelligence do not suffice on their own. 'It was intelligent and rational thought that the Germans used so methodically to destroy human life in World War II' (Frymier, 1969, p. 42). Education is concerned with more than the development of cognitive and manual skills. Children need to learn how to be loving, and this is too important to be left to the chance that parents may do something about it, and do it in the right way. The fact that modern man has the power to destroy all life does not mean 'that children will automatically learn to think and behave positively rather than negatively. They have to be taught' (Frymier, 1969, p. 43), and positive thought and behaviour depend more upon emotional maturity than upon logical reasoning. As Frymier stresses, 'there are no packaged programs, no teacher's manuals, and no texts on teaching love as a unit. We are our best resource. Each of us. It is by what we are, our attitudes and the behaviour that reflect them, that we teach about love. Or teach about hate' (ibid.).

The love required begins with the acceptance of each pupil as a person, recognizing his integrity and cherishing him because he is the person he is, not as a potential jewel in the school's crown. It has nothing to do with licence or permissiveness. The loving teacher responds honestly to his pupil's actions (without indulging in the luxury of being shocked, feeling hurt or moralizing) so that his pupil can learn how his actions are truly experienced by others. He teaches his pupil to value himself highly by giving him positive evidence that he too values him highly, even though he may not approve all he does. A child can learn to recognize the worth-whileness of other people, and learn how to love only if he is sustained by a positive, self-accepting attitude. The pupil whose attitude towards himself has been damaged or distorted will need to test the quality of the love offered him before he can dare to accept the hope it holds out; and it is the willingness to attempt to bear the cost of this testing that is the distinguishing characteristic of the teacher who is genuinely concerned for his pupils' development.

Delinquency

Any teacher who believes that delinquency is something he reads about in newspapers, but that does not concern him professionally, lives in a fool's paradise. This applies as much to the primary teacher as to his secondary colleagues, for the seeds of delinquent behaviour are sown in the early years. Certainty that his class contains no detected delinquents gives a teacher no reason to believe that the problem is unlikely to be represented, for a large proportion of the crimes committed remain undetected. Yet,

> We know that between a third and a half of detected crimes in England and Wales are committed by people under the age of twenty-one — most of them male and showing the greatest frequency of offences between the ages of fourteen and fifteen. One young man in five has at least one conviction for an 'indictable' offence (i.e. excluding malicious damage, common assault, motor vehicle offences and certain others) before he reaches twenty-one years of age; at eighteen the proportion who have been convicted is about one in eight. The great majority of convictions are for thefts, breaking offences, frauds and other offences relating to property; crimes of violence and sexual offences together constitute only about one tenth of indictable crime (Trasler, 1970, p. 180).

The comparatively low incidence of known delinquency among the children of middle-class families may well be attributable to the greater efficacy of their child training practices. Certainly, children coming from homes with a casual or disorganized life-style appear to be far more likely to be delinquent than those from homes in which positive efforts are made to mould and control the children's behaviour in terms of learning to inhibit violent acts towards others, to respect others' property and to distinguish it accurately from their own, to keep clean and be reasonably quiet under normal conditions, and to behave with a degree of modesty. Gordon Trasler (pp. 184–5) concludes that 'the little evidence that we have suggests that the risk that a household will produce a delinquent son is related to the style of life of the family rather than the father's occupation or income (although there is, of course, a close connection between these things)'. Research conducted in the USA by F. I. Nye (1958) suggests that the quality of the relationships in the home is more important than whether or not it is a broken home. The delinquents he studied saw their parents as unhappily married and quarrelling frequently; they reported their relationships with their parents as tending to be characterized by mutual rejection and they felt a wide difference between their own and their parents' moral and religious values. The reverse was found to be the case among non-delinquent children. The same seems to be true of delinquents in the United Kingdom (see e.g. Wright, 1971, pp. 79–100).

H. E. Malewska and H. Muszyński (1970), for example, report that children admitting to stealing are more likely to have parents intolerant of their needs and uninterested in them, more violent in their punitive sanctions for misbehaviour, quick tempered, and given to hitting their children and shouting at them than are children who, on self-report, do not steal; the parents of the latter being more likely to use persuasion than compulsion, and to be more affectionate and willing to praise their children. On the other hand, *Tostig*, in his 'Current Account' column in *New Society* (15 July 1971), writing of his experience in social work, reports:

> The truth of the matter is, of course, that the vast majority of delinquents have not come from broken homes or even bad homes in the conventional way; they just come from indifferent homes. In a very real sense most persistent offenders can be described as orphans *with* parents. One of the interesting ironies that confirms this theory is the fact that though probation officers deal with bad marriages as well as bad people, the bad marriages rarely seem to produce bad people – at least bad people who break the law. My guess is that endlessly quarrelling parents usually create neurotically good children. The average offender, on the other hand, is nurtured in apathy and expects apathy from those who supervise him; all too often this is what he gets.

Yet another view is suggested by Trasler (1970, pp. 184–5), who interprets the evidence available to him as showing that family stress, both before and after separation of children from parents through divorce, legal separation, mental illness, and so forth, provides a background in which delinquency is more likely to occur.

It is well known that many more boys are delinquent than girls. This does not mean that girls are less affected by their home background than boys, or that the effects of their home background are less likely to have an influence upon girls' behaviour in school. On the contrary, Nye (1958) concludes that delinquent behaviour in girls is rather more affected by the quality of home life than it is in boys. He suggests that this is because girls satisfy more of their needs in the family and tend to think of themselves as future home makers rather than as future careerists; they are also likely to be under closer supervision than are boys. Because of this he believes that disruption of family ties has more far-reaching consequences for girls than for boys. On the other hand, because girls are more closely integrated into family life, it probably follows that they have less opportunity to be anti-social outside the home and so have less opportunity to engage in delinquent behaviour (see Jessor et al., 1968). Nevertheless, according to Wright (1971, p. 84), 'disorganisation and other pathological features within the family are a more frequent cause of delinquency among girls than among boys. . . . It seems that to a greater extent than in boys, delinquency in girls can be construed as a protest against, or an escape from intolerable home conditions.'

Again, according to Nye (1958), so far as anti-social behaviour is concerned, the influence of the father is more critical than that of the mother. This is not because the mother's role is less crucial in relation to delinquent behaviour, but because mothers are more consistent in their attitudes and behaviour towards their children, and 'form a more homogeneous group both in their definition of their duties and obligations of their status and in their fulfilment of the parental role' (p. 123); on the other hand, badly behaved subjects were much more likely to see their fathers as dishonest people, and the more delinquent subjects saw their parents, especially their fathers, as generally unjust and inconsistent (p. 81). The matter of honesty, justice and consistency in the home is most clearly shown in the use of sanctions and the offences against which sanctions are invoked. It would seem that the specific nature of the disciplinary techniques employed is relatively unimportant, so long as the parents are seen to be fair. Nye suggests that the strictness or leniency with which they are enforced, and even the use of corporal punishment, does not make any difference. Trasler also suggests that the successful rearing of non-delinquent children is closely connected to the effective use of sanctions, in the sense that they have educative value.

The school a child attends may also be a significant factor regarding the risk of delinquency. It is there that children select most of their friends and are made aware of worlds beyond their family and neighbourhood. Despite the intrusion of television, with its insubstantial images that fail to distinguish between fantasy and reality, it is probably true to say that children define their positions in society, or have them defined for them, chiefly through the formal and informal education they receive at school. Reporting his research, M. J. Power concluded that particular schools may heighten or lessen the risk of delinquency to which a child is exposed through his home and neighbourhood conditions; 'the school a child attends may protect him from the risk of delinquency even though he lives in a highly delinquent area — and conversely, that a school may heighten the risk for children who do not come from such a background' (Power et al., 1967, p. 543). This conclusion has been reinforced by Crescy Cannon (1970, also Cannon, 1971), whose analysis of 440 recorded court appearances in a London borough over a period of six months showed that the only definite pattern to emerge was that which appeared when the information was broken down by schools. Each school had its own distinctive pattern with regard both to the prevalence of delinquency and the type of offences committed, as well as the mean age at the time when offences were committed. 'The fact that schools are unique in the kinds of offences their pupils commit suggests that school cultures play an important part in shaping children's attitudes to both non-conforming and "respectable" behaviour. If, for example, class background were decisive, then we should expect similar schools to exhibit similar patterns of delinquency. Which is not borne out in this research' (1970, p. 1004).

Trasler (1970) suggests that delinquents tend to be those children whose verbal facility is below their measured level of practical ability; and that their educational attainments also tend to be poorer than their measured level of intelligence would seem to suggest: that is to say, that they are under-achievers. He suggests further that it seems likely that under-achievement and delinquency both stem from the child's inability to use and understand relatively sophisticated styles of language; which, in its turn, stems from the child's parents' inability to do the same. Wright (1971), on the other hand, would regard this analysis as grossly over-simplified. He divides delinquents into three categories, and regards even his own categorization as an over-simplification. First, the *solitary delinquents* (boys) who are likely to come from higher socio-economic levels of society, to have disturbed family relationships, to be of higher intelligence and to provide greater evidence of emotional disturbances. They are also likely to report greater neglect by their fathers and more disturbed relationships with their mothers than are gang or group members. In other words, they are more likely to be neurotic, that is to say very unhappy, insecure, inadequate and inferior children. Such children tend to come from small, middle-class, intact families, to have a strong attachment to parents who set austere and uncompromising standards and punish in ways that threaten the rejection or withdrawal of love and to have an over-protective, over-anxious mother and one or both parents exhibiting some emotional instability. He also suggests that those children of such parents who do not become neurotic or compulsively delinquent are likely to be very conscientious and tense, to lead extremely respectable lives, and to be very intolerant of what they regard as immorality in others.

Second, the *unsocialized* or *aggressive delinquent*, who is defiant of authority, sullen, malicious and generally hostile to others, is unresponsive to either praise or punishment, showing little sign of guilt or remorse, is always blaming others, and suffers from feelings of persecution. He has few peer friends, but is often afforded leadership through fear and respect. 'His dependence on the gang is not based on friendship but upon the fact that his self-esteem rests upon his aggressive domination of others' (Wright, 1971, p. 90). Such children tend to come from lower-class families in which the parent–child relationship is characterized by mutual hostility, rejection and distrust; in which the parents are punitive, erratic and unjust.

Third, the *pseudosocial delinquent*. The gang constitutes his emotional sheet-anchor, so he conforms unquestioningly to its group norms. His attitude towards authority is defiant, hostile and suspicious, but with no suggestion of violent and uncontrollable impulses. Such delinquency is an adaptive response to the gang as substitute family, that is, an obligatory response to the peer-group pressure it generates. Such delinquents come from homes marked by parental neglect, distance and coldness. Their relationships with parents, especially with fathers, are characterized by mutual indifference, fathers often being absent from home for much of the time. Wright suggests that the gang may be a father-substitute and that membership of the gang may be an attempted flight from a 'female-based' home.

It need hardly be emphasized that a teacher is not a diagnostician, and should be concerned with the symptoms of and background to delinquency only in so far as they help him to avoid making mistakes which could have serious consequences when dealing with individual children with problems. He is not concerned with pigeon-holing or condemning delinquent children. His concern is to be an effective teacher, and whenever he is in doubt about a particular pupil he should turn, if at all possible, to expert help, both for information and for guidance. His sole purpose in making his quasi-diagnosis should be to gain some insight into his pupil's real problems, to see the world as it appears to his pupil, and, with this understanding, to attempt to create a learning situation in which the pupil may have a real chance to experience creative success and possibly take a step forward towards working his own cure. The informed teacher should at least be equipped to avoid adding additional loads to the burden a delinquent pupil already bears. But it must be stressed that although deprivation through environmental circumstances and domestic stresses appear to be closely associated with delinquency, only a small minority of the children affected in these ways become delinquent.

Modern knowledge in the areas of emotional disturbance and delinquency underlines the importance of a teacher's knowing and understanding as much as possible about each of his pupils — and of his sharing this knowledge, rather than his complaints and criticisms, with his colleagues. It also indicates the importance of the delicacy with which he should endeavour to effect his relationship with his pupils. Since the teacher is most likely to express his discipline requirements verbally, it also indicates the importance of the early establishing of a common language with his pupils so that his requirements may not seem to them to be arbitrary. The fact that the child may be under arbitrary discipline at home will not make this task any easier. Above all, however, it emphasizes the importance of his attempting to develop a genuine and warm concern for each of his pupils, no matter how unattractive they may appear to be at first sight; and also the need for this concern to be quite plain to the child.

To be successful in his exercise of discipline he must accept that children with delinquent tendencies regard informing on others to be more seriously wrong than do non-delinquents; so he should be wary of using this as a disciplinary instrument. Likewise, he should remember that, although delinquents tend to place high value on toughness, doing things for 'kicks' and getting quick rewards for little endeavour, they also claim to value highly such values as working hard at school, the reading of good books and the saving of money; so he should not be deceived by a brash exterior, but should endeavour rather to create conditions in which these values could be realized. Again, so far as boys are concerned, since most delinquent acts are committed with the full knowledge and support of peers, group operation being most prevalent between the ages of 5 and 14, he should try to provide sufficient appropriate opportunities for spontaneous peer groupings to discover creative activities which will seem to them to be potentially more inviting and exciting than social deviancy. Since girls do not normally form or have a place in organized gangs they are less subject to peer group pressure, and delinquent influence is normally transmitted to them through individual contact or association — either in school or in such places as coffee bars. Since girls rely more on adult approval than boys do, and are also more ashamed of their misdemeanours than boys, the quality of the teacher's relationship with a girl pupil will always be an important factor in preserving a girl from delinquency if she has delinquent tendencies.

The fact that a child is a known *non*-delinquent may of course mean nothing more than that he has not had the same opportunity for delinquency as those known to be delinquent; or that he has not been subject to the same degree of temptation. Since delinquency is not evidence of chronic emotional disorder, or of psychological damage, often being no more than the outcome of emotional immaturity or of unsuitable but attractive social contacts, a teacher is often better placed than most to help such children; especially since some delinquency is a deliberate attempt to attract remedial attention (see Goodman, 1970, pp. 157–74). Although on average, the majority of known delinquents tend to be of below average intelligence many are not, and it is quite likely that the more intelligent are the more skilful at avoiding detection, or it could be that they are better at getting what they want without recourse to actually breaking the law. Since delinquents tend to do less well on predominantly verbal intelligence tests, it follows that the teacher who concentrates on ensuring that his pupils acquire as high a degree of verbal dexterity as possible is likely to be able to help at least some potential delinquents from being branded as such.

8 The teacher's art

If an inexperienced and unprepared observer were asked what he hoped to witness in a classroom his probable reply would be, a good teacher in action. Pressed further, his answers would indicate that he hoped to pick up tips to help him become efficient, or at least to keep him out of serious difficulties in his own teaching. This is a misplaced hope. He is a different person from any teacher he may observe, and to adopt a technique or stratagem on the grounds that it has been seen to work effectively when employed by someone else is to act unthinkingly. That is not to say that he cannot use it; but the cost will be that of limiting the intellectual and emotional space available to him in his teaching. Under such conditions he would be playing a part, with too much attention focused upon remembering his lines and actions, especially if any pupils demonstrated unwillingness to play their appointed roles. Tips for teachers may seem to have a superficial attraction to the naturally anxious, they may hold out some promise of security; but they should be avoided by anyone who wishes to develop his teaching capacity to the full.

Observing the teacher

What then should he look for when observing a teacher? That is to say, when his attention is focused upon a teacher working with children, rather than upon the children themselves. It is clearly no business of his to evaluate the teacher as a person, or to pass any judgment upon his ability. No matter what limitations may be placed upon the teacher's right to decide whether or not he wishes to be observed, an observer is present only by invitation and an act of generosity on the teacher's part. An observer can justify his presence only if he is there to learn; and there is much that he can learn from any teacher, good, bad or indifferent. His task is to pay attention to whatever the teacher is doing, noting how pupils respond to this activity, to consider why the teacher is doing what he is doing and perhaps to question his choice, and then to imagine how he himself might best tackle the same situation. The teacher, in so far as he is successful in achieving his object, is doing no more than demonstrating in a unique situation, a way of operating which is appropriate to him — the person he is, with the skills, understandings and experience which are subsumed in his being. What an observer witnesses, therefore, is not a model to be imitated, but a stimulus to imaginative reflection. He is there to learn about himself, without having to bear any responsibility for action or its consequences, and not to learn about the teacher he is observing. At the same time, he is able to witness one example of the possible uses of the teaching techniques employed by the teacher. This can be a valuable experience inasmuch as it helps to put some flesh on the bones of what may previously have been encountered only in theoretical form. But it should not be looked upon as though it were a demonstration of *the* correct way of employing a technique; as it is witnessed, it is no more than an extension of a particular person, expressing himself in a way that he believes to be educative.

Observing a teacher in action, with the purpose of learning from the experience, is more difficult than the kinds of observing outlined in the preceding chapters. This is because a teacher is engaged in a multiplicity of activities at one and the same time. It is easy to gain a general impression of what he is doing, but this can supply an observer with little more than ill-defined inspiration. Since typical teacher activities have a complex and dynamic nature that generates a large number of powerful and competing stimuli that may distract an observer's attention, teacher observing must be highly selective. An observer's task is to gather information for future study, and the quality of attention needed is vigilance. As C. M. Stroh reminds us (1971, p. 1),

> there would be no knowledge, no civilization, if man did not have the ability both to focus and to maintain attention. Concerning the first of these abilities, the ability to focus attention, we have found that those stimuli which will have the greatest likelihood of being attended to are the ones which: (1) are the largest (in intensity, size and time); (2) are novel; (3) involve movement; (4) fulfil a need; (5) are of particular interest to the individual; or (6) conform to ex-pectancy.
>
> The second of these abilities, the ability to sustain attention, is what we call *vigilance*. Vigilance, then, can be defined as the process of maintaining attention. Although attention shifts constantly, the shifting is not random; it is guided by certain definite conditions of the external and internal environment.

In the light of this statement worth-while observing of a teacher in action is clearly not easy and requires practised skill. In the first place, the focusing of attention in an environment as rich in stimuli as a classroom demands a high degree of discipline. It is not hard to envisage situations in which the aspects of teacher behaviour to be observed do not relate to the largest stimuli, are neither novel nor conform to expectancy, involve little movement on the teacher's part, and may not be felt to fulfil a strongly felt need, nor to be of particular interest, at the time observing is done. Second, even though the observer's 'internal environment' may be in good order through the exercise of self-discipline, the external conditions may well be such that shifts of attention are misdirected by irrelevant stimuli. Noise, for example, is a frequent element of external conditions in a classroom, and 'noise seems to have a decremental effect on vigilance performance. Furthermore, this decremental effect probably increases directly as a function of (1) task difficulty, (2) noise pitch [by which is meant, the higher the pitch, the greater the effect] and (3) intensity' (ibid., p. 33).

Since the findings reported in Stroh's monograph based on laboratory controlled experiments involving uncomplicated — though not necessarily easy — tasks, it is difficult to determine the extent of their relevance to observing in the classroom. Nevertheless, it is on such findings that the many schemata for systematic classroom observation have been based (see e.g. Withall, 1949; Amidon and Flanders, 1963; Jersild et al., 1939). Such schemata clearly have their uses. The danger in placing too great a reliance upon them lies in the fact that they concentrate attention upon those aspects of teacher behaviour which are most easily recorded; furthermore, the records made are insensitive to the subtle nexus of attitudes and relationships which disclose the true meaning of the recorded statistics. Schemata like that of Amidon and Flanders attempt to overcome this difficulty with the aid of a matrix within which the results are to be plotted. Yet, whilst such a system is an improvement on a simple gathering of statistics, it remains a crude instrument, and conclusions drawn from its use should be approached with caution (see Taylor, 1971, pp. 225–6). Indeed, the same should be said of any conclusions that are drawn from observation, other than those which the observer may make about himself.

William Taylor (1969, p. 160) cites a salutary warning from Zalkind and Costello (1962–3, p. 235), who write:

[Crow] found that a group of senior medical students were somewhat less accurate in their perceptions of others after a period of training in physician/patient relationships than were an untrained control group. The danger is that a little learning encourages the perceiver to respond with increased sensitivity to individual differences without making it possible for him to gauge the real meaning of the differences he has seen.

It might also be added that training based on the use of such instruments as are available tends to reduce awareness of the range of possibly significant behaviour to that which is measurable or recordable within the limits of the schemata employed. A. A. Lumsdaine reminds us that the factors shown up by the use of a particular instrument may not be the most potent, and therefore those of the greatest potential significance to the observer. As he says (1963, p. 666), 'in an extended series of experiments on a number of relevant factors, we should expect that, by and large, the most important or more potent sources of variation would be those that show up as statistically significant, and that, by and large, the unimportant or weak sources of variation would not'. But this will occur only if the experiments meet the condition of 'comparable sensitivity'. In Lumsdaine's opinion, 'this condition is, in general, not fulfilled over the range of educational experiments'. He concludes, therefore, that experimentation with such instruments 'creates a morass of ambiguity and inconsistency which has led some, including the writer, to wonder whether it is worth doing experiments until some basis for achieving comparable sensitivity from experiment to experiment is achieved' (ibid.).

In a similarly critical essay, Norman Wallen and Robert Travers (1963, p. 493) state that 'Research on teaching methods which will contribute to an organized body of scientific information requires that teaching methods themselves be designed systematically in terms of empirically established learning principles.' They list six such principles (pp. 494–500): reinforcement of (partial) achievement of an educational objective, stimulating motivation toward achievement by the introduction of cues, practice in applying principles to problem solving in differing ways, fitting the learner to a planned learning programme, training in imitation and active participation by the individual pupil. These are acceptable so far as they go; but, allowing that they do not constitute a complete list, they provide a slender foundation for justifying the manipulation of teaching procedures on a 'scientific' basis. As the writers themselves point out: 'Numerous attempts have been made to design teaching methods which will achieve such varied objectives as critical thinking, creativity, problem-solving ability, and so forth. Such methods have generally been stated in only the vaguest terms largely because knowledge on which they could have been built has been lacking' (p. 493). Since they advocate the scientific design of teaching methods, in order that teaching can be subjected to 'subsequent research on their effectiveness' (ibid.), Lumsdaine's conclusion suggests that this development — although of interest to researchers — would not self-evidently be to the advantage of pupils.

The decision whether or not to employ such instruments as are available is a difficult one to make. It would appear, though, that they might be better suited to the purposes of self-examination by a practising teacher — using either recordings of his performance, or codified reports made by friends who observe him — than to those of the student teacher. Before leaving this topic, however, it should be noted with Donald Medley and Harold Mitzel (1963, p. 257) that

> Most classroom visitors go to the classroom with definite preconceptions of what they are looking for. They go to the classroom not to find out what effective teacher behaviour is, but to see whether the teacher is behaving effectively, i.e., the way they believe he should behave. . . . No fallacy is more widely believed than the one which says it is possible to judge a teacher's skill by watching him teach. This being so, the use of instruments might be justified in the early periods of observing in a course of initial or post-experience training; if only to direct attention away from such preconceptions.

Student teachers, being on the whole well motivated, are too accustomed to paying attention to the teacher; they need to break the habit when observing. If their observing is to be rewarded by more than a feeling of admiration for that which they have witnessed, they must approach their task fully aware that 'Observation is no aimless relaxation, it is an active, outward-going effort of attention and a recognition of essential characteristics, which consequently enriches our subjective appreciation' (Mock, 1970, p. 110). Or, as Kenneth Barnes puts it (1960, pp. 9—10),

> To observe — to take notice of — is in some measure to experience, and observation therefore implies imagination. No knowledge is possible without an act of synthesis on the part of the knower, some kind of putting together, the imagining of a relationship. There can be no such thing as 'mere' observation, a passive mind receiving an imprint. We bring something of ourselves to the discrimination of the most trivial object in the outside world.

All too often, however, John Holt's description is nearer the mark (1969, pp. 35—6): 'Student teachers in training spend long periods of time in one classroom', as he says,

> but they think they are in there to learn *How to Teach*, to pick up the tricks of child management from watching a *Master at Work*. Their concern is with manipulating and controlling children rather than understanding them. So they watch the teacher, see only what the teacher sees, and thus lose most of what could be a valuable experience.

Focus on interaction

Since a teacher exercises his art in a social context, it is important to be clear about the nature of that context. Getzels and Thelen (1960, p. 82) provide an image of the classroom, as a guide to educational researchers, which may be of use to an observer.

It is not the image of a social system in equilibrium. It is rather the image of a system in motion or, if you will, in dynamic disequilibrium. It is the image of a group continually facing complexity and conflict (if not confusion) and dealing with these realities, not in terms of sentiment but in terms of what the complexity and conflict suggest about the modifications that have to be made in the goals, expectations, needs and selective perceptions of the teachers and learners. It is through this experience of recognizing and dealing with complexity, conflict and change in the classroom situation that we can educate children to take their places as creative and autonomous participants in the other social systems that constitute the larger social order.

It is against a model such as this that the observer should evaluate — and recreate in imagination — that which he witnesses; a social system in which all are participating in learning, exercising their imaginative powers and, as Herman Epstein puts it, 'figuring out what to do next and how to do it'. How often the observer will encounter such a schoolroom is open to question. Speaking of the American scene, Epstein says: 'This is the orientation of problem-seers and problem solvers. It is the most difficult capacity to develop in our brainwashed children and it is a capacity that can be and should have been developed in grade school' (1972, p. 204).

Epstein writes as a university teacher who receives the products of the school system. Whilst holding nothing against the youngsters, he is highly critical of the system; believing that motivated students are successful in spite of, rather than because of it. He adds moreover (1972, p. 203), 'People who have studied the psychology of learning and the strategies of teaching have produced such minimal results that there is almost no point in paying attention to their theories.' There is therefore little to be said for providing a tightly organized schema as a framework for systematic observation, despite the security that such an approach might seem to offer. Despite Epstein, however, we will continue to draw attention to the work of educational theorists, not because what they have to say is necessarily true, but because the student-teacher needs intellectual antagonists with whom to grapple, if his own thinking is to be an improvement on theirs; and, as we have emphasized throughout, the value in observation is to be found in the thinking it generates, not in what is actually seen. Some theoretical framework is necessary if observations are to be interpreted and if contradictions between observations are to be resolved on a more reliable basis than that of sentiment; which, in the context of interpretation, has the status of a theory or hypothesis if it is not replaced by something more trustworthy. As N. E. Miller says (1956, p. 200): 'Pure empiricism is a delusion. A theorylike process is inevitably involved in drawing boundaries around certain parts of the flux of experience to define observable events and in the selection of events that are observed.' But, as he continues,

> Since multitudinous events could be observed and an enormous number of relationships could be determined among all of these events, gathering all the facts with no bias from theory is utterly impossible. Scientists [and an observer should include himself in this category] are forced to make a drastic selection, either un-consciously on the basis of perceptual habits and the folklore and linguistic categories of the culture, or consciously on the basis of explicitly formulated theory (cited, Getzels and Jackson, 1963, p. 576).

Since there is no firmly established theory of the kinds of teacher behaviour that are necessary for learning and growth it is not possible to provide one with any confidence. An observer must formulate his own, based upon his studies as well as upon his limited experience. As a possible starting point he might do well to consider the global conception of C. E. Moustakas (1956, p. 259) who, on the basis of his non-experimental observations, concluded that the conditions of teacher—learner interaction most conducive to learning and develop-ment were met best by interpersonal relationships 'where there was freedom of expression within the limits of the classroom, where each person could state himself without fear of criticism or condemnation, where feelings were expressed and explored, where ideas and creative thinking were treasured, and where growth of self was the most important value'.

According to reported findings, when teacher contacts with pupils are predominantly dominative the pupils are more easily distracted from school work and show either greater compliance to or rejection of teacher domination (Anderson, 1939, 1945, 1946a,b); when greater compliance is evoked pupils find it more difficult to proceed without directions from the teacher, and when a generalized condition of dependence upon the teacher is established pupils become extensively compliant (White and Lippitt, 1960); and, with particular reference to the teachers of younger children, the dominant teacher who curbs pupils' spontaneous ideas to a relatively great extent produces more rebellious and aggressive behaviour among his pupils than a less dominating teacher (Anderson, 1943). None of this is particularly surprising, and an observer should not be content just to note that it is the case. He should be on the look out for the over-tones and under-tones of such relationships. In particular, he should not be blinded by his first impressions; dominative behaviour is not necessarily obtrusive. There is, for example,

> a tyranny of selflessness that can turn the whole love-relation inside out; giving the beloved guilt for breakfast, claustrophobia for lunch and a nervous breakdown for dinner. Beware of this. The willing slave in each of us needs watching and subduing. She can become the egoist in love with her own slavery.

Although Pamela Frankau is referring specifically to the marriage relationship in this passage (1966, pp. 8–9), it has equal relevance to the teacher–pupil relationship. Similarly, he should look to see whether teacher dominance incites resistance, frustration or aggression, and whether any aggression aroused is directed towards a child's peers as well as his teacher. He should also attempt to discover whether Flanders (1951) is right in his contention that a sustained dominative pattern is not only disliked by pupils, but also reduces their ability to recall the material studied and increases their level of anxiety. Furthermore, he should look to see whether it is only the dominative teacher who settles disputes between pupils in favour of the less aggressive disputant, or whether it is customary for all teachers observed to reward the apparent absence of aggression, irrespective of the burden of responsibility or guilt borne by either or both of the contesting parties.

Further contentions worth examining might be: pupils are more inclined to do both their assignments and also extra, non-required, work for an integrative teacher than for one who dominates; or, an affectionate and attentive adult sharing in a task with children leads to good learning performance. Some observers may prefer to start at a more elementary level. For them, a good starting point might be the contacts the teacher makes with individual pupils: not just their number, but their quality – whether they express some kind of approval or disapproval – and their recipients – whether they are directed to a few selected pupils: those who are nearest, most troublesome, academically weakest, most congenial to the teacher and so forth. In this exercise it would be worth bearing in mind some of the findings of J. W. B. Douglas (1967). For example, women primary school teachers are 'less successful in arousing the interest of the boys than of the girls' (p. 100), 'Their assessment of the boys' ability is particularly unfavourable in the manual working classes' (p. 103), 'These views are heavily influenced by the behaviour of the boys in class' (ibid.), and 'It seems that good teaching in the primary schools can make up for the deficiencies in parental interest, so that, in the schools with the best record of grammar school awards, the children whose parents take little interest in their school progress do as well as those whose parents take much interest' (p. 143).

It is not only the statistical surveys that provide suitable starting points, however. The more impressionistic reports, from such as Clegg and Megson (1968) and Cleugh (1971), are just as useful for this purpose, for not only are they not necessarily less reliable than the statistical surveys (they are the work of skilled and experienced observers), they also direct attention toward more subtle aspects of interaction than can be accommodated by most statistical schemata. Dr Cleugh, for example, suggests that her observations have shown that to stress that nothing but the best work is good enough and that standards must be kept high and uncompromised is basically discouraging. Beyond a certain point pupil interest shades into anxiety, and boomerangs, leading to a lowering of achievement. An attitude of don't care or anti-social behaviour which may result from such pressure is no more than a defence against anxiety (pp. 115–16).

The work of psychologists interested in 'behaviour modification' suggests profitable areas for observation; for example, how the teacher copes with disturbing behaviour from members of his class. Since punishing a child who behaves badly in order to attract attention provides no remedy (Madsen *et al.*, 1968), some other approach is required. The approach developed by these workers, based upon experiments in animal training, in training the mentally retarded, and in the treatment of phobias, involves the reinforcement of behaviour held to be desirable, through the giving of rewards. George Goodlet (1972) draws attention to three types of reward which have proved to be successful in improving children's behaviour in experimental situations. These are (a) tangible reinforcement, for example sweets, (b) token reinforcement, for example behaviour ratings on a numerical scale, or curtain rings which can be cashed for some desired reward at a later time, and (c) social reinforcement, the reward of praise and attention. Of these, social reinforcement is clearly the most suitable for the classroom situation.

That the technique works is beyond dispute; and, in cases where a child is so disturbed that he has genuine difficulty in controlling his own behaviour and requires therapy, may be justified. But it is not without its dangers; and this would be the point of particular interest to an observer. For bad behaviour is not necessarily a symptom of psychic

or social disorder; it may be a justifiable response to what is demanded
by the teacher, and to employ the technique under these conditions is
to develop socially undesirable attitudes and expectations. Furthermore, since it is such a powerful technique, it is available as a stratagem
for avoiding genuine involvement with pupils — especially since the
technique has been found to be effective with a whole class, as well as
with individual pupils. As Goodlet concludes (p. 13):

> For young children there is no doubt that social reinforcement is a
> very useful form of control, which can be exercised at no cost by the
> teacher. Older children find their classmates' reaction to their disrup-
> tive behaviour more rewarding than their teacher's attention. Young
> children show the reverse. There is a tendency on the part of the
> teacher to ignore good behaviour and to pay attention, by repri-
> manding, to bad behaviour. By reversing these responses, the teacher
> adopts a powerful weapon.

The fact that the weapon is double-edged should provide the
observer with much to occupy his mind; not least the criteria — and
their underlying presuppositions — invoked in assessing behaviour as
bad and in need of correction. As Goodlet says, in all innocence, 'The
use of reinforcement is particularly important in shaping behaviour' (p.
11); thereby raising fundamental moral and social questions which he
does not attempt to answer. The more subjective approach of Dr
Cleugh, who looks upon education as a total process in which there is a
traffic both of ideas and feelings, not only between teacher and pupil,
and does not therefore abstract class order as a discrete factor, also
shows that positive, direct and approving verbal communications to
pupils are more successful in eliciting co-operation from them than
negative, non-specific and reproving communications. She maintains,
furthermore, that positive, unhurried, specific and encouraging verbal
directions produce better success on the part of pupils in the
performance of their tasks, than discouraging prohibitions. But then she
is less concerned with controlling pupils, than with trusting them
sufficiently to withdraw from them, in order to leave them space within
which to foster their own development. Yet,

> It is not just a matter of leaving alone in a *laissez-faire* way: some-
> how a feeling of active acceptance has to be communicated. Given
> this feeling of acceptance, an individual is encouraged to show more
> of himself. He behaves more freely since he is less cautious and on
> guard. Paradoxically, it may be a good sign if a tense child begins to
> misbehave and allows himself to try out his confidence in his teacher
> (Cleugh, 1971, p. 121).

The importance of the teacher offering something positive to the relationship, other than the information he may make available, is emphasized by the theory of social exchange developed by G. C. Homans (1961); for such information may not be immediately attractive to the pupil. According to Homans, the continuance of social intercourse depends upon recognition of the principle of distributive justice; the parties involved must feel that they are getting roughly equal profit from the relationship. If the distribution of profit is seriously out of balance there will be a strong tendency on the part of the deprived party to break off the relationship; hence, it is the responsibility of the party receiving the disproportionately advantageous share to take adequate steps to restore the balance. Recognition of the principle of distributive justice is not the same thing as the establishing of a democratic regime. The teacher cannot abdicate his responsibility as leader. Indeed, it is likely that a democratic regime would contribute little to high morale and job satisfaction, if it is fair to draw an analogy between the work situation of school and the work situation of industry. The results of an extensive study of leadership styles in industry indicate not only that 'High job satisfaction was associated with being led in the way that respondents preferred to be led' (Sadler, 1972, p. 547), but also that a democratic management style was the least preferred — 2 per cent of the sample placing it first. The significance of this finding is emphasized by the fact that this least preferred style, as defined in the survey, approximates closely to a pattern found in some schools: that is to say, the manager's function was seen as that of defining the problem and of indicating the limits within which the decision had to be made, with the right to make decisions being delegated to the group.

Two further findings are of particular interest to an observer. First, although it was not catered for directly in the inquiry, it became clear that the absence of a distinctive management style was most likely to inculcate the lowest levels of job satisfaction and satisfaction with the company in subordinates, because 'The "no-style" manager is likely . . . to appear inconsistent and unpredictable' (Sadler, 1972, p. 548). Second, the strongest preference was for a consultative style of leadership (60 per cent support, even though over two in three acknowledged that their managers did not adopt this style). This style involves the leader in making his own decisions, but in the light of advice and suggestions obtained through consulting the group. 'The decision is still his, but he does not take it until after he has consulted his staff' (p. 547). It is noteworthy that all the perceptions of managerial behaviour which received ratings significantly above average under consultative style relate to the sorts of behaviour which have particular relevance to the teacher's task. For the sake of completeness, and also because the styles are adopted by certain teachers, it should be noted that the style in which the leader makes his own decisions and issues orders which are expected to be obeyed without question was highly unpopular (7 per cent support), but that a modification of this style, with the leader attempting to persuade his subordinates to accept his decisions, received about half as much support as that afforded to the consultative style.

Although, as Walcott Beatty says, 'Climate in the classroom is something about which we have much to learn' (1969, p. 92), it is obviously an important focus for observation, and needs to be considered in relation to the teacher's style of management; for children, like adults, work best when their morale is high, and the climate of morale in the classroom 'is basically the feelings created in the children by the teacher' (ibid.). Dr Cleugh draws attention to four indicators of high morale which may be taken as a frame of reference: (a) A positive attitude to work, shown by a willingness to tackle a task even though a successful outcome is by no means assured, and an absence of the defensive attitude of inability to cope. (b) Pupils putting their best efforts into their work, and progressing at a rate commensurate with their presumed ability. (c) The absence both of passive swimming with the crowd and an over-driving application to work. There should be evidence that working is an enjoyable experience. (d) Willingness on the part of pupils to apply themselves to tasks which, though not particularly enjoyable in themselves, have to be completed before more enjoyable work can be undertaken: that is to say, there would be evidence that pupils have the capacity to postpone satisfaction (see Cleugh, 1971, pp. 117–19). 'Above all', however, 'a situation of good morale is characterized by trust and confidence' (p. 120).

Since the climate of morale is inextricably linked with the quality of class control, an observer should be mindful of the fact that children require different kinds of control at different stages of their development. This is particularly true of children in secondary schools, for, not only does the pattern of much secondary schooling derive from an era when it was felt that children ought to be repressed, it derives also from the days when, in the main, it was concerned with children under the age of 14 — the period of puberty and early adolescence when many children feel a strong need for the stability provided by a degree of imposed order, in order to counterbalance the emotional instability which is characteristic of this stage in development. Older children in mid-adolescence, on the other hand, have a more pronounced need to develop self- or inner-directedness (see Riesman, 1950), associated with a strongly felt need to earn the respect of adults who will look upon them as being themselves adult. They no longer look for external control as a crutch to support them; they seek rather for help in establishing self-control over the new impulses they experience in themselves, and for help in defining the elements of the conflicts which lie before them — emotional, moral, spiritual, and intellectual — in order to regain at least some of the security they have experienced previously in the worlds they had ordered in the less tumultuous period of later childhood. Furthermore, since individual competitiveness is a learned and not a natural characteristic of adolescence, and most of their self-originated activities take place in naturally formed small groups, they need the opportunity to co-operate with their peers on work where interest is shared.

Yet the need for co-operation with their teachers, as adult to adult, is paramount. Life today is so organized that young people experience very little association with their elders at more than a superficial level, and their understandings of adult society are derived, in the main, from secondary sources — in particular from television broadcasts. Contact with parents, and especially with father, is limited; for many children home is located in an anonymous and impersonal area, isolated from the larger community, as is the school. One of the most marked effects of this condition is the peer group dependence young people have developed for the main influences upon their lives; which cannot be other than removed from the main stream of the community at large. The only adults with whom the majority of young people spend substantial stretches of time are their teachers; and it is from them alone that they can have any real expectation of gaining access to the interests and understandings of members of the adult community. But they can do this only if they are accepted as young adults, and therefore as equals, by their teachers. So long as their school life is ordered as though they were eternally pubescent this door remains closed to them. This places a heavy responsibility upon schools and teachers; a responsibility which is not met by castigating the younger generation for their lack of respect for their elders — their institutions, values and concerns. Without an initiation into these they can know little of them. An observer in a secondary school, therefore, should be especially observant to see how, and with what success, pupils are accepted as adult, and initiated into the real world of adult life, both within the school and through the opportunities created by the school for initiation into the wider environment (see Bronfenbrenner, 1970).

How successful the teaching staff of a secondary school can be in this respect depends not only on themselves, but also upon the extent to which their pupils may have been conditioned to distrust teachers during their primary schooling; not that this can cause insurmountable difficulties. Whatever else a child may learn at school he learns to measure himself against his peers, and to place himself in relation to them according to this exercise in self-streaming. Although this may have a profound effect upon his willingness to move out of the stream in which he locates himself (see Rosenthal and Jacobson, 1968) it need not have any effect upon his relationship with his teacher. If the teacher confirms this self-assessment through streaming within the class, which has an even worse influence upon the child's feelings of self-worth than streaming between classes (see Lunn, 1970), this indicates to him that his teacher – and if his experience continues throughout his primary education, all teachers – has a poor opinion of him. This makes the establishing of a relationship of mutual esteem well nigh unattainable, and the child will bring this understanding with him into the secondary school, where his teachers may find themselves virtually forced to stand by as he either drifts into perpetual infancy or struggles to find his own way into mature adulthood. The problem is intensified in the case of special groups and individuals; the most obvious of whom are the physically abnormal and the immigrant child or child of immigrant parentage, who, although he may not have needs different from those of children native to this country, has them in a more intense and pressing form (see McNeil and Rogers, 1971).

The chief problem facing a teacher is that of deciding where each particular child can make its unique contribution to the life of the school, in such a way that its self-image and prestige are enhanced, so that its relations with others may be deeply personal. In some instances the child may need help in order to overcome his difficulty; yet 'the timid child can be given courage, the uncouth poise, the irresolute determination, and all can be given in the right home or the right school a measure of self-confidence and self-respect. To do this is part of the normal stock-in-trade of the infant school' (Clegg and Megson, 1968, p. 85). Sometimes, of course, it is the teacher himself who needs help. For example, J. W. B. Douglas draws attention to the lazy child, whom he differentiates from the dull child who tends to be idle. 'The lazy children seem to be a special group', he says; 'they do better in the tests than those who are simply described as poor workers, and although there are many backward children among them, more than one would expect are of above average ability' (1967, p. 91). In E. B. Castle's view, if a child's parents describe him as busy and active at home, and the teacher thinks that the child is lazy, 'parents' judgment based on home observation may be nearer the truth than a teacher's view based on school performance' (1968, p. 181). Moustakas (1972, pp. 34–6) even cites the case of a highly intelligent child whose ability was not detected by his parents, let alone by his teachers. In all cases, even those of the dullest children, it is the responsibility of the teacher to discover how to interest the child in being busy at school, so that whatever abilities he may have may be aroused, and he can become an active and respected member of the school community.

The problems posed to the teacher by the presence of such out of the ordinary children in his class are of particular interest to an observer just because their needs are not different from those of other children. Because their needs are more intense, however, they provide a specially fruitful focus for attention.

9 The teacher in action

Little is to be gained from making methods of instruction a chief focus for observation. As I. A. Dodes puts it 'there is no decisive proof that any particular method of teaching (inductive, deductive, individual, group) or any particular philosophy of teaching (teacher-dominated lesson or socialized lesson) will guarantee better results than any other method or philosophy, *so far as achievement is concerned*' (1953, p. 163, my italics). Yet methods of instruction have educational importance and teach other things than those their user may have in the forefront of his mind. Choice of methods depends at least in part on the teacher's personality, and whilst in general 'Teachers and children together need to explore patterns of information new to both of them, and the teacher's skill as a learner is his most valuable skill, the one he needs most to demonstrate in action' (Mason, n.d., p. 17) it is not his only valuable skill. Some have the histrionic skills of a performing artist, and 'having seen some rare beauty or some subtle truth, are anxious to communicate it' (Taylor, 1971, p. 198). In contrast to class-teaching as the longest-running-show-on-earth, there is in the formal lesson at its best 'a vitality, a vividness, a directed force in teaching which no other medium quite duplicates' (ibid.). However, most class lessons are not of a high pitch of inspiration as performance and it is ridiculous to pretend that they could be.

The teacher who insists upon hogging the stage, whatever methods of class-teaching he may employ and no matter how he may ring changes upon his limited repertoire, is acting defensively; supporting himself first, the problem under consideration second, and his pupils third; a procedure that is guaranteed to create inter-personal anxieties in his pupils and to reduce their efficiency. The focus of attention, both in teaching and learning, must be the matter in hand and not the teacher himself. The most appropriate method is that which suits the individual teacher best. If he has to keep redirecting pupil attention to what he himself is doing, either he is using a method inappropriate to his pupils, or, assuming that the matter in hand has genuine relevance and is pupil-related, the matter is not coming alive in his pupils because it is not the focus of his own attention. Of course, if a child has been taught throughout his schooling to respond only to demands for 'compulsory' attention he will be unlikely to associate his natural capacity for what Dewey calls 'reflective attention' (see Dewey, n.d., pp. 89–94) with what happens in school; in fact, this capacity may be atrophied. Yet, the development of reflective attention, which develops from unreserved absorption in immediate experience at infancy, through the development of a sense of worth-while ends and of awareness that activities can become means to the attainment of such ends, to the power to 'conceive of the end as something to be found out, discovered' (p. 90), is what instruction is all about. 'In general this growth is a natural psychical process' of the first twelve years of life. 'But the proper recognition and use of it is perhaps the most serious problem in instruction upon the intellectual side' (p. 91). Since the basis for reflective attention is 'some question, some doubt, present in the mind' (p. 92) – not one put there by someone else – an observer should pay close attention to the relationship between the matter in hand, the methods employed, and the nature and quality of pupil attention. Only if the relationship is right will the teacher be teaching his pupils how to study complex matters without the aid of an instructor.

Whatever methods may be employed the sole justification of teaching is the fostering of learning. To teach, in contrast to indoctrinating, is to stimulate and nourish the autonomous powers of the learner, without which he could not learn to do anything: the power of extraction – of finding the common element in a widely varied phenomenal field, the power to make transformations – without which there could be no language, the power to handle abstractions – words are no more than arbitrary abstract signs, the power of stressing and ignoring – of abstracting, the power of control, organization of materials and co-ordination of activities, and the power to undertake increasingly larger tasks and to accept more complex challenges as a consequence of practice in learning (see Gattegno, 1971, pp. 1–16). Much of the justifiable criticism of so-called child-centred teaching is not criticism of its child-centredness but of the sentimental reduction of Dewey's ideas manifest in much self-styled progressive teaching. An observer should test Barry Sugarman's hypothesis that 'the *vagueness* of "progressive" teaching and curricula fails to provide a sufficiently clear framework for the child and hence increases his insecurity: whereas old-fashioned disciplines and subjects – and marked examinations – at least avoid this error' (1967, p. 395). Activity-centred teaching is vague only when the teacher pays insufficient attention to the individuals being taught. The price to be paid for increased permissiveness in the classroom is increased self-discipline on the teacher's part. He must really know what is going on and must exercise his art so skilfully that what his pupils genuinely choose to do is really worth doing, in itself, and at this time.

Since the development of responsible thinking is central to education an observer will learn much from what is said. He should disregard the spurious impressiveness of the slick recall of 'right' answers from memory and should concentrate upon the quality of the thinking underlying what is said. Thinking takes time, not least because language is a far from perfect tool. Since intellectual powers are developed and understandings deepened by grappling with the apparent or real difficulties generated by the use of language he should pay special attention to what happens when genuine conversation develops, and should note the stimulus to thinking provided by the teacher's contributions. As E. J. Amidon rightly points out (Amidon and Flanders, 1963, p. 3), 'The key to developing more effective classroom verbal behavior is the opportunity to experiment with and practice desired communication skills.' The observer should therefore attend to the example given by the teacher of the exercise of such skills as:

(1) ability to accept, clarify and use ideas, (2) ability to accept and clarify emotional expression, (3) ability to relate emotional expression to ideas, (4) ability to state objectively a point of view, (5) ability to reflect accurately the ideas of others, (6) ability to summarize ideas presented in group discussion, (7) ability to communicate encouragement, (8) ability to question others without causing defensive behavior, and (9) ability to use criticism with least possible harm to the status of the recipient (ibid.).

Since a developed language is used in a great variety of ways, to these should be added skill in

1. the adoption of language that will aid present understanding,
2. the use of language that will not conflict with communication in other areas of the curriculum,
3. whenever possible, the use of language that will allow for future refinement rather than the need to unlearn and restructure as concept hierarchies are developed.

In recent years considerable attention has been directed towards what is known as divergent thinking (see e.g. Hudson, 1966, 1968; Gordon, 1966) or lateral thinking (see de Bono, 1970). The development of this style of thinking should not be ignored by an observer. Like so many other fashionable terms, divergent thinking has become somewhat debased currency, and a habit has developed of classifying people as convergers and divergers, whereas a genuine thinker employs both styles, the relation between them depending upon the nature of the task in hand and the individual's personality make-up. Divergent thinking in any area can develop only if pupils are given opportunity and encouragement to do their own thinking. This demands a teacher who matches the example set by Charlotte Mason who, according to one of her students, 'would not deliver those she loved from the growing pains of thinking for themselves' (cited, Taylor, 1971, p. 129).

'In convergent thinking, the information leads to one right answer or to a recognized best or conventional answer' (Guilford, 1959, p. 470). This is an essential style of thinking, and most traditional school work is directed towards its development; but it is not an exclusive style. Even though it may be the style most appropriate to the majority of adult work situations, it is of no greater importance than divergent thinking for the living of life, and both styles should be stimulated and developed in school. 'In divergent thinking operations', to quote Guilford further, 'we think in different directions, sometimes searching, sometimes seeking variety' (ibid.). 'The unique feature of divergent production is that a *variety* of responses is produced. The product is not completely determined by the given information' (p. 473). The importance of divergent thinking for education, therefore, is that it stimulates flexibility, originality and fluency of expression — in particular, verbal fluency. It helps to draw attention to that which cannot necessarily be expressed with the clinical clarity of analytic language, and draws on experience which, within the conventions imposed by the languages of convergent thinking, would otherwise be excluded. Its language, whatever the subject matter, is the poetic, the peak of human verbal achievement, in which man has traditionally given expression to his most profound insights and experience, from divine prophecy to the peasant-art of keening. Since convergent thinking is inescapably reductive, to confine thinking in school predominantly to this style is to reduce the area of potential human experience and awareness.

Both divergent and convergent thinking are intelligent forms of intellectual behaviour, neither being superior to the other. The only possible criterion for an assessment is appropriateness to the task in hand; but greater appropriateness under particular circumstances does not invest one style with absolute or general superiority over the other. There is a proper place for both styles in every conceivable area of a school curriculum. (For an exploration of some possible strategies for developing divergent thinking, see Gordon, 1966, pp. 33ff.) An observer, therefore, should attend, not only to the use made of divergent thinking by the teacher, but also to the encouragement given to it, the respect with which pupils' contributions are received, the respect afforded to such contributions, and the type of intellectual stimulus given by the teacher. The list could be extended considerably; however, the most important part of the exercise is the observer's imaginative projection of what he might have said in the same situation and his expectations of such a contribution.

The psychology of thinking is a complex field in which much still remains unclear. Nevertheless,

> there is strong support for the ideas that width of attention deployment relates to the ability to utilize incidental cues in problem-solving and that this capacity is a feature of the cognitive style of the creative thinker. Secondly, it seems desirable to distinguish two types of attention which relate to two different cognitive modes: on the one hand, there is a mode of thinking, described variously as 'unregulated', 'global' and 'syncretistic', which is accompanied by diffuse awareness; on the other hand, regulated, analytic thought occurs within focal awareness. A recurrent theme in the literature is that the creative thinker is more able to gain access to the former mode. But, thirdly, he must be able, not only to gain access to it, but to integrate it with explicit, analytic thinking. Measures of adaptive regression and flexibility may reflect this capacity to some extent, although it is doubtful whether they exhaustively define the integrative abilities necessary for creative thinking (Bolton, 1972, p. 197).

Furthermore, and this is of particular interest to the teacher with regard to the type of environment he attempts to create and the life-style he encourages within it:

> As Warr (1970) has commented, the distinction between a measure of ability, defined as an index of how well a person *can* think, and a measure of cognitive style, defined as an indication of how he habitually *does* think, has now become a fluctuating and dubious one. To think creatively must mean to exercise an ability and yet, . . . it seems probable that the exercise of this ability is enhanced or inhibited by one's approach to life and style of behaviour. Ultimately, then, it may be we shall have to revise the concept of an ability which sees it as a determinate quality possessed by the subject in the same way that he possesses a pancreas or a hook nose (ibid., p. 205).

In his concluding chapter Bolton draws upon the theory of cognition proposed by Merleau-Ponty on the basis of his analyses of the phenomenology of perception. On this theory the central point of reference of cognition is the motility of the body. 'Motor intentionality' (Merleau-Ponty, 1962, p. 110) lies at the heart of our perception, habit and thinking, because actual experience is prior to the objective world. Consciousness is therefore a matter of an 'I can', before it

The teacher in action

becomes a matter of an 'I think that'; and the body, as the medium for motor intentionality, is the origin of the worlds which we construct. As Merleau-Ponty puts it (p. 146), 'The body is our general medium for having a world.' The world posited may be a biological world – if it is restricted to actions necessary for survival; a world with figurative meaning – if these primary actions are elaborated upon, as in, for example, ritual dancing; or a cultural world – which is a projection by the body around itself of a meaning which cannot be achieved by the body's natural means, the body constituting itself as instrument for this purpose. Consciousness, then, is not a discrete interior mental activity, but an active process of perception or thinking or of both which animates that which already is within the body's environment. Commenting on this, Bolton draws a conclusion which has important implications when applied to the art of teaching.

> We can no longer be content to study behaviour from a merely external, objective point of view, since such an attitude fails to encompass the intentions which animate behaviour; conversely, we can no longer analyse mental processes, such as perception, feeling or thinking, as though they took place in a self-contained and interior realm, for then we would fail to understand how such phenomena can ever relate to the subject's involvement in a real environment (1972, p. 233).

A number of matters follow from this; not the least important being that competence cannot be thought of in absolute terms, but must be interpreted by reference to the environmental conditions in which it is manifested. Similarly, human adaptation cannot be thought of purely in terms of survival in a given environment; for example, even such an obviously survival orientated practice as the wearing of clothes as a defence against cold weather is also employed to express values, to communicate, to employ a system of symbols for representing perceptions of reality. Hence, human adaptive behaviour must be thought of both in terms of strategies for survival, and also in terms of the construction of points of view, which, as Bolton says, 'by going beyond the here-and-now, enable man to achieve a greater understanding of his environment' (p. 238).

Focus on strategy

Whilst there is little to be said for an observer focusing upon the tactics employed by a teacher, since these are heavily conditioned by variables in the situation, some value may be derived from a consideration of the

112

strategies he employs, so long as the observer's intention is not that of picking up tips for survival in a different situation. His purpose must be to learn something of the complexities and subtleties which influence the effectiveness of different strategies. But he must be careful not to interpret what actually occurs, in terms both of behaviour and learning, as though it were the inevitable consequence of the use of a particular strategy. The relationship between teaching and learning is ambiguous. Teaching is a task which, logically speaking, is satisfied by the activity of teaching: though teaching which leaves pupils' behaviour unchanged or changed for the worse can hardly be looked upon as a worth-while activity. Learning, on the other hand, is the consequence, not of teaching, but of studying. It may, of course, be regarded as a task or process; but not in relation to teaching. The occurrence of learning is neither caused by teaching, nor is it a logical outcome of teaching, for the teacher does not make something happen in the learner. He is not, or at least ought not to be, a mechanic in a social engineering factory. Since teaching is not a manufacturing process there is no method or strategy that will guarantee successful learning, for it is no more than a vehicle for conveying the teacher's awareness of the holy ground of the present moment. As Whitehead says (1950, p. 4), 'The present contains all that there is. It is holy ground, for it is the past, and it is the present'; and, so far as teaching is concerned, it is only in the teacher's conscious awareness until learning has occurred.

Hence, whilst noting the tactics employed by a teacher in the pursuit of his strategy, an observer's interest will be focused upon the learning generated by the exercise. The decision to focus upon strategy must depend, of course, upon the time the observer has to spend with a particular teacher working with a particular class. For teaching according to a strategic plan may involve activities located at different points along the continuum of possible activities, and a single lesson may concentrate upon an activity that would be undesirable if it were used predominantly. In general terms, this continuum ranges from conditioning (which is concerned primarily with shaping behaviour without any reference to pupils' intelligence) to indoctrinating (which is concerned exclusively with the shaping of belief; interest being concentrated upon right answers rather than on right reasons). Whereas what is to be done or believed is the focus of interest at the extremities of the continuum, the question 'how?' dominates the mid-point: 'how do I do this?', 'how do I understand that?', 'how do I believe the other?' To either side of the mid-point are located training, which is concerned primarily with shaping behaviour which is appreciated and understood by the person under training (i.e. teaching to), and instructing, which is also concerned with shaping behaviour, but in which greater emphasis is placed upon the development of the understanding of truths and beliefs (i.e. teaching that and teaching why).

Since teaching is more concerned with the manifesting of intelligence than with the development of conditioned responses, a well conceived strategy will have its centre of gravity at the centre of the continuum, though not all of the teaching activities employed will be located there. It should be recognized that the need for this variation is determined, not only by the particular requirements of the constituent members of a class, but also by technical and social factors. For example, before work of an inquiring nature can be undertaken in certain areas, training aimed at the development of certain specific skills must be given. Such instances are normally clear-cut, and there is little dispute about the appropriate action to take. The determining role of social factors, on the other hand, is less easy to evaluate, owing to the conflict of values within society. Yet a teacher should be aware of the need to preserve society's careful arrangement of cultural patterns, which could be recklessly destroyed if no limits were placed upon learning in the school years of young people. Undisciplined learning leads to iconoclasm not to cultural evolution and development. As Jules Henry indicates from his anthropological studies, 'the dialectic of man's effort to understand the universe has always decreed that he should be alternately pulled forward by what has made him *homo inquisitor* and held back by the fear that if he knew too much he would destroy himself, i.e. his culture' (1960, p. 179). Without substantial shared elements of a common culture the possibility of meaningful communication is removed, and without meaningful communication the possibility of meaningful individual being is diminished, if not destroyed. Even though language is a primary tool for exploration and investigation, it is also, as Henry points out (ibid.), an 'iron matrix' which binds man's brain to ancient modes of thought; and without this matrix, culture would perish.

Any sound strategy for teaching will be formulated in awareness of this dialectic, for, if cultural development is to result from education, children must be firmly rooted in a culture that facilitates communication in school, a culture common to both teacher and taught; the onus being upon the teacher to know and understand the extra-mural culture of his pupils. But, since a teacher's further responsibility is to initiate his pupils into a wider and richer culture than this, he engages in what Thomas Green (1971, p. 4) calls the strategic acts of teaching: namely, motivating, counselling, evaluating, planning, encouraging, disciplining and questioning. Green draws an important distinction between the essential activities of teaching – the strategic acts and the logical acts – and the institutional activities of teachers 'which are in no way required by the nature of teaching itself' (1971, p. 5). By the latter he means such activities as 'duty', marking the register, chaperoning and collecting money. Since such institutional activities occupy a considerable proportion of a teacher's time — according to Hilsum's survey (1972, p. 32) over two-fifths of time spent in the classroom and nearly three-fifths of time spent on school work outside the classroom — they may well obtrude in an observer's estimate of the activities of teaching. But, as Green says, teaching 'does not require the institutional arrangements we associate with schools' (p. 5). By logical acts he means such activities as explaining, defining and giving reasons: the types of activities we understand as determining classroom tactics.

Since schooling is essentially a laying of foundations upon which future learning can be built, it might be said that the underlying grand strategy of the school teacher is one that will lead pupils to lay such a foundation. As Peters (1967) has pointed out, this requires an emphasis upon training and instruction, particularly in the earlier stages of any educational enterprise — whether it is the business of formal education considered as a whole, with the need to develop such skills as reading, writing and computation, or initiation into some more or less specialized area of human activity. Hence, in any sound strategy, there is bound to be an emphasis upon the practice of skills, and upon the bodies of information without which the principles which constitute the conceptual frame of reference of understandings cannot be attained by the uninitiated. This should not be misinterpreted as suggesting that schooling should comprise training in skills and instructing with information alone, for, while the grasping of principles is inseparable from the acquisition of skills and information, it is of greater educational significance. It is to emphasize this that Peters, perhaps confusingly, distinguishes between teaching on the one hand, and training and instructing on the other, so that, in his analysis, ' "teach" unlike "train" or "instruct", suggests that a *rationale* is to be grasped behind the skill or body of knowledge' (p. 19). It is only as the rationale informing a particular form of knowledge (Hirst, 1965) or realm of meaning (Phenix, 1964) is grasped that critical thinking and evaluation can be undertaken, and reasoned dialogue be substituted for 'verbal legerdemain' (Peters, 1967, p. 21).

Since an observer cannot focus upon a teacher's strategy without paying some attention to the tactics he employs, it would be improper to leave this topic without reference to some of the more important of such tactics. Of these the most commonly encountered is class-teaching. L. C. Taylor reminds us (1971, pp. 221–2), it is a very slippery term; for, 'Although we talk about "class-teaching" as though it were a uniform object, we know well enough, of course, that it is a portmanteau term stuffed with the extremes of human divergence.' There are occasions when no other tactic would be preferable.

Nevertheless, whenever an observer encounters a class-teaching situation he should question whether a different tactic might not have been more appropriate. As Phenix says, the form of every discipline is 'inextricably connected with what and how the teacher as mediator teaches' (1964, p. 317). In consequence, 'the teaching of material from any discipline should always be considered specifically in relation to the character of that discipline and not from some supposed principles of teaching in general' (ibid.). This being so, it is reasonable to anticipate, for example, that class-teaching will feature more in the teaching of music appreciation than in the teaching of history or reading. In the class-teaching situation it is all too easy for a teacher to become the slave of a text book, doing little more than reinforcing the ready-ordered, predigested material it contains, in a manner which can only stifle scholarship. Scholarship does not consist in following a well-worn path, but in learning how to ask the important questions, where to obtain essential information, and in testing the ideas put forward by authorities. Text books, on the other hand, focus upon the conclusions drawn within a field of intellectual inquiry, rather than upon the field of inquiry itself. This is the case even with most text books which purport to present a field of inquiry as such, in that successful progress through the book depends upon the successful discovery of predetermined conclusions which must be drawn by pupils. Under such conditions pupils often feel that 'discovery' is a frustrating and time-wasting activity, since progress through such materials tends to be slower than rote-learning.

It should not be assumed that work-cards are necessarily in any way superior to text books. Often they are no more than unbound sheets that would be quite at home within the covers of a text book. It is not enough for such cards to present problems, or to cover a part of the syllabus – like a unit from a correspondence course – or to be useful for keeping pupils occupied. They are truly useful in so far as they help to create a genuine learning situation, in which the pupil is cast in an active role in relationship to the material with which he is working, and so is taken into the field of inquiry itself. That is to say in very general terms, in the fields of mathematics and the physical and life sciences they should concern him with the idea of order, in such fields as history and geography they should concern him with the issues of life and society as they are experienced and discussed today, in the field of languages and their related literatures with human feelings and communication, in religion and philosophy with the idea of meaning and personal response to the universe, and in the arts and crafts with control of the self and of material, and also with self-discovery and communication. Although the text book problem is to be found in some primary schools, the observer is likely to find, with Clegg and

Megson (1968, p. 85), that it is especially in the secondary school that 'the substance of education, which is the development of the total personality, tends all too often to give way to the shadow, which is measurable book-learning'.

The problem in the primary school is less likely to be that of fostering book-learning, but rather that of fostering little, poor, or no learning. It does not suffice to send children on voyages of discovery with little more than a few words of advice and encouragement. They need ample resources, appropriate to their individual needs, readily accessible and easily identifiable. They require a teacher who is skilled at organizing such provision before they enter the room or enter upon the activity. They also need a teacher who notices how each child goes about using inquiry to solve his problem or task; one who is able to understand how an individual's thinking works and to identify the sort and quality of his inner resources of experience and information. Only such a teacher will be able to recognize the sorts of experience an individual pupil requires in order to improve his discovery performance and the opportunities he requires if he is to open up new possibilities for perceiving relationships and dissonances. If a child is invited to explore and discover a world too big for him, if he is not asked the right questions at the right time, and if his experience is not guided to directions potentially fruitful for him, he is likely to be overwhelmed by the immensity of the task of ordering that world, and will give up in despair.

To teach in this way demands considerable powers of observation and of interpreting that which is observed, for the teacher's guide is no longer a set syllabus, or text book, but the children themselves. The teacher stands in for that experience which the children are too young to have gained for themselves and helps them to avoid wasting time and effort on work or materials that are beyond their powers, or stimulates the less daring to test their abilities beyond that which they have already mastered. Hence the teacher's task is to prepare, select, stimulate, encourage and even correct the experiences and interpretations of each child, whilst still leaving the child adequate freedom to suggest areas of working, and specific tasks within areas which interest him. All this demands considerable wisdom, resourcefulness and knowledge on his part, if the children are not to experience a hotch-potch of unrelated experiences and ideas which lack meaning as a whole. It also means that a teacher must know sufficient about every child to be able to arbitrate between what is in the child's interest, and that in which the child happens to be interested.

The problem is intensified in a school that adopts the principle of an integrated day, for there can be no self-contained timetable or detailed scheme of work that covers a period of schooling over several years.

117

This imposes upon a teacher the necessity of keeping informative and full records covering the whole development of each child, tracing his intellectual, emotional and social growth; for, without such records it would be impossible to determine whether he is being stretched by the work he is undertaking, or perhaps even strained, or distorted in his overall development. Under these conditions, testing becomes an important element in a teacher's task, not just for purposes of diagnosis and categorization, which, as Ira Gordon says, is 'a dead-end, meaningless operation' (1966, p. 27). Rather, 'The goal here, and in the utilization of subsequent techniques, is increased insight into the child, so that learning situations can be constructed to foster his intellectual development' (ibid.). There is much for an observer to notice in this type of situation, though he will learn more from focusing his attention upon the children than upon the teacher. Above all, such observation will give him practice in being aware of what is happening in many different places at the same time, involving many different people; and also in learning when to step in with advice to a child, when to stand back, and, perhaps most important of all, when to help a child to draw a particular activity to a conclusion because, although it has been good and useful to him, it has lost its head of steam and become unprofitable.

Careful observation will show how effective the integrated day approach can be − and if the exemplar does not appear to be particularly successful an observer should exercise his imagination and work out how it might be made more successful in that situation. Where it is successful, he will discover with Arthur Razzell (1968, pp. 34–5) that

> Perhaps the most startling feature is the degree of involvement the children show in their work . . . [and that he is in] . . . a room where every child feels that he counts and is wanted; a place where children work for joy and satisfaction of doing a good job on a worthwhile task, unperverted by other incentives; a place where teachers get results by example and inspiration and not by reliance on prizes and punishments.

Such a state of affairs does not just happen and an observer should try to discover the extent and nature of the effort needed to create it.

A form of integration to be met in both primary and secondary schools goes under the name of integrated studies. This is conducted through team teaching: 'A form of organization in which individual teachers decide to pool resources, interests and expertise in order to devise and implement a scheme of work suitable to the needs of their pupils and the facilities of their school' (Warwick, 1971, p. 18). The organization of team teaching can take many forms (see Warwick for details), the most appropriate being dictated by the needs of the pupils to be taught, the possible contributions to be made by teachers who are willing to take part in the scheme, and the various factors (physical, organizational and architectural) that impose the limits within which the work has to be undertaken. In other words, team teaching is neither a slogan, nor some theory of teaching which is a paradigm of good practice, but a tactic which, under certain clearly defined circumstances, may be the most suitable for giving effect to a clearly thought-out strategy.

One of the great advantages of team teaching is that, excepting when a teacher is actually engaged in giving instruction, it gives him increased opportunity to attempt accurate observation of individual pupils, which, if records are kept over a period long enough for recurring patterns in a child's behaviour to emerge, can lead towards greater objectivity in assessment and, in consequence, better prescription to meet the child's needs. Furthermore, assessments can be compared with those made by other members of the team. But such observations do no more than provide a body of information which relates to how a child behaves in certain particular situations, it does not indicate why he behaves in such ways. As Ira Gordon says (1966, p. 65), 'Gathering the data, however, is only the beginning of the process. The inferences to be made are, in the long run, the major concern of the teacher.' It is from these inferences, drawn 'in terms of the child's perceptions of the present situation' (p. 67) as observed by members of the team, that answers (hypotheses) are formulated regarding questions about how to foster improvements in his learning and other behaviour. When observing team teaching, therefore, there is much to be learnt from a consideration of the mechanics of the operation, of whether the best is being extracted from the opportunities afforded by the technique; and of the sorts of opportunity for observation by teachers it provides.

Another tactic involving the withdrawal of the teacher from being the focus of pupil attention is that of group teaching; the advantages and disadvantages of which have received little attention from researchers, apart from those working with adult students (see e.g. Abercrombie, 1970). The arguments made in favour of such an approach are that it makes work less tedious so more is done and more learning takes place, peers have a hand in bringing troublemakers to heel and, since individual efforts are a contribution toward a group goal, it elicits greater enthusiasm and motivation, particularly if successful contributions are rewarded by favourable attitudes on the part of peers. Furthermore, it is held to foster the development of such social skills as perceptiveness regarding the expectations of others, and the ability to fulfil them, or at least to evade them gracefully; and also

119

to foster the development of a secure self-image which is relatively free from anxiety. On the other hand, it is argued that it may make pupils other-directed (see Riesman, 1950), that is to say, extra-sensitive to the expectations of their peers, and that the lack of formal structure can lead to the adoption of insufficiently stringent criteria of adequacy regarding contributions. However, since the teacher is not expected to sit silently to one side, but is a member of the group, these arguments do not have much force. If the social climate is healthy, contributions will tend to approximate to the highest standard set and, so far as the pupil who feels under pressure not to deviate from the attitudes of his peers is concerned, if the teacher intervenes firmly on behalf of deviant pupils, he should be able to establish the principle of tolerance on the one side and of standing up for what one thinks right on the other—two lessons that are central to any process of socialization in a democratic society.

In this type of situation an observer will gain more from observing pupils, or the group as a whole, than the teacher; for 'The group system of teaching focuses attention on the interaction between all partici-pants, students and teachers, not on the polarized interaction of a student with a teacher' (Abercrombie, 1970, p. 4), since a primary aim of the system is to assist the discovery of basic but unacknowledged biases and assumptions (p. 3), as well as the fostering of independent thinking (p. 11). Dr Abercrombie draws a distinction between group teaching and a tutorial, since in the latter the teacher's function is to correct his pupils' mistakes and omissions. In observing group teaching it is probably best if the observer does not participate in any way in the group activity, since if he were involved in the interaction he would be unable to observe it objectively. His purpose in observing should be to discover how effective such group activity is, under the prevailing conditions, in assisting the intellectual, social and emotional develop-ment of the participants, and how far it assists them 'to change their own behaviour, to make it more effective' (p. 20).

The success of the tactics described in the preceding paragraphs depends to a great extent upon the quality of the discussion and activities generated by pupils; as is also the case when discussion is engaged in in a more formal class situation. In many schools the only times pupils are encouraged to talk is in the context of a formal class discussion. The fact that these are often conducted with little sign of enthusiasm and interest suggests that an observer should pay particular attention to the dynamics of any discussion he witnesses; for when talking is not officially permitted by the teacher most lively children show great interest in conversing with their neighbours, even when they know that they may be punished for it. The stimulation of educative discussion clearly demands considerable insight and artistry on the teacher's part; especially if that which he wishes his pupils to discuss does not seem to them to lie close to their interests, for genuine discussion occurs only when the matter under discussion is felt to be of real significance in the lives of the participants. Once again, little research has been undertaken in this field with children but, from his work with adults, R. W. K. Paterson has shown that 'True discussion cannot be directed, or even guided' (1971, p. 47), and it is probably at this point that many teachers fail. A discussion is not just an exchange of views or ideas, particularly when these are inert bits of information, but 'a genuine exchange of personal perspectives' (p. 48); hence, the teacher's part in a discussion situation demands sensitivity and resolution, if he is to prevent himself and others from steering the discussion to a predetermined destination.

A guided discussion cannot be more than a spurious exchange of verbalizations, since 'authentic self-disclosures and self-commitments' (Paterson, 1971, p. 48) are inherent in all genuine discussion. If pupils are unaccustomed to making such disclosures and commitments in their other school activities they may well find it uncomfortable, even difficult, to engage in discussion in class. They cannot be expected to transform themselves from being dry rationalists to engaged advocates of their deepest convictions at the teacher's whim. Apart from other considerations, such self-disclosure makes one vulnerable to teasing, even to ridicule, when the more open conditions for discussion are closed again. Thus children accustomed to engaging in educational activities in which their feelings are not taken into consideration may well be lethargic about, even hostile to, the possibility of genuine discussion, feeling it safer to keep up the pretence of being non-persons, the role they are customarily expected to play. Yet, as Michael Oakeshott emphasizes (1962), the integrated outlook of the whole man is brought about not by courses of instruction, but through conversation, and conversation bears no relationship to a directed discussion.

The purpose of a conversation is the creation of a common world within which each individual can make his own contribution and also learn from the shared experiences – in particular how other individuals perceive and interpret their worlds. Abercrombie (1970, p. 14) quotes from a report on free group discussion (i.e. conversation) in a class on human biology by S. A. Barnett (1958). In this he reported that students who displayed an emotional bias in discussing an excerpt from an essay on control experiments 'were *eventually* corrected *by other students*, and the latter *gradually* formulated their thoughts on the subject during *uncontrolled* discussion'. This bears out Peters's contention (1967, p. 21) that the ability to engage in genuine conversation is something that has to be learnt, it is an 'achievement'; but one which is not possible without knowledge, understanding, objectivity and sensitivity to others. It is also the most natural of all learning situations; in fact, most informal learning occurs within the context of conversation. The reason for this is self-evident. 'To be a conscious self, a person, is to be haunted by the need to give meaning to one's experience and by the need to compare one's own solutions with the solutions arrived at by others' (Paterson, 1971, p. 40).

Formal education is, or ought to be, a recognition of those needs, and is a project which is, or ought to be, consciously directed towards their fulfilment, by means of a common search for the meaning(s) of the phenomena under consideration. If this is the case, then Paterson is correct in stressing that discussion is not just one educational method among many.

> It is rather the educational activity *par excellence*, an educational end-in-itself, and to participate in discussion is to share in one of the educational ultimates to which the accumulation of factual knowledge, the use of teaching aids, and the practice of educational techniques are nothing but the useful and necessary preliminaries (pp. 40 and 45).

Should an observer have the good fortune to encounter a genuine conversation in school time, he should be careful to note the enabling function fulfilled by the teacher; sometimes as a stimulating participant, sometimes as a resource, always knowing where relevant information may be found, but never dominating — even though his pupils may be homing in on a wrong conclusion or attitude at a given point in time. To such a teacher this is no more than an indication of his need to provide further experiences which may lead to a reconsideration of the conclusions and attitudes being adopted.

Since the art of meaningful and educative conversation needs to be learnt, and creative conversation depends to a large extent upon the ability to ask pertinent questions of oneself and others, it follows that the ability to converse in this manner is fostered by the experience of good questioning by teachers; thus the art of questioning is a proper focus for an observer. Though Gurrey may overstate the case by claiming (1963, p. 43), 'The art of questioning, then, is the teacher's most valuable gift or acquirement', he is right to stress that 'much thought and effort should be given to further its use and improve its quality'.

Educative questioning should not be confused with verbal testing, which has as its purpose no more than a trial of a child's ability to recall information from memory. The latter tactic may be an important preliminary to educative questioning, particularly in work with younger children or with children who have difficulty in concentrating. As

Gurrey says: 'Questioning can hold a fly-away mind to the point, where "teacher-talk" will carry it away in a windy gust' (ibid.). Educative questioning, on the other hand, is questioning which helps a pupil to learn how to probe his presuppositions, to make more explicit the principles he may apprehend only dimly, to clarify and structure his thinking, to refine the exactness of his knowing, to discover that some questions are more worth asking than others, to discover unsuspected paths for exploration, and so forth. Such questions are unlikely to be answerable with a simple yes or no, or with a right or wrong answer — except in certain discrete areas like simple computation. The aim of such questioning is to build up the child's confidence in his powers of independent thinking, and to encourage enterprising and perhaps creative thought. Under such conditions there can be no such thing as a wrong answer to a question; there is always an answer from which something can be learnt, an answer that places the child in a new situation from which he has to advance in his thinking. The teacher's responsibility does not require that he counter with the judgment 'wrong', but rather that he help the child to ask further purposeful questions to clarify the next steps in his investigation; in other words, that he opens up new possibilities for the child's inquiries.

Educative questioning depends upon the teacher having accurate knowledge of his pupils' store of memorized information, and upon the availability of adequate resource materials; for, if previous instruction has not provided an adequate preparation, questioning can force a child into a state of anxiety, and lead him to practise errors, to give up trying and to rely upon guesses, or to engage upon strategies which may help him to spot the 'right' answers (see Holt, 1969). Allan Fromme poses a number of questions that an observer may find helpful in his observing (1969, pp. 13–14):

What *does* the child hear when he is called on? What does he feel? What are his fantasies and wishes? What does he try to do? What kinds of habits is he developing? What effect does he have on the teacher? What does the teacher think and feel and do as he awaits the answer? Does he understand the meaning of the child's answer or see it merely as right or wrong? Does his relationship with the child have the intimacy ideally necessary for intellectual growth or is it a dull, contractual one which fosters non-learning as much as it does learning?

To this list should be added the most important questions of all: what questions would the observer have asked if he were in the teacher's position and why? Also, what sorts of answers would he have anticipated? And to what use would he have put them?

123

When observing a question and answer session an observer can learn much about the weaknesses of the tactic by watching the children as they put up their hands — if this is the custom in the school — to indicate willingness to give an answer. He is likely to find a small number always to the forefront, followed by a larger number who, having looked to see that they are not the first, raise their hands and then nod sagely when a 'right' answer is given. This is particularly likely to be the case if the teacher is in the habit of calling upon children who clearly seem not to know the answer. Should the teacher call upon one of the middle group, the answer is likely to be given in a quiet voice — a sure sign that the pupil is afraid of giving a 'wrong' answer — in the hope that the teacher, expecting the right answer, may assume that the mumble is correct or nearly correct, and then repeat the awaited answer for the benefit of the rest of the class. He may also notice a number of pupils who are impulsive in answering questions — a reaction indicative of a defensive attitude to schooling, adopted by some children who, having met repeated failure, expect to go on failing. If he is in the presence of a sensitive teacher, he will notice that he does not accept such answers until a period of time — perhaps as much as twenty seconds — has passed, in order to allow time for reflection, having given previous warning that he intends to adopt this tactic (see Schwebel and Bernstein, 1970). Such a teacher will be interested in developing reasoning, rather than with receiving right answers, and, whatever answer he receives, will show interest in the reasoning that led to its being given. No matter how interesting he may find a particular question and answer session, however, an observer should not forget to question the appropriateness of the tactic within the educational strategy of the teacher, and in relation to the work that precedes and follows upon the session.

10   The teacher's authority

Effective work in the classroom on the part of both teacher and pupils is closely related to orderliness. But what is meant by order? And how is it evaluated? It is not difficult to tell whether a classroom is noisy or quiet, whether the pupils seem to be working, or whether the teacher seems to be in control of the situation. But such information does not tell an observer much. If good order meant no more than that the teacher is in charge and has his pupils under control it would be easy to obtain with a little force and determination. Since the only justification for classroom activities is that children are being educated, the question of order constitutes a very real problem for many teachers.

It is similarly a problem for an observer, for the constituent elements of good order tend to be elusive and cannot be indicated in the abstract with much clarity. It is quite possible to compile a list of possible teacher statements, attitudes and practices and to suggest to an observer that he watch for and enumerate the instances of each given lesson; but such labours provide little of use to one who wishes to become a better teacher as a result of his observing. For authority is not that which follows upon the exercise of disciplinary measures, as is often thought; rather disciplined (but not drilled) conduct is the consequence of properly exercised authority. This being so, it will be more helpful to provide clues to be sought out in an analysis of order in a classroom under observation, and to mention information that an observer needs if his analysis is to be more than superficial. Since the quality of the order in a particular situation is a product of the balance of powers present in the room, the most accurate analyses can be expected only with first-hand knowledge of the participants. Nevertheless, even though a particular class and its teacher are not well known, a firm grasp of what lies behind good order will enable an observer to learn much of value from the time spent observing with discipline as his focus.

The nature of the teacher's authority

By virtue of his office the teacher is *in* authority in his classroom. This does not mean that he is *the* authority, but that he bears responsibility for the exercise of authority. But what is authority in this context? We might say 'authority is present when something is correct or to be done because an individual, or body of men, who has been given the right says so' (Hirst and Peters, 1970, p. 114), and that an authority is he who determines what the 'rules' are, who interprets the rules in a particular case, or who enforces the rules. On the other hand we might say that an authority is one whose skills we can attempt to emulate, whose precepts may help us to do the right thing or may give us a framework of action (Wilson, 1967a, p. 101), agreeing with Frank Musgrove, that 'the powerful teacher will promote teacher-centred or pupil-centred learning according to the outcome he wants. . . . But whether the teaching mode adopted is "democratic" or "authoritarian", it is likely to be effective if it is the expression of the teacher's power to decide' (Musgrove, 1971, p. 21), for clearly the teacher must have power and must be in control. But none of this takes us far. The attempt to analyse the nature of the teacher's authority shows it to be far more complex than appearances suggest, and that, although Musgrove (p. 29) may be right in claiming that 'teachers are relatively powerless because they have little to offer that their pupils urgently want', no teacher, except in the most exceptional circumstances, has grounds for doubting his latent capacity to maintain good order, the successful exercise of his authority depending more upon his readiness to pay the price of preparing *himself* properly, than upon what others can teach him or upon charismatic power. Indeed, the teacher with a really powerful personality can be at a disadvantage when he attempts to create an educationally stimulating order, in that his powerful presence may inhibit his pupils' initiative.

An important element of a teacher's authority derives from his office as final arbiter and delegated representative of the community in the classroom. It is his responsibility to see that the educational purposes of the school are achieved within his jurisdiction, and in so far as his authority extends, that the administration of the school as a unit is facilitated. The teacher who depends upon this element of his authority for good order is very likely to be authoritarian with his pupils. In a school with rigorous entrance standards and a high regard for traditionally conceived academic excellence no harmful consequences may be evidenced in his pupils who, rightly or wrongly, will have been led to believe that their teachers can give them that which they need to be successful in life, and so are prepared to be compliant with little protest, even though the relevance or significance of the teacher's gifts may seem obscure. But in many schools pupils are not under pressure to accept that which the authoritarian teacher wishes to impose on them. Rather, they are aware that he needs what they alone can provide, namely, the absence of disruptive noise and confusion and the evidence of his teaching ability provided by examination successes. In such a school he is likely to find himself driven to adopt a harsher and more repressive approach than even he would like (see Musgrove, 1971, pp. 31–2). In a strongly repressive teacher's classroom an observer is unlikely to see much direct evidence of harshness, since his pupils will have been well drilled to be on best behaviour when visitors are present, though hard-edged directions like 'pay attention' are likely to be heard.

The second element in a teacher's authority is the skill he possesses in his subject area, for in the classroom he is not only in authority, he is also *an* authority; one who has achieved some kind of mastery in a given field. The power he derives from this depends in great part upon the field of expertise. Subjects like mathematics carry a great weight of authority with pupils because of their vocational relevance, others, on account of their intrinsic interest, are recognized as powerful by a proportion of pupils. In such subject areas most teachers can anticipate a degree of co-operation from most pupils. But subjects not immediately relevant to job or career prospects, particularly if they are not examined, provide little support for a teacher's authority purely on the basis of his academic skill. The authority derived from such skills, though valuable, is not without its dangers. A teacher over-sensitive to the fact that he is in authority may be afraid of admitting ignorance or of being unable to provide a snap answer off the cuff, and this fear can easily lead on to an authoritarian attitude, as can the nature of some subjects, particularly the physical sciences, with their large body of (for school purposes) incontrovertible fact. Closely related to the authority derived from academic skill is the authority a teacher derives from his experience and understanding, that is, from his skill as a teacher. This develops from his ability to learn from past successes and failures in the classroom, without taking them as a sure guide to future practice, and from his knowledge of his pupils, so that he is aware of their problems and of their impending successes almost before they themselves are.

With these three elements in the teacher's authority go three more which, though less obvious, are no less important. First there is the authority deriving from his commitment to what he is doing; to the belief that his pupils are worth teaching, that the body of knowledge he is handling with them is valuable in itself, as is the experience afforded to those initiated into the field of activity that presumably excites him. Disbelief cannot be concealed from pupils, neither can the infection of enthusiasm. Second is the authority deriving from consistency between a teacher's behaviour towards his pupils and his inner motivation, from the harmony between his personality and his communications. Pupils are highly skilled, well practised observers of teachers, and are not easily deceived by, for example, the hollowness of insincere praise, artificial enthusiasm, or the pretence that what is of no real significance to the teacher is somehow important. Third is the authority deriving from openness or vulnerability, the absence of defence-mechanisms and the willingness to allow young people to be real partners in their own education. This last is perhaps the most elusive for it depends upon the teacher's ability to accept quite naturally, but not to hide behind, the authority deriving from his function, skill and experience. Whether or not teachers are born rather than made, access to this element depends ultimately upon willingness to accept pupils as real (if immature) people, rather than as potential evidence of professional skill, or as crosses it is a teacher's misfortune to have to bear.

How the teacher exercises his authority

The nature of the teacher's authority being so complex, it can be exercised in a variety of ways, and no simple recipe for its most effective use to meet all situations can be given. A teacher is neither a benevolent despot nor a child-grower. His first responsibility is to sustain the enterprise of education, and in order to do this he needs certain minimal conditions of order. This means that when rational methods of persuasion are ineffective, he must issue commands, or at least make strong requests; for the pseudo-progressivist who shrinks from using legitimate authority is no improvement on the authoritarian. But the way in which authority is exercised has educational significance; whatever a teacher may intend, his pupils will take the values expressed by his use of authority to be the values he regards as truly adult, disregarding other values to which he may pay lip service. For our educational aims reside ultimately in our attitudes towards children, in the methods used in teaching them, the discipline devised to foster growing up and the punishments and encouragements used to this end.

Authority is a form of power, and the ways in which power is exercised in organizations and societies suggest that there are three basic kinds of power (see Etzioni, 1961); *coercive*, based on the use of force (which is inescapable in any society that seeks to maintain certain minimum standards of behaviour), *remunerative*, based on rewards and penalties, and *normative*, based on an identity of values and attitudes between those who wield and those subject to power. This last is linked to moral involvement and becomes fully effective only as a response to a person because of the qualities he possesses or is believed to possess, or because of a personal relationship established with him. All three have their place in school, but good teaching and learning thrive in a situation in which the third predominates. A teacher observed in such a situation will be seen to be firm in his dealings with pupils, expecting high standards from them within the limits of their abilities, but also to be genuinely interested in the whole class, co-operating with the children, though unwilling to stand any nonsense, in helping them to develop self-control and so to grow up. He will clearly know and have confidence in himself as a person, accepting the full responsibility vested in him by school and community. His class will show that it understands and agrees with the limits he imposes, both upon his overt exercise of authority and upon their behaviour, and that within clearly defined limits he is both open to influence from his pupils and willing to encourage them to make their own decisions. In this way the full potential of forces within the classroom will be harnessed to satisfy both the fulfilment of personal needs and the mastery of worth-while tasks. An observer could expect to see the teacher drawing out any child of a withdrawn disposition in such a way that it will grow in self-confidence, unaware of being the object of special attention, and restraining the exuberance of a more ebullient child without dampening its confidence and enthusiasm.

The teacher who exercises his authority effectively demonstrates to his class that he knows what is going on, is sympathetic yet detached, that whatever happens he will never withdraw sympathy or support and has clearly asked himself 'how would I like this to happen to me?' before dealing with any trouble. He cannot be described as a permissive, a controlling or even a punitive teacher; for as circumstances demand he may be any of these. He is a provisional authority; one who can be dispensed with in so far as his pupils are sufficiently self-disciplined to be able to accept responsibility for their own behaviour and studies. Despite the blandishments of those children who admire him as an authority figure and wish to identify with him as such, rather than prolong the period of pupil dependence they offer him he will use this a-rational bond of 'calf-love' to transfer the child's interest from himself to those worth-while things that excite and motivate him; yet he will do it delicately, so that the child's confidence in him is not disturbed. The teacher and an outside observer may be aware of the child having made an error of judgment, but the teacher will conceal this from the child himself, and with luck, from his peers.

Discipline in an educational context

'Everybody, unless he is an intelligent parent or a trained teacher, knows all there is to know about discipline. . . . Most people assume discipline to be the same thing as punishment, and this is the major error' (Castle, 1968, pp 201–2). Although a trained teacher might not make so elementary a mistake the evidence suggests a lack of agreement among teachers regarding the nature of discipline. Some, for instance, have not grasped that good discipline presupposes noise, bustle and activity, if they are not distracting. Many fail to recognize that in traditional schooling we use force to impose on adolescents, in their most active years, a relative stillness few adults could sustain, and such 'discipline' is not necessary for educational reasons.

Discipline derives from the Latin *discere*, 'to learn', its root idea being submission to rules which structure that which has to be learnt. The close connection between discipline and learning is emphasized by the terms *discipulus*, 'disciple' – one who learns from his master; and *disciplina*, 'training', 'learning', 'living under the rule of inner compulsion', 'feeling the stimulus of parental example', and so forth. Discipline is, therefore, submission to an authority such as the rules immanent in a way of thinking or necessary for learning something, or to the one who may determine a disciple's task and so forth. It is not an imposition, but is essential to learning. Subject areas are disciplines because the learner submits himself to the rules implicit in them. As he progresses his consciousness becomes structured by their procedures; the mark of progress being an increasingly disciplined approach to the subject. Hence, an educated man is one who adopts an appropriately disciplined approach to things, and discipline is 'the sum of experiences in our lives that enable us to grow up' (Castle, 1968, p. 203). That which the teacher seeks to achieve through the exercise of his authority is self-discipline by his pupils in worth-while pursuits. But, since a self-disciplined approach to complex matters is not innate, one of his major concerns is the creation of physical, mental, moral and social conditions that will help children to grow up to become autonomous persons of integrity and courage.

Since self-discipline cannot be learnt without the experience of bearing responsibility (for responsibility has to be *felt* before it can be understood), whenever possible a teacher will encourage pupils to exercise their own judgment, giving them every practicable opportunity to accept responsibility for their own behaviour, for the successful performance of their studies and, whenever necessary, for the well-being of their less fortunate or less successful peers. Should they fail in this he will be prepared to support them, without undue recrimination. Nevertheless, the younger his pupils the more frequently he may have to invoke discipline external to them, that is to say, the acceptance of rules which he dictates. But he will be sparing in this, because such manipulation of children into doing what others want easily degenerates into playing upon their desires and fears. Circumstances may sometimes demand that he impose discipline with the support of sanctions, creating artificial connections between desire and extrinsic reward or aversion and punishment, but since this is educationally speaking the least valuable kind of discipline, he will do it infrequently. It is, of course, easy to overstress the dangers implicit in imposed discipline. Self-discipline is often more burdensome than young people can bear; furthermore, that which one admires, respects, or wishes to emulate in others, exercises a powerful form of external discipline upon the self, which (if the model is good) few would designate as harmful. But whenever obedience is demanded of a child its justification must be made in terms of reasonableness. Obedience demanded for the sake of obedience is valueless in educational terms. It may produce behaviour convenient to others, but the underlying emotion will be bad.

The exercise of discipline

The creation of conditions in which learning is not hindered is so obviously necessary that it requires no further elaboration. However, the motivation behind a teacher's requirement of discipline is by no means so obvious. Although an observer's judgment will inevitably be subjective, he should try to formulate the attitudes that appear to lie behind the practice of the teachers he observes. For example, restrictive demands may well originate in such educationally worthless attitudes as love of power, laziness, obsession by the examination system, or fear of losing control once and for all (suggesting a deep suspicion of the impulses of youth). All these suggest a lack of self-confidence, the overcoming of which involves taking oneself less seriously, becoming less egocentric, and finding others more interesting than oneself; that is to say, achieving maturity through learning how to love. As Willi Schohaus warns (1932, p. 43):

> For those who are not sure of themselves, the problem of authority easily becomes a highly personal matter. Their wavering self-confidence makes it necessary for them to fight for their personal position, when all that is needful is to establish in the children a happy respect for all those high aims which all of us as human beings are bound to honour. It requires a good deal of personal assurance to be able to endure children being children in all their unbroken strength and natural delight in criticism.

School discipline is not an end in itself and has value only in terms of its consequence. It exists for the sake of the children, and not vice versa, and discipline that does not further development, and increase the benefits and happiness of life for pupils, is worthless. External controls are certainly necessary, for self-discovery needs external authority as a catalyst, but the right approach is remedial, positive and educative, rather than penal and negative. All too often, however, classroom control is effected through fear and anxiety; for these render most children more malleable. Fear, however, inhibits constructive thinking and working. Strangely enough many teachers regard the well-behaved docile child, who does what teacher wants, perhaps without even needing to be told, as the model pupil, even though they might claim that they admire an inquiring mind, independence of thought and adventurous thinking and doing, above all else.

The long-term aim of discipline in schools is the development of social awareness and responsible autonomy in children, in other words, the development of self-discipline. The capacities necessary for this development may originate in the early stages of personality development, they need practice and experience if they are to develop. Since acceptance into social organizations depends upon having learnt to impose limits on egotism and the cravings of impulses and frustrations, school discipline should foster the realization that the needs, opinions and efforts of others ought to be respected, the teacher's aim being to use his power to create opportunities for his pupils to learn how to create conditions agreeable to all and so to experience the freedom known only to the self-disciplined. It should be possible for an observer to say 'everything that the school demands of the child in the way of reasonable discipline, serves the development of his moral will' (Schohaus, p. 39). For as Norman Williams rightly stresses (1967, p. 307),

> It is not possible to say that one's job is to teach reading, or arithmetic, or French. In all these activities we may advance, or retard, the child's moral development; we educate more frequently and more effectively by what we do and what we are than by what we say. . . . We are furthering or hindering a child's moral progress every time we foster his self-respect by giving real responsibility, or remain uninterested in trivial problems that loom large to him, or make arbitrary decisions overriding his developing ability to think for himself. We are all moral educators, whether we like it or not.

A child can learn genuine self-discipline only through self-generated activity and experience, and not through impositions by another authority, for he has to learn to evaluate the consequences of his own actions for himself and others. This has important implications for teaching objectives, for as John Wilson says (1967b, pp. 404—5),

> there is a strong presumption, to say the least, that teaching the

child to express himself orally and encouraging him to take part in rule-governed group activities are necessary methods of moral education: and from this one might be reasonably inclined to go on to the more specific opinion that, from the point of view of moral education, it would be better if more time were spent on teaching children to describe, explain and argue and less time on getting them to copy things down from the blackboard.

Responsible behaviour begins when the individual, even the smallest and least competent of children, feels that he is engaged upon a job of which he can say 'it all depends on me'. This delegation of authority to pupils is not only important from the point of view of the development of responsible behaviour, it is also essential if the teacher is to be free to employ his time and skills efficiently.

No observer will spend long enough with a particular class to be able to notice the development of self-discipline in pupils. As a full-time teacher, however, he will notice that as the capacity for reasoning develops there is a steady movement towards autonomy and self-direction, and the child develops the ability to make moral judgments without experiencing debilitating guilt. Should he decide that his behaviour has been faulty, he will simply engage consciously in inhibiting such behaviour. This, of course, presupposes that the child will have had considerable experience of discussing the claimed wrongness of his offences (and the rightness of any ensuing penalties) with adults, especially his parents and teacher. A teacher's function in helping the child to achieve moral autonomy may be less than the parents', but he can reinforce good practice and do something towards making up for parental failure in this respect. In any case, he should do nothing that might inhibit the child's development of moral autonomy.

Authoritarianism

Although it is not confined to such institutions, an observer is most likely to encounter authoritarianism in traditional schools; that is to say, those that interpret their functions as feeding pupils with right ideas and instilling approved moral standards in them. In class the teacher takes the initiative and pupils are expected to be led and to learn. Discipline is imposed according to prescribed quasi-immutable rules. Pupils are expected to endure rather than enjoy school, in the knowledge that by doing what is good for them they are being prepared for the future. What is good is generally assumed to be that which conforms to the school's view of the good man and citizen. Whatever its virtues in a static society, such an approach to schooling is singularly inappropriate at a time of rapid social and environmental change.

Although an authoritarian teacher may do little to help his pupils to develop as autonomous persons, he is not necessarily ineffective. If examination results are an acceptable criterion, he can often claim to be highly effective; though he is less likely to instil much love of learning in most of his charges. Similarly, he may not necessarily stifle individual initiative, for he will consistently reinforce potential for leadership in his pupils, provided it does not conflict with his own status or leadership function. It should be remembered that decisive intervention by a teacher, when either social or academic behaviour is bad, is not necessarily authoritarianism. It may be the most appropriate way, in many situations, for a teacher to fulfil his duty of giving adult support to his pupils as they work through the stages leading up to acceptance of responsibility. The essential character of authoritarian behaviour or intervention is dictation of *all* the rules, effective discussion does not come into question.

Among the more obvious reasons why some teachers adopt an authoritarian stance are uncritical acceptance of tradition, interpreting the teacher's task in terms of teaching a subject rather than of teaching children, failure to recognize that experience of mutual respect and agreement is a more effective stimulus to understanding than rote learning, belief that the teacher's supreme duty is to suppress his pupils' inescapable and evil inclination to disobedience, and the belief that there is no place in the classroom for pupils' emotion or feelings. The authoritarian inevitably initiates an unnecessary struggle with his pupils, in which either his dignity and the enjoyment of his job or his pupils' proper independence and integrity must be the loser. A teacher cannot establish authentic relationships with his pupils unless their feelings and emotions are taken seriously, and if he is unable to acknowledge his own feelings publicly, particularly those aroused in him by his pupils' expressions of feeling or emotion, he cannot have much confidence in his personal authority, and will have little alternative to hiding behind the rules of which he is dictator. Furthermore, because the children's emotional needs are not met but repressed, they become aggressive toward each other. Because of inhibition few, even among the strongest characters, are likely to achieve full potential. Lack of practice in being self-disciplined will leave them over-dependent upon teachers and, although they may perform well at school, they will have difficulty in organizing their own work and in organizing their thinking in unexplored regions. Having learnt that doing the right thing as defined by authority is being good, children will learn that making mistakes is being both wrong and bad, and feelings of anxiety, even of guilt, will prevent the creative use of errors (i.e. unconventional acts or statements) as stimuli to learning.

The teacher's authority

Authoritarian teachers purchase a quiet life not only at the cost of their pupils but also at that of their less authoritarian colleagues, for, if at all possible, children who are suppressed 'let off steam' once the pressure is off. The columnist *Tostig* recalls in *New Society* (10 December 1970) the art master of the highly repressive school he attended as a boy who could not keep order at all. Although he did not welcome the ensuing chaos and violence he did not retaliate in kind. 'The other masters clearly viewed the art teacher with mild contempt. They failed to realize that in the ecology of the school his role was crucial; he took the anger that was largely created by their rigidity and inflexibility.' The apparently ineffective disciplinarian should not therefore be condemned out of hand. The ineffective order in his classroom may have its origins elsewhere; and he may be teaching something positive and beneficial about human values in the apparent disorder. People rarely forget those teachers who make a profoundly human impression upon them. As *Tostig* remarks, 'Years later, when I met old schoolmates, they often spoke affectionately of the art master.' Should authoritarianism be linked with vagueness, inefficiency, and the failure to give necessary information in good time, the effects are worse still. The confusion created by the teacher who will not tolerate disorderliness leads to his blaming the class for his own faults, thereby arousing resentment and setting up a vicious circle of mutual distrust and recrimination leading to rudeness on both sides, whether or not it is expressed openly. The teacher who is rude to his pupils shows them that he either despises or is afraid of them. He is inviting them to defend their self-respect at least with cheekiness, if not by learning to despise his subject along with himself. Though he may force them through their examinations he is likely to kill their interest.

Some writers (e.g. Musgrove, 1971, p. 20) suggest that high morale fostered by non-authoritarian attitudes is an alternative to high productivity, and that good relationships between pupils and their teachers may be a serious impediment to educational attainment. But this is to assume that every non-authoritarian teacher adopts a *laissez-faire* approach. Under certain circumstances the authoritarian may produce better short-term results, scholarships won and examinations passed, but the non-authoritarian is more likely to foster a life-long love of learning and capacity for self-education, not to mention moral autonomy. Concern for high standards and the ability to achieve them are not the prerogative of the authoritarian.

Freedom and discipline

A serious difficulty facing an observer trying to evaluate the quality of

135

discipline in a classroom is that of determining whether the pupils do what is right because the teacher demands this, or whether he takes the risk involved in encouraging them to *want* to do what is right. Freedom always entails the possibility of risk, and it is tempting to the teacher to interpret the responsibility of being *in loco parentis* in terms of protecting pupils from risk. But

> the role of adults is not to protect adolescents from all adversity and from every difficult experience. It is their obligation to let youngsters do their own experimenting – without freedom to experiment there is no learning of responsibility. Obviously this freedom entails risk. But the only alternative to the risk of freedom is the swaddling cloth of over-protection. But at the same time, it is an adult's role to guide and to give temporary assistance when a young person is faced with overwhelming odds. Youngsters still need discipline and control and can't be left entirely to their own whims and interests. 'Until they are ready to ship out alone, they need to feel that the help is in strong, capable hands' (Rubin, 1969, pp. 37–8).

The *laissez-faire* teacher compounds the risk to his pupils, for 'as soon as a teacher, with whatever good intentions, abandons his responsibility of providing a framework of effort and activity for his subject, some other factor will take his place. Today commerce intervenes', and as a result the child's 'expression is not free or personal; it is resolved by alien and often shoddy influences, and in it there is no trace of his innate sensibility and awareness which the exponents of freedom intend to encourage' (Mock, 1970, p. 90). Children are not naturally free. From the start of life they are restricted by personal insecurity and frustrations due to incompetence. Throughout childhood and much of adolescence their experience is limited by the culture of their home environment and this determines not only their physical habits but also their rational thought and imaginative scope. An important element of the teacher's task is, therefore, the de-culturalization of his pupils at every stage of their development, the provision of a constantly enlarged world that each child can explore in body, mind, and spirit, and make his own through imaginative understanding.

The authoritarian may claim that he too de-culturalizes his pupils and provides them with defences against commercial influences. But, having learnt little or nothing through their own initiative, they will lack the resources to deal sensitively and creatively with problems and situations in later life. He will have done no more than replace one limiting culture by another. The person educated in a free environment, in which the effort and achievement, though assisted by adult stimulus and suggestion, have been his own, will find freedom 'in his personally controlled and organized creative imagination and in his imaginative relationships with everybody and everything around him' (Mock, 1970, p. 91). There is no conflict between freedom and true discipline. A school may be a relaxed, friendly, informal and seemingly happy place, with little obtrusive supervision of the children and no restrictions on talking, but this will be because an underlying discipline is accepted by the whole community, and this sets them free to persevere with their work and restricts talk to that which is relevant and not just noise. The children will be aware that only certain types of behaviour are appropriate in school because the teachers will have played a highly skilled and sensitively sympathetic part in helping them to accept high standards; not least by living up to high standards themselves.

Although, from time to time, all teachers have difficulties over discipline, discipline problems are particularly associated with the *laissez-faire* teacher (who often creates problems for his colleagues) and the authoritarian (who stimulates pupils to defy legitimate authority). Whenever there is a threat to authority there is a discipline problem for the authoritarian, since his frame of reference precludes the possibility of interpreting such incidents as defiance, disagreement or refusal to obey as inevitable commonplaces in community life with young people. Far from constituting a personal attack, in a typical instance even the concept of problem need not enter the discussion, for such difficulties can nearly always be resolved by fair interpretation and adjudication. As Herbert Kohl suggests (1970, p. 78), 'a good habit for teachers to develop', and especially for observers, 'is to begin to ask "why?" of all the rules and breaches of discipline that occur in the classroom. Why must students never call out? Why must they line up in the same way every day? Why mustn't they talk to each other? Why must they line up, raise hands, do homework?' It is also a good habit to reject trite answers to such questions.

The non-authoritarian teacher in an authoritarian school has a special problem in that his pupils, being unaccustomed to freedom in the classroom, may find it a threat. Being used to doing what they are told and having never thought about what they might enjoy doing if they had the freedom to do so, they are likely to suspect the teacher who offers them freedom of being unsafe to take seriously. Either they will suspect a concealed trap, or they will doubt his ability to teach. To dispose of this threat they will test his offer to the limit, certainly to the point of testing his nerves and patience. If he does not feel sufficiently strong as a person to demonstrate that he too is a person, with as much right to be angry, frustrated, impatient and distrustful as his pupils, he is likely to be victimized by them. It is his responsibility to take the initiative by acknowledging his feelings publicly, explaining them, and by affording his pupils reciprocal rights. As Kohl says (p. 81), 'if the teacher remains a silent, abused witness to student authoritarianism, a time will come when the teacher has had enough and will take back the freedom he offered the students'.

To avoid this outcome requires more than openness and tolerance from the teacher. It is his responsibility to ensure that there is no confusion about the limits of freedom available and the high standards expected as a consequence of the agreements he and his pupils have made with each other; for, if he doesn't, and still emphasizes in the classroom his common humanity with the pupils and his common uncertainty in the face of problems, the pupils will not take kindly to being demoted to the status of children in other relationships within the same institution. Indeed they may write off that classroom relationship as a 'soft sell' (Schools Council, 1965, p. 22). Even in non-authoritarian schools discipline cannot be left to chance. Pupils need the support to be derived from the authority of their elders, particularly when they are engaged in open-ended exploration in their studies. Under these conditions they are likely to experience conflicts of responsibility, both within and among themselves, and 'if pupils could not look to their teachers for guidance they might look to their peer group rather more than was desirable and this might lead to "unsatisfactory attitudes" ' (Schools Council, 1971, pp. 24–5) – that is, attitudes unsatisfactory for their development.

The relationship between freedom and discipline being so important and controversial, an observer should gain experience in as many schools and with as many teachers as possible. From this wide experience he will be able to discover the wide range of interpretations put upon the term discipline, and the qualities each brings out in children. Since discipline is not a purely personal matter between an individual teacher and his pupils, he will need to take into consideration the general quality of life of each school in which he makes his observations before drawing any firm conclusions. Reading and hearsay may lead him to an intellectual conviction that a free approach is the only one proper to a genuine teacher, but only extensive and critical observation, supported later by experience of teaching, can lead to the emotional conviction essential to real understanding of, and commitment to, the style that liberates him and enables him to provide a liberating but disciplined environment for learning.

Morale in the classroom

Morale is an elusive quality and it is not possible to suggest activities and attitudes that will guarantee good morale in a classroom. When attempting to make his assessment, however, an observer should bear in mind that the quality of morale is determined more by the teacher than by the pupils. The more supportive he is with encouragement and kindness the less likely he is to be rewarded with disorder. The teacher who sets a high standard for his own work and behaviour is likely to see these reflected in his pupils. On the other hand, no teacher can expect his pupils to be interested in a programme of work in which they can arouse no real interest, no matter how important he believes it to be. If he wishes to begin such a programme and first sets out to generate interest by stimulating the children's natural interest in new things he is likely to succeed, for good morale depends upon their being committed to doing well and being thought well of by their teachers, which is most likely if the teacher is considerate and courteous.

A teacher expects his class to respect him, likewise the class expects him to respect them. This means paying careful attention to detail, not allowing anything important to any member of the class to go by default, that class work should be a co-operative endeavour, with the teacher being aware of and meeting the needs of each individual, concentrating attention on his pupils' good qualities and not on their limitations. Mutuality of respect requires that every child should feel that he is known for the person he is, that suitable work should be provided for him and that he should know that his teacher is confident that he can do that work, and that the work prescribed should be intrinsically satisfying as well as having a remote purpose, so that even the least able child can expect to achieve some identifiable success and, more importantly, feel he has achieved it.

Just as academic success depends upon full understanding of the rules governing a particular form of activity, so social success depends upon full discussion, leading to understanding, of the rules setting the limits to acceptable behaviour and defining the area available for social experimentation. Since a school is a highly artificial community with a ludicrous age and authority structure its members are best able to cope with its absurdities by accepting that school life is a form of game playing. Children have no option to being in school so it is important for their self-respect that they should share in determining the conditions of their being there. Unless they are totally alienated, part of the school game consists in encounter with teacher. This is conducted according to strict rules, even if they have not been discussed and defined, for 'children seem to have an instinctive calculus as to what they can get away with' (Cleugh, 1971, p. 99). Edward Blishen (1969, p. 153), summarizing the comments of a large number of children, reminds us that 'school-children hate being out of control, obviously enough, because that turns schooling into a farce, long periods of it are wearisome and demoralizing'. Like adults they dislike prolonged chaos, for a disorderly situation bewilders and frustrates, whereas a secure regime facilitates both work and play. But a healthy desire for discipline will not buy discipline at any price, particularly in the secondary school. Discipline based upon trust is what is looked for, because this is the most effective way of preserving self-respect, and pupils' dislike of prefects stems from this concern for trust and trustworthiness. When they are presented with reasonable demands for discipline pupils normally respond with reasonableness, good faith and good humour. As Etzioni says, 'levels of alienation are closely associated with the degree of coercion applied' (1961, p. 49).

Frank Musgrove suggests on the other hand that 'Etzioni's thesis is a serious over-simplification', and that 'Whether or not coercion alienates depends on the purposes of the school and the way in which pupils define the situation in which they find themselves' (1971, pp. 41–2). He rightly suggests that 'pupils commonly demand rigour in learning and discipline' and that 'The function of the school is to provide a testing ground' (p. 43). The key factor is certainly the purposes of the school, but the key question is the social acceptability of those purposes. If pupils are aware that they are being prepared for life as members of a social élite, or, as Musgrove puts it, for 'difficult and arduous duties ahead', and they approve of this aim (as they will if they have been exposed to no other), they are likely to regard anything but unsympathetic toughness as an indication that authority is 'going soft'.

The narrowness of Musgrove's approach is shown by the fact that he appears to believe that the alternative to rigour can only be the 'manipulation of prestige symbols': by which he seems to understand honours, grades and citations, the personal influence of the teacher, 'talks' with the principal, scolding and sarcasm, the demanding of 'apologies', and similar means which are based on appeals to the pupil's moral commitments and on manipulation of the class peer group's climate of opinion. It is unlikely, however, that such forms of control – with the exception of the personal influence of the teacher – would be treated with less derision in a non-authoritarian school than, as he claims, they would be in a social élitist establishment. He appears to suggest, furthermore, that the acceptance of a rigorous discipline in élitist schools is explicable finally in terms of Festinger's so-called (but see Bannister and Fransella, 1971, p. 13) theory of cognitive dissonance (Festinger, 1957), for according to Musgrove (1971, p. 44)

people who have gone through a great deal of pain and trouble to attain something will be reluctant to concede that it was not really worth it, if that should prove to be the case: they will over-estimate its value to bring it into line with the effort they have expended. If what they have gained is membership of a not very attractive community, they will reduce their dissonance by exaggerating its appeal.

A more damning indictment of social élitist schools would be hard to conceive.

The experience of failure is part of the teacher's job. Generally speaking failure is specific; part of a lesson is unsuccessful, or he has a poor relationship with a particular class. But pupil misbehaviour that stems from the healthy naughtiness of high spirits, the misbehaviour that is a 'cry for help' over some distressing personal problem, or the misbehaviour stemming from a child's lack of experience in playing the school game, should not be classified as failure nor be confused with misbehaviour resulting from bad morale. Children having much opportunity for observing and comparing notes, are very perceptive of their teacher's strengths and weaknesses. If they are enterprising and he inexperienced it is hardly surprising if they set up a diversity of awkward situations in which to test him. Having no legal rights and little redress against unjust discipline, misbehaviour is often nothing more than a demonstration of their independence by pupils who have more to offer or who are in greater need than the school acknowledges. Rather than condemning unco-operative pupils as an act of solidarity with the teacher, an observer should try to find answers to such questions as, has the teacher any right to penalize attempts to preserve individual identity? Should he not rather try to change things so that every child's energy can be fully directed towards some more profitable learning activity? Why do teachers value docility in their pupils so highly? Is it essential for them to 'cover their syllabuses'? Since badly behaved children are least likely to succeed in the tests designed to show mastery of the syllabus would it not be better to forget the syllabus and remember the child?

The adult who always does what he is told without demur is described as a 'doormat', and it is customary to think most highly of oneself when one's self-selected and generated efforts are crowned with success. Are children in school different? Shouldn't their independence be valued highly and an attempt made to understand the particular causes of any periodic ill-discipline? Isn't the why more important than the what? Why are children who cause trouble so resented? Because they make trouble for the teacher himself? Because the teacher feels threatened by it? Because his powers of imagination have atrophied so he can no longer remember what it is like to be a child? Because he is afraid of losing control if he permits his word of command to be questioned? Besides attempting to account for any bad behaviour he may witness an observer should also look out for other signs of poor morale, such as restlessness among the pupils (normally a sign of boredom, of having insufficient to do that is seemingly worth doing), the ineffective invoking of irrelevant rules (thereby increasing the risk of pupils ignoring sensible rules), lack of opportunity for pupils to experience success and achievement, or the teacher's indulging in favouritism or injudicious familiarity with a minority of his pupils. Such immature behaviour is as disruptive of morale in a particular classroom as are bad inter-personal relations among the staff, which cannot be concealed from pupils in the school as a whole.

A particularly common cause of poor morale is the teacher's failure to be clear both in teaching and in giving instructions, so confusing pupils and depriving them of the possibility of job satisfaction because the obligations laid upon them are confused or meaningless. Good morale in the classroom is, of course, a product of moral behaviour appropriate to the situation, and the moral worth of such teacher incompetence is low. Individual personality characteristics play an important part in shaping moral behaviour, but so too does social influence. Derek Wright (1971) draws attention to four elements in the latter that may provide a useful set of reference points for an observer. *Social facilitation*: 'the tendency for an individual's performance of a well-established pattern of behaviour to be enhanced when others are watching him or doing the same thing in his presence'. *Effect dependency*: 'the fact that our self-esteem is dependent upon the approval and acceptance of others', in class, particularly of the teachers. *Information dependency*: 'the fact that, when uncertain what to do, we frequently have to make use of information that others, deliberately or inadvertently, supply us with', hence, the importance of the teacher's being clear if he intends to adopt the dominant role. *Responsibility defusion* or *loss of identity*: the condition the individual is likely to experience when he is a member of a large and unstructured group, in which his sense of himself as a separate person is temporarily weakened or lost (p. 27). Wright also stresses (ibid.) the importance of the fact that 'sometimes people actively resist group pressures because they have morally evaluated the group's norms and found them wanting'. In the school context the group could be either the school itself, a particular teacher's class, or a peer group.

Other significant factors, less easily perceived by direct observation but no less important, relate to poor morale in individual pupils. For example, conflict between ego ideal and actual performance, which when serious can generate guilt (Williams, 1967, p. 255). All factors are not so deep or disturbing as this. Some, though of immediate importance to the child, may not be particularly significant; such as resentment of homework for its intrusion into time that should properly be devoted to leisure activities, or conflict between a home culture that values and gives status to physical strength and the ability to fight bravely and the verbalized aggression characteristic of school culture, or between a culture that regards the immediate expression of aggression as normal behaviour and school which does not. Parental divorce is, of course, an important factor. It has been estimated that, even at the 1969 rate, more than half a million children under school leaving age will have this experience during the decade 1971–80 (Chester and Streather, 1971). Since the separations preceding possible divorce occur most frequently in the first seven years of marriage many children suffer in this way when they are most vulnerable. The extent of the problem is larger than the figures might suggest for a clear correlation between parental divorce and poor socialization in offspring has been established, in the case of both non-delinquent and delinquent children, and it seems reasonable to expect a similar consequence in families with separated or out-of-love parents. Strikingly, parental death does not appear to affect the level of bereaved children's social adjustment significantly (Megargee *et al.*, 1971).

Naturally an emotionally stable home is no guarantee of social adjustment or adaptability in children. Highly permissive parents are unlikely to guide their child's behaviour, and the child may well interpret this as indicative of rejection or indifference on their part. Certainly he will have little opportunity to learn any stable norms and values and so to develop a stable self-image. If they are highly restrictive their child is often likely to identify himself as being naughty and, in time, as being a naturally bad child, a self-image he is likely to live out in school (see Williams *et al.*, 1971). An important consequence of the poor emotional background of many children is that they are likely to compete for the teacher's attention in order to test his commitment to them, and to project onto him many of the feelings of frustration experienced in their home life. Hence the importance of sympathetically discussing a troublesome child's behaviour with him, and also of knowing as much as possible about his background. Even if all his pupils are emotionally healthy no teacher can expect their full co-operation at all times; the deferring of reward is not instinctive, and healthy growing up involves being from time to time both bold and bored.

The hard core problem

'People are not asocial because they want to be but because they cannot be social'; 'The so-called professional criminal, the man who chooses deliberately to offend, is a very rare bird – if he exists at all' (*Guardian*, 7 April 1971), in the opinion, tested by extensive experience, of Professor A.-M. Roosenburg, Professor of Forensic

Psychiatry at the University of Leyden, Holland, and Director of the Henri van der Heuven Klinick in Utrecht. Although speaking of adults convicted for violent criminal offences, her words are applicable to serious offenders in school, who no more need restraining than do the psychopathic offenders in Dr Roosenburg's clinic. Her aim is to create an awareness in them that they belong to the same community as everyone else, having the same responsibilities and so forth. For example, an absconder is given no chance to return of his own volition: 'You shouldn't swindle them. It's no good trying to say we're nicer than the police.' Furthermore, she stresses the importance of avoiding giving offenders any sense of being 'special', or of the clinic being a soft option. The teacher needs to adopt 'the mental hygienist's point of view in recognizing and diagnosing cases of pupil maladjustment. Too often mental symptoms are overlooked because the teacher is more sensitive to those student characteristics which are related to unsatisfactory disciplinary conditions in the classroom than those which may connote emotional disturbance' (VanderMeer, 1948, p. 199). Not that he should try to be a psychiatrist, for in cases of serious disorder professional help is required. The teacher should, however, be aware of the probability of some psychic disturbance lying at the root of some pupil indiscipline, and should try to create conditions and opportunities similar to those created by Dr Roosenburg in her clinic. For example, opportunities could be provided for physical expression, other than the limited ones provided by PE and games. The professor describes mime as 'an excellent training for de-personalized people', and Judo as being 'very good for people who are all aggression and poor at self-control': 'basically you've got to struggle to get them out of themselves. Many are so depressed and anxious. They are people who never expect themselves to succeed. Somehow you've got to make life challenging for them, and create a situation in which they begin to wonder "can it be true? can I do something with my life?" ' (ibid.). There may be no place for Judo in the normal classroom situation, but it should not be impossible to provide real opportunities for pupils to discover their many-faceted selves.

Emotionally disturbed children do not inevitably behave badly. As J. Kounin and his associates have shown in an unpublished report (see Gordon, 1966, pp. 3–4), although in general their behaviour is the least appropriate in school, class or group activity, it differs according to the group they are in, and more significantly, with different teachers. As a rule, the better behaved the group they are in the better their own behaviour. 'Relatively well-behaved disturbed children were in classrooms with relatively well-behaved children in general, and vice versa.' 'All in all we concluded that the behaviour of the emotionally disturbed child was not irrevocably caused by "inside" the child variables only, and that an attempt to delineate situational variables about teacher style and activity settings could be promising.' This suggests that the initiative remains with the teacher.

11 The place of punishment

Punishment, which should never be confused with discipline, is all too often a preoccupation of teachers. This comes about whenever a teacher forgets that although

> knowledge is good, knowledge unsought is not true knowledge . . .
> no boy full of sap and vigour would reduce himself to the rank of a
> servile listener for five hours a day without some stimulus . . . to ask
> a child to concentrate its mind on lessons learned under conditions
> of silence and inertia is to ask more from it than it is, in general, in
> its power to give. That is why punishments and rewards play so large
> a role in the administration of a school conducted on traditional
> lines (MacMunn, 1921; cited, Taylor, 1971, pp. 132–3).

These words remain as true as when they were first written. Nevertheless, although the need to punish indicates some absence of good discipline and, usually, failure of some sort on the teacher's part, it is not easy for a teacher to contemplate giving up his power to enforce and to punish; if only because the removal of restraints – whether in terms of punishments, grading, referral to higher authority or even the awarding of poor marks – disturbs the security provided by custom and is therefore likely to generate disturbance. It follows that any declaration of an irrevocable intention to desist from punishing in some form or other is a dangerous enterprise.

Punishment is simply a device to which resort is made for the purpose of maintaining some kind of discipline. To be relevant and effective it must involve some kind of unpleasantness, even of pain though not necessarily physical pain. It must be inflicted on an offender solely as a consequence of some agreed breach of rules, and always by someone in authority. Even if the punishing is delegated for some reason to a third party this individual must have some recognized and accepted authority within the school. Even when these conditions are met, punishment should never be allowed to be the focus of attention, since its infliction is intended only to signify the temporary withdrawal of esteem by a respected adult, and the unacceptability of some behaviour or other. If this is not the case, punishing is degraded to an interference with personal liberty and an unwarranted act of aggression; which in its turn may stimulate the pupil to be aggressive; it can even become a ludicrous action making the teacher ridiculous in the pupil's eyes. There are, nevertheless, bound to be occasions in the life of every institution containing a large number of young and inexperienced people when some form of punishment is called for. Whenever an observer witnesses the infliction of punishment, or the threat of punishment, he should ask himself what lesson it is supposed to teach, whether the punishment in question is likely to succeed in teaching it, whether in fact the particular form the punishment takes can be justified in the circumstances, or even perhaps whether the use of punishment in that particular situation can be justified. If his answer to any of these questions expresses doubt he should go on to consider what more appropriate action the teacher might have taken.

According to John Wilson, if punishment is to have any educational function it must be regarded primarily as part of the child's moral education, having the purpose of aiding him towards moral autonomy, which will enable him to act not only reasonably (which does not mean the same as conforming to teacher expectations or community norms) but also intentionally, accepting responsibility for his actions. 'If a person is to act morally, he must know what he is doing, and must do it freely — that is, it must really be *he* who does it, and not some form of duress or compulsion that makes him do it' (1967a, p. 46). Moral action requires intentionality. A person cannot be made to act morally; he can only be made to behave in ways which might be called moral if he were fulfilling his own intentions. In so far as he is responding to compulsion he is only play-acting, being not himself, unless he has deliberately chosen to play that role. Such behaviour may keep him out of trouble, or from being a nuisance to others. But, as Wilson says of a child conditioned to fulfil someone else's wishes (p. 47), 'Certainly it is "well-behaved" in a sense: but in another sense it is not behaving or acting at all; it has no choice', and so cannot be said to be engaging in moral action.

If the function of punishment is to assist the moral education of a pupil, it follows that it can only be inflicted upon one who has certain real responsibilities and obligations which he has failed to fulfil, either through culpable ignorance or indifference. A child who fails to fulfil an obligation is commonly held to be to blame. But, unless he has reached a certain stage of moral development, this is unreasonable. He must at least be able to comprehend what being to blame means, and have reached the point of being able to recognize that certain actions are indeed blameworthy. Young children who do not have a general understanding that actions can be required of them by others, cannot be held to be responsible for performing certain specific actions. Failure in such circumstances cannot be called irresponsible, for such children have no 'sense of responsibility'. Having a sense of responsibility implies being aware that one has certain responsibilities and obligations, even though the fulfilling of them may be unpleasant. A responsible person 'need not want to act as he does, but he must act intentionally since a man would not be said to have a sense of responsibility if he *accidentally* discharged his responsibilities, or if he discharged them only because he had to if he was to achieve some other end' (Hare, 1970, p. 55). However, 'we expect a person with a sense of responsibility to admit when he is "to blame" and not to attempt to evade his responsibility. He may feel that he was justified in acting as he did, but his justification may be rejected by others. He may continue to believe that his punishment is unfair' (ibid.).

A capacity for intelligent action is a necessary condition of bearing responsibility, and a sense of responsibility can be increased and refined throughout life, but it does not require a life-time's development. It is possible for a young adult to have a highly developed sense of responsibility if he is provided with the right conditions for its development. Similarly, the exercise of responsibility does not presuppose a high level of academic intelligence, for any pupil who can make the attempt to learn what skills and knowledge are needed in order to be able to undertake a particular responsibility can develop an appropriate sense of responsibility; for the acquiring of such a sense is not a purely intellectual task. The developing of a sense of responsibility cannot be equated with the learning of a set of rules which, with certain possible exceptions that are generally agreed, apply in all cases. For, since changing circumstances can create new opportunities for action, the exercise of responsibility consists in determining, in the light of moral principles and the prevailing conditions, what the doer's responsibilities happen to be. When responsibilities are in conflict he also has to determine which takes precedence over the others.

Some authorities (e.g. Niblett, 1954, p. 92) suggest that pupils can be taught a sense of responsibility by being given responsibilities. This is not necessarily so, since they can only be real responsibilities if the pupil knows what a responsibility is. It is possible that the use of blaming procedures against him regarding such 'responsibilities' may drive home that what he considered to be merely a request by the teacher was something else. In this way he may come to grasp the concept of a responsibility and eventually, though by no means necessarily, develop a sense of responsibility. Whether or not it is morally defensible to use punishment in order to teach responsibility Hirst and Peters doubt whether it is effective. For them punishment, when it is used as an aid to moral learning, is nothing more than 'a dramatic way of underlining a rule, or marking it out as important'

(1970, p. 128). They see punishment as essentially a deterrent and not a reformative or, in any positive sense, a formative measure. Furthermore, they suggest that evidence is lacking of punishment being successful even as a deterrent measure, which suggests in its turn that punishment, as such, has no educational value, its only justifiable purpose being the upholding of the rule of law. That is to say, it is a lesser evil than the absence of the rule of law.

Willi Schohaus, on the other hand, claims (1932, pp. 106–7) that punishment

> is intended to help the pupil not only to give up his fault from the surface but to overcome it from within his personality. To acquire such complete mastery over it, it requires above all unbroken courage, happiness and self-confidence. These are indispensable factors for this moral struggle, but they are nevertheless actually weakened through guilt provoked by the wrongs suffered by the children. It is essential for us to remove this feeling of guilt before we may restore the individual to his former moral energy. And here we reach the one reasonable educational significance of punishment. Punishment is a means of *atonement* which may cancel inhibiting pricks of conscience. Punishment, therefore, should be no vehicle of oppression, but one of *liberation*. Where it attempts anything else it will produce an anti-educational effect. . . . From this it may be gathered that a reasonable punishment is only possible in relation to a child who is sensible of his wrongdoing and is filled with remorse and consequently in need of atonement.

Notwithstanding this, he too believes that the only justification of punishment is the safeguarding of the conditions necessary for learning to take place.

The dangers of punishing

An obvious danger in punishing is that of attacking symptoms rather than causes; the only result being that the children are hardened rather than helped. The paying of the penalty for a misdemeanour by accepting punishment has nothing to do with, and should not be confused with, the removal of its cause. Furthermore, if punishment is wrongly used it can stimulate indiscipline and, even though its use may secure good classroom order if enough fear is generated, any unjust, unfair or brutal punishment is likely to encourage rapid unlearning of the punisher's subject matter, if not immediately, then as soon as the threat of further punishment for forgetfulness is past. The indiscipline stimulated may well be experienced by those teachers who are not naturally inclined to rely upon punishment for good order rather than by the punisher, for pupils are likely to take advantage of the absence of repression for releasing the tensions built up by the punitive teacher. In consequence, such teachers may be driven to adopt a more punitive role than they would prefer, purely to retain the opportunity for relatively uninterrupted work in a purpose-orientated atmosphere.

It is often remarked that many children are alienated from the purposes of school. One of the most potent sources of such feelings of alienation is a punishment system that corroborates the pupils' conviction that education is something that others impose upon them, and that school is not, as its name implies, a place of leisure or re-creation apart from the hard grind of the necessities of daily life, but a coercive corporation in which they neither have, nor wish to have, any real part. For his punishments to avoid this alienating effect, it is essential that a teacher should be just and impartial in maintaining the rule of law, and that he avoid the slightest suspicion of being unsympathetic to offenders as human beings. That is to say, although he may have to punish an offender, he must still respect him and show that he understands his point of view and his personal difficulties — this should of course be evident from his attitude to his pupil.

Punishment, as it is generally exercised in schools, is unlikely to lead to any increase in self-control in most pupils, unless there is a genuine bond of respect for each other as persons between both pupil and teacher, so that both are partly on the other's side. Even then, however, the most likely outcome will be that the pupil will just take more care to avoid being found out in the future. More significantly, of course, if such a bond of respect exists, the teacher's disappointment or disapproval is likely to be a sufficient sanction in itself — though, of course, this should never be capitalized as a form of moral blackmail — thus obviating the need for recourse to an instrument of punishment. When punishing becomes inescapable, however, a teacher's success in using a sanction without alienating his pupils, either from the school or himself, depends almost exclusively upon the nature of his relationship with them. If he is really interested in them and engages with them with sensitivity and understanding, if he really listens to what they have to say — whether it is to the point or not, even if it is of no particular interest to him — if he strives to get behind their words, gestures, expressions, and general behaviour, to what they are really trying to convey through these, that is to say, if he can sufficiently get the feel of being in the pupil's place and see the justness of the punishment he is about to inflict from the pupil's point of view, he stands a fair chance of counteracting, or at least diminishing any possible feeling of alienation.

A former Professor of Child Life and Health at the University of Edinburgh specifies three points regarding the infliction of punishment which, although he relates them to the parent—child relationship, are of significance to a teacher (Ellis, 1962, p. 388),

1. The effects of punishment will depend to an overwhelming extent on the basis of the parent—child relationship.
2. When the parent—child relationship is a satisfactory one, based on mutual affection and respect, punishment is likely to be most effective and least necessary.
3. When the parent—child relationship is unsatisfactory and the child feels insecure and unloved, punishment fails to achieve its object because it is interpreted as one more evidence of parental hostility. This in turn tends to lead to excessive and repeated punishment to which the child reacts either with defiance or an apparently 'don't care' attitude. This 'don't care' reaction is the despair of many parents who fail to realize that it stems from something deeper than a reaction to punishment itself. It is really the child's defence against something which is in fact intensely painful and damaging, namely, the basic lack of parental affection.

This third point has further significance for a teacher, since the child's attitude towards parental punishment tends to persist into later life, being projected onto his teachers. Since, later still, this attitude is projected onto any adult having authority over him, the role of the teacher in his upbringing becomes increasingly important; for,

since a hostile attitude can, at least to some extent, be overcome during the early school years, and a healthy attitude damaged, a very great responsibility rests on teachers at the nursery school or infant-class level. . . . If the child's confidence and affection can be won as soon as possible after entering school, his attitude to learning (receiving instruction and direction and giving attention and interest) will be started on the right lines. This in turn will greatly ease the task of teachers at later stages. If on the other hand, the child's hostility is aroused or confirmed when he first enters school, he is much more likely to carry through an attitude of hostility and defiance into the later school years becoming one of those whose main object seems to be to upset the class and make the teacher's life intolerable (Ellis, 1962, p. 389).

It would be unreasonable, however, to conclude that punishment is inescapably demoralizing, and that it must inevitably negate or frustrate the development of moral responsibility. Children have to come to understand the practice of blaming and, although this does not mean that they must themselves be blamed, one way of initiating the child into this is that of adopting blaming procedures against him, being serious about that which is blameworthy, but not holding the child to be to blame for what lies beyond the limits of his sense of responsibility. He can be held to blame only in so far as it is reasonable to expect him to be responsible. According to Hare (1970, p. 57), blame and punishment, so long as they are judiciously used, do not conflict with the development of a sense of responsibility, 'since an understanding of what constitutes a fair punishment and what makes a person to blame is part of having a sense of responsibility'. But he also stresses that if a pupil is to develop the attitude that a person must discharge his responsibility simply because it is a responsibility, particularly in the area of those responsibilities which are imposed or fall upon him in contrast with those which he takes upon himself through personal choice, the danger of his developing a response which is mere habit can, and should be, offset by the teacher's indicating and making clear the rationale and justifiability of the required actions. 'We should not create the impression that our responsibilities are *all* a matter of our own decision' (p. 58).

The act of punishing

When considering the infliction of a punishment an observer should remember that no child is cheeky, lazy or disobedient, quite like another child, or for the same reasons; and that no teacher responds to his pupils according to a single pattern. Unless he knows well both the teacher and the pupils he is observing, he will be at a disadvantage when attempting to evaluate the appropriateness or the effectiveness of a particular instance of punishing. He should, however, achieve some degree of objectivity if he bears in mind the conclusions drawn by Piaget (1932, pp. 195–325) from his research into the development of moral judgment in children. According to Piaget the young child assumes that moral rules are external to him and that they are rooted in authority; that is to say, he is a moral realist, one who tends to regard duty and the value attaching to it as self-subsistent and independent of the mind, imposing itself regardless of the circumstances in which the individual may find himself. He feels a genuine need for his misdeeds to be balanced by some kind of punishment, but the form the punishment takes can be quite arbitrary; that is to say he feels the need to expiate his offence through some kind of suffering, and even to feel that the greater the punishment the more suitable it is. He is likely to think of

virtue essentially in terms of obedience. When punishment is administered it is automatically acceptable to him because it has been decreed
by a person in authority whose justness is unquestioned. If, on this
understanding, a child does not own up to his fault, it is quite
acceptable for the whole class to be punished if some other member of
the class does not give him away. His need for punishment is often so
strong that when some misfortune follows closely upon a misdeed that
has not been discovered, he is likely to construe it as a punishment; as
though natural forces were in league with those in authority to ensure
that those who disobey suffer for their disobedience.

The older child has a more rational kind of morality; one of
co-operation or reciprocity. He is aware of other people's points of view
and realizes that moral rules grow out of human relationships. He is
beginning to develop moral autonomy and is able to work out the
consequences of wrong acts. He is conscious of the need for reciprocal
affection among equals and, similarly, is coming to realize that this can
be brought about only by evolving guiding principles for achieving
mutually agreed and valued ends, and not through simple obedience to
authorities. (Personal development is rarely a uniform process over the
whole spectrum of human development of course, and many adults
retain some elements of infantile moral realism in their thinking
throughout their lives.) To the older child the purpose of punishment is
no longer expiation, but to bring home to the offender the nature of his
offence and to deter him from repeating the offence. Therefore the
punishment must be tailored to fit the crime, which he often thinks of
in terms of an eye for an eye. Some recognize that a particular
punishment does not have the same degree of severity for all children
and that, as a consequence, the offender's circumstances and needs
should be taken into account when a suitable punishment is being
considered. Punishment in their view, however, must only be given for a
real offence, and punishing by proxy, for example, the punishing of a
whole class for the offence of an undiscovered culprit, is always wrong.
As the child grows older, so the central importance of authority
diminishes and the desire for equality increases; so that justice is no
longer identified with authority, but is regarded as something above
authority.

The most crucial element in punishing resides in consistency on the
teacher's part; he must keep his promises. It is beyond doubt that the
certainty of a particular piece or manner of behaviour being rewarded
with a mild punishment is a far more effective sanction than an
uncertain possibility of sporadic severe punishment. What a child has to
learn is that the way others respond to him is in large part determined
by his own behaviour, that it is open to him to exercise some control
over the behaviour of others affecting himself. Consistency by the

teacher, therefore, not only secures for the pupil assurance of living in a calculable, if not particularly comfortable, world, it also confirms for him the fact that he has some real power to influence his social environment.

When assessing problems in this elusive field an observer should bear in mind that some teachers are their own worst enemies. Quite innocently, they wish to be liked by their pupils, who value warmth and friendliness in their teachers (if it is not impertinent). This desire and their responsibility for discipline, if they conflict, can generate serious anxiety in them; as a consequence of which they will tend to regard overt acts of misbehaviour, such as stealing, cheating or lying, as being more threatening to good order than the more serious attitudes that underlie the poorest, though not necessarily the most disruptive, behaviour, such as hypersensitivity, suspiciousness and fearfulness. In consequence they are liable to pay more attention to decorum, and to punish indecorous behaviour, than to the educationally more important emotional well-being of their pupils – even though mental health is not a primary aim of schooling (see Wilson, 1968, pp. 83–97). Of course, it is much easier to punish than it is to care effectively; and, since withdrawn children tend to cause little overt trouble, it is easy to put them out of mind as 'model' pupils – those only too anxious to please.

It is not possible to produce a calculus which would show when a particular piece of behaviour ought to be punished, or even to state with any degree of assurance what sort of behaviour ought to be punished, for the need for punishment and the appropriateness of a particular punishment, are determined, to a considerable extent, by the circumstances within which behaviour occurs. The only real test of appropriateness is that the particular punishment in a given situation can reasonably be expected to contribute to the reformation of the individual punished, and to improve the social behaviour of the group of which he is a part. Even so, the evidence of a right decision is, in the nature of the case, unavailable until after the event. Research into punishment by parents (see Trasler, 1970) seems to show that those successful in child-training have used sanctions easily associated by the child with the behaviour that gave rise to punishing, that are acknowledged by the child to be unpleasant, even painful, and that have been employed consistently. It is also clear that the prohibited actions have been easily and accurately distinguishable by the child from the permissible. When this has not been so the child has been made anxious about possessions and behavour in general, and conse-quently has been inhibited rather than liberated by his punishment. Successful child-training is closely associated with parental ability to explain to a child exactly what his disgraceful deed was and, in the case of young children, with consistent summarizing of prohibited behaviour by a few general concepts, such as stealing is wrong, telling lies is wrong; so that, surrounded by a general atmosphere of trust, the child has been encouraged to translate the idea of prohibited action into new situations, and also to perceive similarities between superficially different actions which are governed by the same prohibition. It goes without saying that it is always punishable behaviour that is shameful and not the child, and a punisher's behaviour should never suggest that he is ashamed of a child or that the child should be ashamed of himself.

From a psychological point of view, the aim of punishment is the provoking of the least degree of anxiety required to stimulate a child to inhibit unacceptable behaviour and to foster the development of self-control. Any punishment that makes the victim angry with his punisher rather than with himself for meriting punishment is unlikely to be appropriate. To avoid the possibility of this reaction punishment must be backed up by firmness, kindliness, consistency, reasoning with the culprit about the blameworthiness of his action and, when necessary, explanation of the punishment in terms that are understandable by and acceptable to him.

It is likely, then, that suitable punishments will be those requiring the performance of tasks related to the fault and, when appropriate, making some reparation for any hurt given; though in some instances it could be that renunciation of a pleasure or some curtailment of liberty would be more appropriate. Nevertheless, a child's reaction to punishment is not determined solely by the specific penalty. The quality of his relationship with the punisher is of as great, if not greater, importance.

A likelihood of the punishment misfiring will persist, however, if consistent punishment for failure in performance is not supported by equally consistent recognition of success. This means treating a pupil as a mature person, within the limits of his experience of responsibility, so that he can learn to see himself as a mature person, able to perform mature deeds, and with whom it is possible for an adult to have a mature relationship. Since he is almost certain to be regarded as a non-adult for far too long at home, if he is to grow into a mature person his school must ensure that he learns that those who break community cannot interfere with the rights of others with impunity, and that neglect of obligation entails unavoidable consequences. School punishments should, therefore, act as reminders of these truths. Hence, deprivation, in that it makes its point less ambiguously, is probably more suitable than imposition, which can more readily be misinterpreted as an act of spiteful revenge.

Of all punishments used in schools two stand out as least satisfactory. Sarcasm is the more common. It may be effective, but it tears down a child's defences, strips him of his self-respect and debilitates his powers of recovery. Adults often forget that to be made to feel a fool is far more damaging to an inevitably self-conscious adolescent than it is to someone more hardened by life's knocks, or who has learnt to brush sarcasm aside with the contempt it deserves. The other is corporal punishment, which, particularly when it is administered or awarded publicly or by a person with whom the victim has no strong bond, does nothing to reduce any child's general level of aggression. Since corporal punishment is commonly reserved for punishing acts of aggression its victim can only interpret it as a repaying of like with like, as being an assault on himself. What is more, this act of aggression is perpetrated by one who is supposed to be a model of how adults behave when they are being truly adult. In other words, corporal punishment for aggression is a first class lesson in the rightness of the offence for which it is awarded. Furthermore, since it treats symptoms rather than causes, it frequently provokes retaliatory aggression, and there appears to be little evidence of its effectiveness in bringing about permanent changes for the better in children's behaviour.

This is not to say that occasional smacking within the context of the home does any real harm, if by home is understood a happy and united family; it may in fact be beneficial, in the sense that it relieves an irate parent's pent up feelings which are inhibiting the expression of affection to the child. But the emotional climate of a classroom is never likely to be sufficiently positive for the teacher to dare to put it at risk in this way. Of course, in a 'beating' school corporal punishment is unlikely to have serious consequences because beatings, being part of the context of life, are regarded as part of the we—they dimension of the school game. However, it is difficult to recommend its use on such grounds. If corporal punishment is rarely used, however, it is just possible that a beating might have some vicarious deterrent influence on witnesses and thereby be justified. More probably the victim would be regarded as a hero and be encouraged to continue causing trouble, having demonstrated his power to brutalize the teacher. No matter how just his cause, no one feels more human for having beaten a child.

The punishment of delinquents presents a teacher with special problems, for many of them have a strong tendency towards fatalism. They feel powerless to influence their social environment and have already learnt to dissociate their own behaviour from the rewards and punishments that come from others; so, punishment can have no positive effect upon them. 'To them it seems that the only way they can elicit a predictable response in others is through provoking their angry indignation by acts of theft and vandalism' (Wright, 1971, p. 99 but see Goodman, 1970, pp. 157–74). This suggests that the only possible line to take is that of administering reward and punishment in the same way as to non-delinquent children, thereby demonstrating consistency to the class, but a teacher should also make opportunities, probably outside class activities, for delinquent pupils to establish an experimental but genuine and personal bond with him. This is most likely to occur if the opportunities provided encourage them to take the initiative and teach him something, or demonstrate some ability he does not have to the same degree. Such an invitation is, of course, not without its own dangers.

The timing of punishing

Clearly the ideal is that punishment should never be required; discipline being maintained purely through the enthusiasm and efficiency of the teacher in conjunction with the commitment to learning of his pupils. Often, of course, one or more of these conditions is lacking. Even so, no teacher should be in a hurry to punish. Even mature adults find self-control under trying conditions difficult to maintain over long periods. When youngsters go beyond acceptable limits they need help more than punishment, though circumstances can arise in which a hard-pressed teacher appears to have no alternative to punishing. Under those circumstances he is unlikely to do much damage if the imposition of the punishment is a response to (a) the simple recognition of and disapproval of an offence, (b) the reactive anger which follows upon being made the victim of another's misdeeds, or (c) anger felt empathetically on behalf of other victims; but *never*, according to Derek Wright, when it is a reaction to blaming the offender. By 'blaming' he does not mean the simple recognition that the culprit has committed an offence and has therefore earned a punishment but, 'a reflex response of aggressive condemnation of others when they infringe the moral code in some way. It is the same kind of intolerance which when directed towards ourselves we call guilt' (Wright, 1971, p. 105). The danger in this kind of blaming lies in the teacher's being offended for the sake of the moral code itself, and in taking the offence as an affront to his own sense of right and wrong; in other words, of taking it as a personal attack when it was clearly not intended as such by the offender, who is therefore mystified and confused by the reaction.

Blaming in this sense 'implies some kind of personal involvement in the fact that someone else has done wrong which is distinct from our reaction to the effects of the transgression. And the most plausible link between ourselves and the offender which brings about this personal involvement is that we too want to commit the offence but restrain ourselves' (ibid.). Whilst acknowledging the existence of entirely respectable and rational grounds for seeking to punish those who break important moral rules, Wright points out that 'moral anger' is often the strongest element in a reaction to wrongdoing by others. By moral anger he means a supplement to fierce reactive anger on behalf of whoever has been wronged, 'which can sometimes unleash punishment fantasies of a quite barbaric kind. Yet even when this is not the case it is felt to be quite intolerable that people can do these things and escape punishment' (p. 194). Hence 'it is frequently obvious that real concern for the victim has receded into the background. . . . It certainly seems that moral anger can be an alternative to or escape from empathic distress at the victim's plight, a way of drowning it out' (p. 195). Even when there is no victim, or the offender himself is the chief victim, 'there are people who feel compelled to declare their disgust and disapproval of such things and who want to see the offenders suffer in some way, if not through legal means then through shame or social ostracism' (ibid.), as, for example, unmarried mothers. Excepting those rare offences that shock virtually everybody, for most people only certain selective kinds of behaviour spark off such fierce and intense indignation. 'It is as if the person's security has been put at risk and he can only feel safe again when the offender has been punished' (ibid.). That is to say, it appears that he needs certain moral beliefs which contain and stabilize his own desires and fears, and that when he sees others flaunting these beliefs he feels a threat to his personal security and equilibrium.

A genuine offence should, of course, be recognized by awarding a punishment; even though it may not finally be imposed; either because the pupil has made adequate restitution or has come to appreciate the nature of his offence. There are two basic reasons for this: (a) we tend to dislike the people we have harmed, especially when we cannot offer any compensation to the victim, and the victim is powerless to retaliate or will not; and (b) transgression produces both a desire to balance the offence with a good deed, and the desire to avoid the person harmed – it also produces a tendency to resolve the conflict by thinking less well of the victim as if in some way he deserved what happened to him. The awarding of a punishment provides both a means of restitution, and also puts the blame where it belongs, on the offender. Having decided that a genuine offence has been committed and that the culprit not only merits punishment but also needs it, since the nature of the offence precludes the making of suitable restitution, a teacher has to select a sanction that will generate enough anxiety to stimulate both behavioural inhibition and the learning of 'constructive post-transgressional responses' (Wright, 1971, p. 123). If it is to have the desired effect it should be administered as soon as possible after the offence has been committed, because the offender, if he accepts that he has offended, is already in a state of anxiety that needs resolving, for he has damaged his relationships with both his self-image and the outside world. The positive way of resolving the anxiety is through the moral inhibition following upon confession, reparation, punishment and so forth. To delay punishment, or to generate an excess of anxiety by excessive punishment, is to encourage grievance or guilt rather than moral inhibition.

Guilt, which takes the form of self-blaming, self-hating or self-rejection, is an internalized means of resolving anxiety by associating it with a specific kind of thought, the origin of which is located in a particular experience of wrongdoing. If there is a time lag between the offence and punishment, the offender is likely to have already resolved his anxiety through guilt, particularly if he is introverted, and the punishment will do little more than stimulate resentment or increase guilt. Similarly teacher talk at the time of the imposition of a sanction can increase guilt, if, instead of attempting to define the nature of the wrongful act and the reasons why it is wrong, it is personalized and emphasizes the worthlessness and wickedness of those who do such things. Such talk, and all but the most temporary withdrawal of the teacher's approval, generates an anxiety that can only be resolved through self-blaming; that is to say through guilt, and not through being punished.

Of course, guilt, in itself, is not bad; it is a second line of defence in one's moral life, and it motivates one to do something about one's transgressions. But it should not be so strong that it cannot be dissipated by reasonable atonement. If a teacher suggests that the wrongness in an offence lies in its affront to him personally, rather than explains how the deed is destructive of some good the child himself recognizes, it leaves the culprit with the added anxiety of not knowing what good deeds, or how many of them, will be needed to undo the unreal hurt done to his teacher. A child forced to bear a burden of guilt greater than he can dissipate through good deeds will either become hardened and morally stunted or, if he has a tendency that way, may develop a neurosis. A child with a poor self-image, forced to experience an excess of guilt unjustified by any offences he may have committed (pathological guilt), will just have his self-estimate reinforced by punishment (see Wright, 1971, pp. 103–6 and 118–25).

An observer who witnesses the infliction of punishment should try to understand the system operating in the school, and to evaluate whether it is satisfying the intentions that inform it, before considering possible alternative strategies. Punishing is the most distasteful of the many duties a teacher may be called upon to perform; and it would be instructive to the observer if he were to notice the effect that punishing has on the teacher, the ways in which he endeavours to recreate good relationships that punishing may have disturbed, and above all, the ways in which he not only accepts his pupils' attempts to do this but also endeavours to create opportunities for them to do so.

12 Into teaching

It would be foolish to pretend that observation, reflection and analysis are all that are required for the making of a teacher; indispensable though they may be in preparation for and as a continuing practice throughout a teacher's career. The transition from student-teacher to teacher-student is not accomplished without considerable experience of teaching and, although the needs of individuals may vary, there are few who need less than five years' experience before they can regard themselves as a master teacher. Nevertheless, a student's initial experience of teaching is likely to have crucial significance for him, if only because through it he receives the first clear indication of his particular weaknesses. Although it will also disclose some of his strengths his weaknesses will probably dominate his attention, because they signify potential vulnerability. There is no danger in this, so long as he has prepared himself adequately for the task of becoming a teacher in more than name. The student who commences his initiation in a state of preparedness, having been sensitized by his observation, reflection and analysis, will enter each new experience aware that he is engaging in a series of experiments which, from one point of view, he has designed in order to discover how he can best teach. His approach will therefore differ from that of the students of whom Edith Cope writes (1971, p. 107):

> They value the experience [of teaching practice] because it enables them to simulate the behaviour of the fully fledged teacher in the situation in which the teacher normally works; they are frustrated by it whenever it interferes with or undermines that simulation by bringing to the forefront their status as students.

Like the truly fledged teacher, the student-teacher will not engage in play-acting when working with children. Despite his proper concern to learn about himself in terms of self-protection, self-adequacy, subject matter adequacy and his ability to facilitate creative interaction in his classroom he will not, unlike Marc Belth (1965, p. 75), expect his concern with such matters as pupils' learning, their progress, the ways in which he can accelerate this progress, and individual differences between children, to develop at some later date; for he will have developed this concern and its related understandings through his systematic observation prior to teaching. Because he knows that successful teaching is the product of knowing oneself honestly in the teaching situation, of building upon one's strengths, and of building up new strengths, rather than the simple possession of certain specific skills and the mastery of particular techniques and strategic plans, he is unlikely to experience the conflicts revealed by Cope's analysis (1971, pp. 46–7) between worrying about his tutor's assessment of him and the needs of the children, between trying to impress his college supervisors and avoiding disrupting the established pattern of teaching of the classes he takes, or between anxiety about discipline and fear of being firm with children.

Least of all is he likely to experience any real conflict between the desire to experiment and fear of failure, for his experimenting will be the expression of a reasoned approach, based upon self-knowledge and formal studies, both of which will have been refined in the light of his observations. Because he understands the nature of his task he will not be tempted to personalize any failure he may experience, though he will be prepared to acknowledge responsibility for those elements in the situation that can fairly be laid on his own shoulders. Failure leads to loss of self-confidence only when there is a serious discrepancy between a person's self-image and the person he is in reality, or when he has badly misinterpreted the realities of his situation. If he makes a practice of engaging in honest self-assessment, reflective observation, and careful self-preparation before a lesson, rather than simple preparation of a lesson through which his pupils are to be railroaded, and then enters the teaching situation with a degree of courage and common sense, there is little danger that the experience of failure will undermine his confidence. Rather, even after a successful lesson he will engage in an analysis which might disclose comparative degrees of failure, in order to learn how he might be even more successful in the future.

No moral blame can be attached to honest failure, and to look upon failure as being in any way shameful is to encourage concentration upon what is easy and familiar. If accounting failure as blameworthy were anything more than a cultural distortion no baby would take upon itself the heavy experience of failure that accompanies its experimental attempts to predict and control its environment and to make sense of its experience. Indeed, failure provides as much satisfaction and as many opportunities for learning as does success, until praising and blaming introduce feelings of shame into the situation. In the teaching situation blame can be attached only to such failures as mistaking a pupil of below average ability for a below average person, or failure to ask oneself at all times, 'What, at this moment of time, does this child require of me?' Inability to provide a satisfactory answer to this crucial question is neither shameful nor blameworthy; but it does indicate an area where the teacher has more to learn.

The greatest difficulty regarding failure in teaching is that it discloses itself in persons other than the teacher, and may be due to factors totally unrelated to him. For example, the new teacher in a school with a rapid staff turnover may experience a high degree of failure in his early days in the school, his pupils will not be convinced that he will stay long enough to make it worth their while to settle down and really work for him. This, of course, is a factor likely to weigh even more heavily against a student on teaching practice, since he will be known to be no more than a bird of passage. Similarly, many children having learned to feel guilty about failure will fear it and will avoid the possibility of failing by doing little or nothing; for in that way they at least remain in control of the situation. Hence, the tyro teacher must be realistic about his chances of particular kinds of success with particular pupils in his real situation. According to E. B. Castle (1968, p. 191), 'if well done, the teacher's job is one involving not only a high degree of sheer professional competence but also the rare gifts of sensitive observation and the imaginative perception that enables him to unravel the tangled skein of a child's bewilderment'. But these 'rare gifts' are in fact self-taught skills, and it is the teacher's attitude to life (the values he demonstrates in his dealings with pupils) that is his chief means of stimulating pupils to order their own world. Even in a school that supports and sustains him in his efforts the tyro teacher is bound to suffer some degree of failure and frustration, and should beware of the danger of working off his frustration on those of his pupils who seem to refuse to be well motivated.

Because the experience of failure and frustration is inescapable in the teaching situation, it is essential that the teacher's value and belief systems are not only well and reasonably founded, but also well developed. If this is not the case it is likely that he will damage his pupils, quite apart from any damage he may sustain himself. On the one hand he may find himself driven to join those of his colleagues who so distort the value of school and schooling that it becomes an end in itself; a little world set apart and containing all that is really valuable in life. To pupils this is no more than an unreal world inhabited by unreal people who know nothing about life and how it is lived by those who have no part in the sanctuary of school; hence, what they have to say is devalued, whatever its true value. On the other hand he may find himself driven toward cynicism or even nihilism, particularly so far as school is concerned. In this case teaching becomes little more than a means of obtaining a wage packet, to be earned with as little effort as possible.

As Victor Frankl points out, 'It is an inherent tendency in man to reach out for meanings to fulfil, and for values to actualize' (1969, p. 398), whereas, the reductionism of contemporary scientism, and this includes much educational theory, is covert nihilism. Children come to school seeking the meaning of their own lives and the meanings of things. If they find that their teacher's teaching activity is fundamentally meaningless to him, or is based upon values which they cannot share at a meaningful level, the frustration of both teacher and taught can only be compounded. As Frankl says, a reductionist view of life leads to an existential vacuum stemming from existential frustration; which, in more serious cases, is now leading to the development of new manifestations of neuroticism of a type he has termed noogenic neurosis. 'We may define the existential vacuum', he suggests, 'as the frustration of what we may consider to be the most basic motivational force in man, and what we may call, by a deliberate over-simplification, *the will to meaning* – in contrast to the Adlerians' will to power and to the Freudians' will to pleasure' (p. 400). As he says, 'being human is always pointing beyond itself, is always directed at something, or someone, other than itself. Be it a meaning to fulfil or another human being to encounter' (p. 401).

Awareness of this, and the real discovery of and living out of meaning, is essential to teaching, not only in the positive sense of finding teaching an enjoyable activity, but also if deep frustration and fear of failure are to be avoided. For, if failure is not to be interpreted as failure to preserve the invulnerability of one's self-image, it can be understood only in terms of failure to be or to act meaningfully; which, in Frankl's terms, is to enter the existential vacuum. He explains the causes of this phenomenon by saying that,

> in contrast to animals, man is not told by drives and instincts what
> he *must* do. Nor, in contrast to man in former times, is he any longer
> told by traditions and values what he *should* do. Sometimes he does
> not even know what he basically *wants* to do, but instead he just
> wants to do what other people are doing – which is conformism. Or
> else he just does what other people want him to do – which is totali-
> tarianism (p. 399)

the only other alternative being a decline into noogenic neuroticism. Under present conditions, in other words, to be a teacher involves not only knowing what one wants to do, but also why and how one wants to do it, knowing the meaning of doing it and why its meaning is more than just a private meaning, and also having the spiritual resources for this meaning to develop out of personal experience. If he bases his teaching upon such a foundation the teacher need have no fear of failure, for he will not fail at the only point that matters, namely in reaching out beyond himself toward the discovery and creation of new meanings and meaningfulness.

This is not to say that a tyro teacher adopting this approach will not have difficulties. He may, and if he does they may have their origin either in himself or in some of the particularities of his circumstances. But such difficulties will not cripple him with anxiety; he will not evoke anxiety in his pupils, nor will he be tempted to explain away his difficulties in simplistic terms of his having problems with discipline – a diagnosis so devoid of positive significance as to be vacuous. Difficulties never disappear, though they become less apparent as a teacher learns from his experience how to evoke a continuing quality of active co-operation in his pupils. The student-teacher who feels threatened by his vulnerability because his inner resources are not developed may be most conscious of having problems of discipline, even to the point of being unaware of having other more serious problems. But, as M.F. Cleugh says (1971, p. 88), comparing the inexperienced teacher with the 'popular teacher with all the prestige of many successes behind her',

> even if she had no difficulty in the actual management of the chil-
> dren, she would still be faced with a lack of active co-operation,
> which the other teacher gets, apparently without effort. It is this last
> phrase 'apparently without effort' which seems so unfair to the
> young teacher. It all looks so easy!

It is not easy, however, and to dismiss another's success in terms of it being easier for him is no more than self-indulgent forgetfulness of the hard work that has gone into self-preparation, and into learning how to create a working relationship with children. Nevertheless, as Cleugh acknowledges, 'Nothing succeeds like success, built up over a time, it is a great morale-raiser, both for teacher and for children' (ibid.).

Discipline constitutes a problem for many teachers, not so much because discipline is problematical – though there are occasions when it is almost impossible to know what a particular child's needs are – but because they fail to look realistically at themselves. Disciplinary problems are an indication that pupils lack confidence in their teacher – and why should they have any confidence in him until he has demonstrated that he is worthy of such confidence? – and such confidence is not fostered by a teacher who lacks well-placed confidence in himself, his powers and his personality. All too often it is felt that self-confidence will grow if the teacher has a clear understanding of effective teaching procedures, is exact in planning and framing pupils' tasks, and is sensitively aware of his pupils' needs and weaknesses. This is no more than a part of the truth for, although

Gurrey is right in claiming that the young teacher's 'confidence will grow when his responsibility for his classes is felt more strongly', and this will be an effect of greater technical competence, confidence at a deeper level will grow only 'as his whole personality develops' (1963, p. 51). This is the crux of the matter, for pupil confidence depends far more on who the teacher is, than on what he does; and there is no better way of causing frustration and hostility than attempting to behave in a manner which is in conflict with one's fundamental personality structure. As Herbert Kohl insists, 'There are several ways to experiment in the classroom. It depends upon who the teacher is. One ought not to try something basically incompatible with one's personality' (1970, p. 69).

To put the matter another way, disciplinary problems, that is to say difficulties which defy the discovery of any adequate answer, stem from the teacher's inability to recognize and deal with the feelings he himself has in difficult situations. As John Wilson puts it (1967b, p. 430), 'We lack the confidence to behave spontaneously towards our children – not because we are in genuine doubt about what is best to do, but because we are uncertain about what we feel and whether we should be feeling it.' Since, in the final analysis, the teacher has nothing to offer to his pupils but himself, and lack of confidence is a product of uncertainty regarding oneself, the need for honest self-knowledge is beyond dispute. Such self-knowledge, however, is not arrived at by picking the self to pieces like a specimen on a dissecting table; that way leads only to over-indulgent self-awareness and scrupulosity. Rather, to borrow from R. G. Collingwood (1946, p. 10), 'Knowing yourself means knowing, first, what it is to be a man; secondly, knowing what it is to be the kind of man you are; and thirdly, knowing what it is to be the kind of man *you* are and nobody else is.' The acquisition of such knowledge may be a painful process, in that it leads to the shattering of illusions, but it can lead also to encouraging discoveries. Whatever the outcome, however, 'To be able to admit that there is something wrong with *us* without at the same time representing this wrongness as a lack of moral virtue or an inability to accept a package-deal "faith to live by", is to take a very useful and important step' (Wilson, 1967b, p. 430). It is important, not only because it is the first step towards the further development of a teacher's personality, but also because it creates the possibility of a positive change in the nature of the life in his classroom. Though, as Kohl stresses (1970, pp. 69–70), 'A crucial thing to realize is that changing the nature of life in the classroom is no less difficult than changing one's own personality, and every bit as dangerous and time-consuming. It is also rewarding.'

Since entry into the teaching situation places a student-teacher in an unaccustomed situation which demands relationships of which he has had little or no previous experience, it is to be expected that it will lead to considerable personal reorientation. For this reason, if for no other, it is important that he should not be in a hurry to undertake a substantial amount of class-teaching, for not only does such over-involvement provide an excuse for not thinking important matters through in the light of experience, it also has inherent dangers and can inhibit the student's development. Although his words have a modern ring, it is nearly thirty years since A. W. VanderMeer wrote that 'When a student teacher first enters the school, it should be as an observer. This should gradually give way to greater and greater participation' (1948, pp. 235–6); and emphasis should be placed upon gradually. As he says, 'The directed teaching experience [student teaching] should come as a culmination of experience with children in which the prospective teacher has taken a less responsible role' (p. 202). Further support for gradual initiation comes from Sarah Brook (1904, p. 37). 'The period from childhood to maturity', as she says,

> is so full and rich of experiences, so marvellous with both physical and mental development, so roseate with dreams, hopes, and aspirations, that the student of eighteen or twenty is completely out of touch, ordinarily, with children. Life has been so strenuous as to afford no time for intimate associations with the outgrown self of childhood. Consequently the incipient teacher must now be encouraged to renew acquaintance with the past self and to observe children daily.

This is not something that can be best done whilst endeavouring to instruct group after group of children in a teacher–pupil relationship. Hannam, Smyth and Stephenson rightly comment (1971, p. 75),

> The anxiety the new teacher feels in the classroom, faced by a group of adolescents whose behaviour is unpredictable and potentially hostile, inevitably reduces his capacity to perceive clearly and to judge objectively, and it is not unusual to find student teachers operating in the classroom well below their capacity outside it.

As we have seen, much, if not all, of his anxiety can be negated by adequate self-preparation. Though he may have some feelings of apprehension, these are no more than indications of sensitivity to the situation, similar to those experienced by a performing artist before appearing on the stage, and unlike anxiety, lead to a heightening rather than to a diminishing of performance. Like the performer, the teacher is in authority in his situation and, if he is clear about the nature of his authority, can respond and act in a spontaneous and responsible way.

The fact that he may be a student-teacher in no way excuses him from accepting this authority – even though the class teacher may be present as a long-stop. As Bertrand Russell says (1916, p. 146), 'Where authority is unavoidable, what is needed is *reverence*'; and, with particular reference to the teacher, 'The man who has reverence will not think it his duty to "mould" the young. He feels in all that lives, but especially in human beings, and most of all in children, something sacred, indefinable, unlimited, something individual and strangely precious, the growing principle of life, an embodied fragment of the dumb striving of the world' (p. 147).

Reverence implies neither fear nor sentimentality, but rather whole-heartedness and total acceptance of responsibility for what one is doing, because 'the life of another has the same importance which we feel in our own life' (p. 227). So the reverent teacher does not feel sorry for himself and resentful toward the children if they are behaving badly. To be reverent in such a situation means to take charge, to take the risk of attracting the children's momentary displeasure and to replace it by providing educative experiences that are more pleasurable. It does not include dependence upon punishment as a means of self-protection; though not only prudence, but also responsibility, dictate that a student-teacher should accept the pattern of sanctions and punishments established by the class teacher; modifying its application, if he feels this necessary, within the limits of his ability and the climate of the school. However, Kohl's warning (1970, pp. 79–80) that 'the first year, during which a teacher tries to integrate conflict into the classroom rather than suppress it, can be extremely difficult' should not be ignored. As he says, 'One must use one's intuition in dealing with conflict' (p. 78).

Being in authority implies starting work promptly, having everything that is needed ready to hand, and anticipating work of a high quality up to the limits of the ability of each individual child – even though a student may not have taught the children before he should have little difficulty in finding work they have done previously that will indicate previous levels of achievement. It is sometimes said that a student-teacher should be more repressive at first than he intends to be later. If, however, he is strict regarding the quality of his own work and performance, such advice is unlikely to be necessary; for when children are interested misbehaviour is rarely a serious problem. Nevertheless, since there is certain to be some doubt about what may qualify as misbehaviour with a new teacher, he should give clear warning as to what he will regard as tolerable, and then be consistent about this.

It would be foolish to attribute all bad conduct or failure to work or attend to a tyro teacher's inability to interest or control a class; though it may indicate failure to adopt an appropriate approach. Children whose home lives are empty, whose out-of-school activities are basically purposeless, and who have experienced few if any satisfying achievements, either in or out of school, are likely to be unstable, inattentive, easily distracted and listless. Should a student or inexperienced teacher be given a class of such children, without having adequate opportunity to get to know them beforehand, he may well experience real difficulty if he cannot find an approach that saves them from boring themselves; for such children have little self-respect, and it is this, together with habits of perseverance and attention, that needs to be developed before they can find much school work attractive. Such teaching is difficult and depends upon an intimate knowledge of the children and constant individual attention. It is no disgrace for an inexperienced student to acknowledge his limitations if he should encounter little success in working with such children and should turn to his older colleagues for help – indeed, it is never a disgrace for a learner to ask for help and advice. Little is gained by embarking on a war of attrition with a troublesome pupil, even though he may be defeated in the end. One thing is quite certain, if a teacher finds a pupil to be a problem, the pupil similarly finds the teacher a problem, and such problems do not disappear by being ignored – even though the pupil may tire of the game of teasing teacher. An answer, satisfactory to both parties, has to be sought out and implemented, and responsibility for this rests with the teacher.

An important aspect of teaching which receives little attention in this country is the keeping of informative records. This is of particular importance in schools that have broken away from a rigid timetable of discrete subject-orientated periods. It is of similar importance to every student or newly fledged teacher who, having much to learn, is likely to forget all that is not immediately relevant. To be useful, such records should be easy to keep yet informative to any third party, simple to understand and constructive. The best are cumulative, recording each child's achievements, interests, aspirations and personal qualities, and indicating past achievement, present progress, and the direction of overall development. Class records should also show the method of organization and type of work undertaken, the progress and attainment of each individual in specific topics or subject areas, the strengths and weaknesses of each child indicating where special help is required, and relevant data regarding each child's physical and social development. Such recordings should be made at evenly spaced intervals of time; not too infrequently to be valueless but not so frequent as to make the task a burden that will soon be put to one side (Rance, 1971; Gordon, 1966).

Two further aspects of special importance to pupils are also often overlooked. All too often school reports consist of no more than an assemblage of uninformative platitudes suggesting that Mary could do better if she tried, that Mark is a lazy boy, and William shows no interest. Such reports do little to stimulate helpful dialogue between partners sharing in a child's education. They should report work achieved, progress made, and enlightening and constructive comments on these. A more useful report on William, for example, might begin 'I have been unable to capture his interest, or to find materials that will stimulate it', or 'I have failed to discover whether he really understands what we are doing, and, if he doesn't, why not. . . .' Such a report, quite apart from being an honest assessment of the situation, could lead to a fruitful dialogue in which William's parents might well provide the clues needed by his teacher. Similarly, the teacher of a pupil who was experiencing considerable success could use his report for suggesting ways in which the child's parents might facilitate greater success, or extend his experience in directions not catered for in school. Second, pupils receive regular reports in the form of comments on their work. Often it is claimed that these are disregarded and so are a waste of time; as they are if they are uninteresting or uninformative. But, if they provide evidence that the work has been taken seriously and found to be in some way meaningful to an adult, they are not. A pupil is not interested to learn that his teacher considers his work good or bad, but he is in serious critical or complimentary comment indicating why he thinks this. Similarly, he appreciates evidence of whether his teacher agrees with, dislikes, or cannot understand what he has written; together with some indication of what the teacher thinks the pupil means by what he has written; for it may mean something quite different to its author. If conversation is the epitome of education, all reporting or commenting should initiate discussion, rather than pronounce judgment.

Difficulties

Every young teacher can expect to encounter some difficulties which, on account of his initial insecurity, will tend to dominate his awareness. Many of these can be avoided if he is prepared for them; but without worrying about them, for this would focus attention where it is of least use. Despite rumours to the contrary it is almost impossible to meet with real disaster in school, and when it does occur it is almost certainly because some teacher has panicked and lost his sense of proportion. Quite apart from the fact that practically all children are basically nice — and it is part of the teacher's task to discover where their niceness lies if it is not immediately apparent — they know that they have to attend school and are rarely willing to create conditions intolerable to themselves. Allowing that circumstances may sometimes dictate the need for instantaneous action without due reflection, difficulties can only be resolved when their sources have been accurately located, and the teacher himself is only one of these. On the assumption that he has prepared himself reasonably there is normally no reason for a teacher to be ashamed of experiencing difficulty.

One source of difficulty is peculiar to the teacher in training, namely his supervisors. This is particularly so in schools that are organized on the basis of Frank Musgrove's contention, that 'The basis of authority lies in conquest' (1971, p. 30). The student who does not wish to dominate his pupils is likely to find that his approach breeds some confusion; so, to placate the class teacher, he may feel under pressure to adopt a more authoritarian approach. Sometimes such pressure is brought to bear subtly; especially when a student has experienced some degree of failure in a lesson. The class teacher, forgetting that any teaching technique has the teacher himself as one of its more significant components, may suggest or imply that it would work better if it were used as he himself uses it. This may or may not be the case; but the suggestion is simply an invitation to the student to abandon the experimenting that could lead him to discover the ways in which he can teach best. To give such advice is to provide a crutch rather than positive support and encouragement. A student should be able to expect that his supervising teacher will not condemn his failure, but will ask for an explanation of what he was trying to do, why he was trying to do it that way, the results he expected and why he expected those results. In the light of such explanations they would then attempt to work out what was or went wrong with the plan, and possible ways of improving it. Most frequently it will be discovered that there were faults in preparation because the student was not clear about his intention, that neither his technique nor his materials, nor his skill, had been properly put to the test, so his options remain open.

A supervising tutor may also be a cause of difficulty. On the one hand students sometimes panic unnecessarily when their tutors come to observe them, and, in attempting to impress, instead of concentrating upon working with the children, they produce an unimpressive 'performance'. Clearly the tutor's presence may have some effect upon classroom climate, but, even though he may need to make an assessment, his primary purpose on a visit will be to help the student, and his assessment will take into account all that has happened when he has not been present.

The remedy lies in the student getting on with his proper job. On the other hand, a student may find his loyalties torn by having to work with a supervising teacher who is scornful of tutors because they are no longer involved directly in the classroom situation; regarding them as being stuffed with unrealistic theory. Apart from the fact that some tutors are inevitably better than others, this criticism does not stand up to examination.

> There is no evidence to support the notion that only those who continue teaching in the lower schools [i.e. primary and secondary] can offer effective guidance to prospective teachers. Trainees need not just one model of excellent teacher, but many kinds of models. The person who is tied to his own teaching assignments cannot observe enough different models of teaching to help his students analyse the elements of effective teaching (Chase, 1964, p. 41).

A student supervised by such a teacher should simply avoid being drawn into argument, and learn all he can from the teacher's better inspirations. To resist such pressure, however, requires considerable inner resources, for 'Power exists when men have needs and the resources to meet these are scarce. Compliance is exchanged for gratification' (Musgrove, 1971, p. 32).

Other teachers in the school can also unwittingly cause unnecessary difficulties to an unsuspecting student; particularly through their advice and information about classes and pupils. He should be careful not to take such well-meaning statements as gospel truth lest they turn into self-fulfilling prophecies (see Rosenthal and Jacobson, 1968). He needs a glossary to enable him to translate such information into more meaningful categories; such as, for example,

difficult	— non-conforming, non-producing
disturbed	— unwilling to conform for reasons the teacher cannot fathom
dull	— not particularly interested in pleasing teacher
good	— conformist, productive, unquestioning
lazy	— cannot see the point of doing the work set, or of getting into trouble by questioning its worth-whileness
scheming	— gets more enjoyment out of trying to outwit teacher than out of the work set
troublemaker	— unable to contain his irritation at the seeming stupidity and meaningless of school tasks

Bad classes and pupils tend to act badly if they are expected to act badly. They get into the habit of conforming to expectations and often don't know how to respond to a new teacher who does not expect them to behave badly. In order to discover what he understands by acceptable conduct they behave badly, and the unthinking new teacher finds the prophecy fulfilled. His more thoughtful colleague expects this, and so prepares materials and activities that may help him to discover what is relevant to their needs and interests. Being prepared to give his pupils a chance to develop new ways and to adopt new standards he does not expect the transformation to occur overnight. A new teacher should therefore listen to what other teachers have to say about his future pupils, as well as noting any achievement or test scores that may be recorded about them, but he should not pay undue deference to such information; nor should he make too firm decisions about the nature and complexity of the work he proposes to do in the light of it. He should trust his own observations, and, if he needs further information about pupils so as to avoid meeting them with built-in expectations, he should talk with them out of class, watch them at play and in their unsupervised interaction with other pupils, share in their extra-mural activities, and, above all, listen to them and take them seriously as persons. He cannot expect to be uninfluenced by the opinions of other teachers, and should take care to avoid shocking any pupil who is trying to change his ways, by disclosing that he had expected worse behaviour from him than that which he is actually producing. For example, to praise a pupil with a poor reputation for making a good *new* start is to show him that he had been categorized by his new teacher before he had even been met. Similarly, a pupil with a reputation for dullness who is excessively praised for giving a good answer to a question is being told that he was expected to be dull. Children having such experiences soon revert to satisfying long-standing expectations, if only to protect themselves from feelings of embarrassment, if not of anger.

Despite the emphasis placed by many upon the importance of praising children it contains a hidden danger. The child who has done good work knows it without needing to be told so. Although such praising may make him feel good at the time, if it is too generous it may boomerang and make him feel bad when he subsequently experiences failure, as he inevitably will, even though his teacher may say nothing about it. Similarly, encouragement expressed in terms of assurances that he can succeed in a task because he is clever will have a back-lash should he fail. It is far less dangerous and more helpful to say what it is one likes about a piece of work and why one likes it, without praising the child for having done it. Likewise the child will derive deeper satisfaction from being asked to talk about the enjoyment and satisfaction he derived from the execution and successful completion of the task than he could from flattery or praise. Furthermore, such conversation would encourage and help him to formulate criteria for value judgments. Closely related to this danger is that of establishing a correlation in a child's mind between ignorance and stupidity, whereas the genuinely intelligent person is the one who knows how to put the information he has, whether it is little or much, to good and appropriate use. Knowledge does not inoculate against stupidity; indeed, the shallow cleverness of the well informed is often more stupid than the wisdom of the thoughtful, though relatively ignorant, person. Cleverness, which is no more than an innate capacity, is no more praiseworthy than physical beauty — despite the rewards paid to both by commercial interests in society. A teacher should neither praise cleverness nor bask in the reflected glory of his clever pupils, but should ensure that it is put to good and thoughtful use.

Certain difficulties originate in the inevitable loneliness of an inexperienced teacher, particularly a student on teaching practice. He, more than most, will experience a strong desire to be liked by his pupils; for, not only is his position lowly, if not nebulous, he is also faced with the task of establishing a different relationship to the fundamental social groupings in a situation in which he has participated since his early years. To do this successfully he must be quite clear about the kind of relationship he can establish with pupils without being untrue to his own nature or to the leadership and authority function he must be prepared to accept and live with. He has to accept the fact that, as a teacher, he can no longer be more than on the boundary of any classroom group.

> As the teacher he is both inside and outside the classroom group, and must be able to relate to his class without either dominating it or submitting to it. As work leader he is a member of the class; yet his special role as a staff member in the context of the school's responsibilities, must, on other occasions, set him apart from it. If he chooses to operate from too remote and dictatorial a position (or if his pupils succeed in pushing him out beyond the boundary) there can be no shared enterprise between himself and them. If, on the other hand, he seeks popularity at the expense of being an effective leader (or if the class succeeds in pulling him right inside the boundary), he will lay himself open to being exploited by the class members (Richardson, 1967, pp. 3–4).

He is unlikely to discover his proper relationship if he does not know why he is teaching what he is teaching, and why he is teaching it in the way he is.

As a general rule children have no liking for a teacher who tries to establish a sentimental relationship with them; though they will be unscrupulous in exploiting such a situation. Similarly, they regard the authoritarian, and the arbitrary and inconsistent disciplinarian, as enemies, and will try to find ways of defying them. What they hope for is a teacher who is fair, honest, easy to talk to, and who sets himself high standards of behaviour and performance. They do not dislike strictness that facilitates satisfying work, though they abhore strictness that is simply a defence against the just consequences of incompetence or indifference. Similarly they dislike a soft teacher whose softness signifies fear of the consequences that could perhaps follow upon any questioning of his authority if he exercised it. In their view, a teacher who lays aside his authority is unworthy of them and ought not to be a teacher. Establishing a right relationship is clearly no easy task, and the beginner can expect it to take him some time to discover that which is most suitable. If it were true that 'Most older children carry around with them well into their teens a stereotype of a teacher as a somewhat remote figure whose main interest is not in them as people but in difficult and recondite matters, and whose main concern is to discipline them' (Hirst and Peters, 1970, p. 101), the new entrant might feel tempted to revert to such a type. But it isn't, and, so long as he does more than 'manifest enthusiasm and competence' and responds more positively to his pupils than simply disabusing them 'of the impression that he is entirely remote from them as a human being' (ibid.), he will succeed, in time; for, as they gain confidence that he is a genuine person, they too will assist in building up a proper relationship.

Good relationships will not drive away all difficulties, however. 'Human beings are the most awkward species on earth, the most uneven in development, the most beset by obstacles that are not intrinsic to the task' (Bruner, 1969, p. 178). There can be sudden fluctuations in the emotional temperature of a class, even if it is normally highly co-operative, and a teacher needs to be sensitive to this if he is not to be taken by surprise and allow an unsettling situation to grow worse. According to Geoffrey Yarlott (1972, pp. 113–14)

Situations can develop almost without warning, if the teacher is in-experienced or new to the class, when emotional contagion can spread like wildfire. It is as though the whole class were sponta-neously moved by a common desire to find out how far they can go with this new teacher (Morrison and McIntyre, 1969, p. 110).

On the face of it, their lawless behaviour looks like a deliberate flouting of authority, but it is really the pupils' means of testing out the security of the school. It is as if the pupil is saying 'I hope you can hold me' not 'You can't hold me!' (Ashwell, 1962).

Children do not really enjoy misbehaving, at least, after the initial thrill of the first moments. Having made their initial gesture they begin to feel ridiculous, and uncertain about what to do next. They need to be rescued before desperation drives them to further and more ridiculous excesses. Hence the importance of the teacher's remaining calmly in control. Firmness and consistency do not inhibit kindness; taken together they disclose genuine concern. Nor should it be thought that to express disapproval is to be authoritarian. The point to be remembered in moments of crisis is that spontaneous disruptive behaviour is simply a sign that the class, or some of its members, are desperately unsure of themselves, and it is the teacher's responsibility to indicate clearly the behaviour he will accept, so long as it is reasonable, and to be satisfied with nothing less. It could be that a dramatic situation would best be prevented from turning into a traumatic one, by abandoning any preconceived lesson plan and engaging in honest discussion of the situation and what lies behind it. But the teacher must then avoid giving any impression of acting as judge or prosecuting counsel.

The student-teacher, conscious of the threat of being under judgment from all quarters, is especially liable to interpret as hostility any refusal of his pupils to respond to his efforts. 'In an attempt to forestall any active expression of hostility', as Hannam, Smyth and Stephenson indicate (1971, p. 20),

> he may resort to threats, unrealistic punishments and arbitrary be-
> haviour inconsistent with his real personality. This will eventually
> arouse actual hostility in the class, and once this has happened and a
> sense of grievance has become rooted on both sides, any possibility
> of communication between the children and himself becomes more
> and more remote.

It requires courage and imagination to relate meaningfully to other people's children. Hence the prevailing tendency to attach simple labels to them, or to sort them into a limited number of pigeon-holes; for labels are applied only as a kind of decent cover to hide the obscure reality of a human child who is not understood and cared for (Williams, 1967, p. 233). Sometimes, of course, a child consciously adopts a repulsive mode of behaviour; providing himself with a convenient label, because, although he feels the need to be loved, he also feels that he cannot be. Yet, as John Wilson says (1967a, p. 208), echoing Collingwood (1946) and Henry (1960),

> if we value individual human beings, and are interested in promoting
> their rationality and freedom, then it is excessively dangerous to
> look at their behaviour only from the outside, so to speak. We have
> to ask what they are doing, in the sense of how they intend their
> own actions and what they are trying to do, in a manner more like
> the historian's or the anthropologist's than the scientist's. Only then
> can we understand what they are doing from a viewpoint which will

enable us to help them, rather than from one which will enable us only to manipulate or cause changes in them.

This is because science can deal only with the abstract, and by means of a scientific approach 'we cannot aspire to more than . . . a limited "explanation of the principles" involved' in understanding 'the abstract relations which govern our mental processes' (Hayek, 1969, p. 332). But knowledge of the principles involved, and even analysis of particular pieces of behaviour, are unlikely to be of much help to the teacher concerned for the rationality and freedom of a particular child, for, as Bruner acknowledges (1969, p. 162), 'We know extraordinarily little about systems [of action] that acquire their organization in contrast to those that have much of it *built in* from the start.' The wise teacher, therefore, is one who does not subscribe too enthusiastically to the UNESCO credo (1972, p. 116), 'What once was an art – the art of teaching – is now a science, built on firm foundations, and linked to psychology, anthropology, cybernetics, linguistics and many other disciplines.' Rather he will accept with Rush Rhees (1969, pp. 3–4) that whilst

> There may be any number of scientific 'aids' to education . . . this does not mean that the work of educating itself is scientific, or that its problems can be solved by scientific methods. 'Classifying' children by any number of tests is not educating them. And even if we grant that the study of psychology may make a teacher wiser and more alive to various difficulties, the difference between a good teacher and a poor one is still not a matter of being more or less infused with the scientific outlook. Nor is there any reason to think that men in former ages must have been poor teachers if they disregarded it.

Just as science cannot provide an infallible guide to successful teaching, neither can it provide the answer to the average young teacher's most burning anxiety: the superstition that the first requirement of success is to control the children entrusted to him. Unless he is in a school in which relations are explosively bad and as an inexperienced teacher has no business to be in such a school, he need not expect that his pupils will run riot at the earliest opportunity. In any case, order for its own sake is meaningless. Children do not generally resist or resent worth-while work, or reasonable strictness. They are troubled, however, by fussing over trifling details and by the lack of any common ground between themselves and their teachers. In general, the problem posed by naughty children is that they have more liveliness than the teacher is prepared to acknowledge or cater for.

The problem of the maintenance of class order recedes the more a teacher is conscious of the fact that pupils, like all people, have different moods that must be responded to appropriately. It recedes further, the more his relationships with his pupils are unforced, and this includes being naturally humorous. Frank Musgrove suggests that 'Humour breaches control, and a teacher may have difficulty in plugging the tidal wave of laughter and merriment which greets his joke' (1971, p. 47), failing to note that a tidal wave indicates an abnormality in the relationship. He rightly notes that 'Humour, like flirtation, makes proposals possible without loss of face or dignity if the proposal is rejected' (p. 49), but such inordinate laughter is both a joke at the teacher's expense, which he would be wise to interpret correctly, and an indication that a possible creative opportunity has been lost (Koestler, 1964). Whenever a problem of order arises, its satisfactory resolution depends upon the correct identification of the problem, which will be found, in the final analysis, to be moral rather than scientific or technical. As Paul Tillich stressed constantly, 'Science and the arts, politics, education — all become empty and self-destructive if, in their creation, the moral imperative is disregarded' (1969, p. 10), for, 'The moral imperative is the command to become what one potentially is, *a person* within a community of persons' (p. 11); and it 'exhibits itself in scientific and artistic honesty to the extent of self-sacrifice; in one's commitment to humanity and justice in social relations and political actions; and in the love of one toward the other . . .' (p. 10). This ethical dimension is no optional extra for a teacher, since 'The forms and structures in which love embodies itself are the forms and structures in which life is possible, in which life overcomes its self-destructive forces. And this is the meaning of ethics . . .' (p. 95). The way into teaching, if the teacher is prepared to follow it to the end, supported by the power generated by reason and imagination, will be found to lie in the recognition of educating as an ethical activity, and in the identification of those forms and structures available to him into which he can enter and live with and for (but not through) his pupils.

Bibliography

ABERCROMBIE, M. L. J. (1970) *Aims and Techniques of Group Teaching*, SRHE Working Party on Teaching Methods Publication 2, Society for Research in Higher Education, London.

ALLPORT, G. W. (1954) *The Nature of Prejudice*, Addison-Wesley, Cambridge, Mass.

AMIDON, E. J. and FLANDERS, N. A. (1963) *The Role of the Teacher in the Classroom: A Manual for Understanding and Improving Teachers' Classroom Behavior*, Paul S. Amidon & Associates, Minneapolis.

ANDERSON, H. H. (1939) 'The measurement of domination and of socially integrative behavior in teachers' contacts with children', *Child Development*, vol. 10, pp. 73–89.

ANDERSON, H. H. (1943) 'Domination and Socially Integrative Behavior' in R. G. Barker, J. S. Kounin and H. F. Wright (eds), *Child Behavior and Development*, McGraw-Hill, New York.

ANDERSON, H. H. and BREWER, H. M. (1945) 'Studies of teachers' classroom personalities. I. Dominative and socially integrative behavior of kindergarten teachers', *Applied Psychology Monograph No. 6*, American Psychological Association, Stanford University Press, Calif.

ANDERSON, H. H. and BREWER, J. E. (1946a) 'Studies of teachers' classroom personalities. II. Effects of teachers' dominative and integrative contacts on children's classroom behavior', *Applied Psychology Monograph No. 8*, American Psychological Association, Stanford University Press, Calif.

ANDERSON, H. H., BREWER, J. E. and REED, M. F. (1946b) 'Studies of teachers' classroom personalities. III. Follow-up studies of the effects of dominative and integrative contacts on children's behavior', *Applied Psychology Monograph No. 11*, American Psychological Association, Stanford University Press, Calif.

ARBLASTER, A. (1970) 'Education and Ideology' in D. Rubinstein and C. Stoneman (eds), *Education for Democracy*, Penguin, Harmondsworth.

ASHWELL, V. C. (1962) 'Teachers as observers', *New Era*, vol. 43, pp. 107–8.

BAGLEY, C. and EVAN-WONG, L. (1970) 'Psychiatric disorder and adult and peer group rejection of the child's name', *Journal of Child Psychology and Psychiatry*, vol. 11, no. 1, pp. 19–27.

BAINES, G. (1971) 'Learning in a Flexible School' in J. Walton (ed.), *The Integrated Day in Theory and Practice*, Ward Lock Educational, London.

BANNISTER, D. and FRANSELLA, F. (1971) *Inquiring Man: The Theory of Personal Constructs*, Penguin, Harmondsworth.

BARBIANA, Some members of the School of (1970), *Letter to a Teacher*, trans. N. Rossi and T. Cole, Penguin, Harmondsworth.

BARNES, K. C. (1960) *Creative Imagination* (The Swarthmore Lectures for 1960), Allen & Unwin, London.

BARNETT, S. A. (1958) 'An experiment with free discussion groups', *Universities Quarterly*, vol. 12, pp. 175–80.

Bibliography

BEATTY, W. H. (1969) 'Emotions, the missing link in education', *Theory into Practice*, vol. 8, no. 2, pp. 86–92.

BELTH, M. (1965) *Education as a Discipline: A Study of the Role of Models in Thinking*, Allyn & Bacon, Boston, Mass.

BILLS, R. E. (1969) 'Love me to love thee', *Theory into Practice*, vol. 8, no. 2, pp. 79–85.

BION, W. R. (1970) *Attention and Interpretation: A Scientific Approach to Insight in Psycho-analysis and Groups*, Tavistock Publications, London.

BIRLEY, D. and DUFTON, A. (1971) *An Equal Chance*, Routledge & Kegan Paul, London.

BLISHEN, E. (1969) *The School that I'd like*, Penguin, Harmondsworth.

BOLTON, N. (1972) *The Psychology of Thinking*, Methuen, London.

BRENNER, M. W., GILLMAN, S., ZANGWILL, O. and FARRELL, M. (1967) 'Visuo-motor disability in school children', *British Medical Journal*, vol. 4, no. 5574, pp. 259–62.

BRONFENBRENNER, U. (1970) *Two Worlds of Childhood: US and USSR*, Russell Sage Foundation, New York (Allen & Unwin, 1971; Penguin, 1974).

BROOK, S. C. (1904) 'Relation of Theory to Practice' in C. A. McMurray (ed.), *Third Yearbook of the National Society for the Scientific Study of Education*, University of Chicago Press.

BRUNER, J. S. (1969) 'On Voluntary Action and its Hierarchical Structure' in A. Koestler and J. S. Smithies (eds), *Beyond Reductionism: New Perspectives in the Life Sciences*, The Alpbach Symposium, Hutchinson, London.

BUBER, M. (1961) *Between Man and Man*, trans. R. Gregor Smith, Collins/Fontana, London.

CANNON, C. (1970) 'Schools for delinquency', *New Society*, vol. 16 (2 December), p. 1004.

CANNON, C. (1971) 'The culture of delinquency', *The Times Educational Supplement*, no. 2934 (13 August), p. 4.

CASTLE, E. B. (1968) *A Parents' Guide to Education*, Penguin, Harmondsworth.

CHASE, F. S. (1964) 'The education of American teachers' in *Freedom with Responsibility in Teacher Education*, Seventeenth Yearbook of the American Association of Colleges for Teacher Education, The Association, Chicago.

CHESTER, R. and STREATHER, J. (1971), 'Taking stock of divorce', *New Society*, vol. 18 (22 July), pp. 153–5.

CLEGG, A. and MEGSON, B. (1968) *Children in Distress*, Penguin, Harmondsworth.

CLEUGH, M.F. (1971) *Discipline and Morale in Schools and Colleges*, Tavistock Publications, London.

COARD, B. (1971) *How the West Indian Child is made Educationally Subnormal in the British School System: The Scandal of the Black Child in Schools in Britain*, New Beacon Books for the Caribbean Education and Community Workers Association, London.

COLLINGWOOD, R. G. (1946) *The Idea of History*, Oxford University Press, London.

CONNELL, J. Z. (1948) 'Faculty–Student Relations in Teacher Education' in *The Education of Teachers, as viewed by the Profession*, Official Group Reports of the Bowling Green Conference of the National Commission on Teacher Education and Professional Standards, National Education Association of the United States, Washington.

COPE, E. (1971) *School Experience in Teacher Education: A Study of School Practice in Two Colleges of Education*, University of Bristol.

DEARDEN, R. F. (1967) 'The Concept of Play' in R. S. Peters (ed.), *The Concept of Education*, Routledge & Kegan Paul, London.

de BONO, E. (1970) *Lateral Thinking: A Textbook on Creativity*, Ward Lock Educational, London.

DES (1967) *Children in their Primary Schools* (The Plowden Report), Central Advisory Council for Education (England), HMSO, London.

DES (1969) *The Health of the School Child* (Report of the Chief Medical Officer of the Department of Education and Science for the Years 1966–8), HMSO, London.

DES (1971a) *Potential and Progress in a Second Culture: A Survey of the Assessment of Pupils from Overseas*, Department of Education and Science Education Survey No. 10, HMSO, London.

DES (1971b) *The Education of Immigrants*, Department of Education and Science Education Survey No. 13, HMSO, London.

DEWEY, J. (n.d.) 'The Child and the Curriculum' in J. J. Findley (ed.), *The School and the Child*, Blackie, London.

DODES, I. A. (1953) 'A science of teaching mathematics', *Mathematics Teacher*, vol. 46, pp. 157–66.

DOUGLAS, J. W. B. (1967) *The Home and the School*, Panther, London.

ELLIS, R. W. B. (1962) *Child Health and Development* (3rd edition), Churchill, London.

EPSTEIN, H. T. (1972) 'An experiment in education', *Nature*, vol. 235 (28 January), pp. 203–5.

ETZIONI, A. (1961) *Complex Organizations*, Free Press, Chicago.

FESTINGER, L. (1957) *A Theory of Cognitive Dissonance*, Row Peterson, Evanston.

FLANDERS, N. A. (1951) 'Personal–social anxiety as a factor in experimental learning situations', *Journal of Educational Research*, vol. 45, pp. 100–10.

FRANK, A. (1954) *The Diary of Anne Frank*, trans. B. M. Mooyaart-Doubleday, Pan Books, London.

FRANKAU, P. (1966) 'The Meaning of Love' in *The Meaning of Love*, BBC Publications, London.

FRANKL, V. E. (1969) 'Reductionism and Nihilism' in A. Koestler and J. S. Smithies (eds), *Beyond Reductionism: New Perspectives in the Life Sciences*, The Alpbach Symposium, Hutchinson, London.

FREIRE, P. (1972) *Pedagogy of the Oppressed*, trans. M. Bergman Ramos, Penguin, Harmondsworth.

FROMME, A. (1969) 'Introduction' to J. Holt, *How Children Fail*, Penguin, Harmondsworth.

FRYE, N. (1967) *The Modern Century* (The Whidden Lectures 1967), Oxford University Press, Toronto.

FRYMIER, J. R. (1969) 'Teaching the young to love', *Theory into Practice*, vol. 8, no. 2, pp. 42–4.

GALTON, F. (1892) *Hereditary Genius*, Macmillan, London.

GATTEGNO, C. (1971), *What We Owe Children: The Subordination of Teaching to Learning*, Routledge & Kegan Paul, London.

GETZELS, J. W. and JACKSON, P. W. (1963) 'The Teacher's Personality and Characteristics' in N. L. Gage (ed.), *Handbook of Research on Teaching: A Project of the American Educational Research Association*, Rand McNally, Chicago.

GETZELS, J. W. and THELEN, H. A. (1960) 'The Classroom Group as a Unique Social System' in N. B. Henry (ed.), *Yearbook of the National Society for the Study of Education*, vol. 59, part 2, pp. 53–82, University of Chicago Press.

181

GOLDBERG, M. L., PASSOW, A. H. and JUSTMAN, J. (1966) *The Effects of Ability Grouping*, Teachers' College Press, New York.

GOODLET, G. R. (1972) 'Classroom behaviour', *New Society*, vol. 20 (6 April), pp. 11–13.

GOODMAN, P. (1970) *Growing Up Absurd*, Sphere Books, London.

GORDON, I. J. (1966) *Studying the Child in School*, Wiley, New York.

GOULD, R. (1965) 'Introduction' to *N.U.T. Annual Guide to Careers for Young People*, NUT, London.

GREEN, T. E. (1971) *The Activities of Teaching*, McGraw-Hill, New York.

GUILFORD, J. P. (1959) 'Three faces of intellect', *American Psychologist*, vol. 14, pp. 469–79.

GUILFORD, J. P. (1967) *The Nature of Human Intelligence*, McGraw-Hill, New York.

GURREY, P. (1963) *Education and the Training of Teachers*, Longmans, London.

HANNAM, C., SMYTH, P. and STEPHENSON, N. (1971) *Young Teachers and Reluctant Learners*, Penguin, Harmondsworth.

HARE, W. (1970) 'A sense of responsibility', *Teacher Education* (Toronto), no. 3, pp. 52–9.

HAYEK, F. A. (1969) 'The Primacy of the Abstract' in A. Koestler and J. S. Smithies (eds), *Beyond Reductionism: New Perspectives in the Life Sciences*, The Alpbach Symposium, Hutchinson, London.

HEBB, D. O. (1966) *A Textbook of Psychology* (2nd edition), Saunders, Philadelphia.

HENRY, J. (1960) 'A Cross-Cultural Outline of Education' reprinted in J. Henry, *Essays on Education*, Penguin, Harmondsworth, 1971.

HILSUM, S. (1972) *The Teacher at Work*, National Foundation for Educational Research in England and Wales, Slough.

HIMMELWEIT, H. T. (1970) 'Why we cannot afford to stream', *Comprehensive Education*, vol. 16 (autumn), pp. 12–3.

HIRST, P. H. (1965) 'Liberal Education and the Nature of Knowledge' in R. D. Archambault (ed.), *Philosophical Analysis and Education*, Routledge & Kegan Paul, London. (Also in Hirst (1974), pp. 30–53.)

HIRST, P. H. (1974) 'Realms of Meaning and Forms of Knowledge' in P. H. Hirst, *Knowledge and the Curriculum: A Collection of Philosophical Papers*, Routledge & Kegan Paul, London.

HIRST, P. H. and PETERS, R. S. (1970) *The Logic of Education*, Routledge & Kegan Paul, London.

HOLT, J. (1969) *How Children Fail*, Penguin, Harmondsworth.

HOMANS, G. C. (1961) *Social Behaviour: Its Elementary Forms*, Routledge & Kegan Paul, London.

HOWSON, G. (ed.) (1969) *Children at School*, Heinemann, London.

HUDSON, L. (1966) *Contrary Imaginations: A Psychological Study of the English Schoolboy*, Methuen, London.

HUDSON, L. (1968) *Frames of Mind: Ability, Perception and Self-perception in the Arts and Sciences*, Methuen, London.

HUDSON, L. (1972) *The Cult of the Fact*, Cape, London.

HUNT, A. (1970) 'The Tyranny of Subjects' in D. Rubinstein and C. Stoneman (eds), *Education for Democracy*, Penguin, Harmondsworth.

HUTCHINS, R. M. (1970) *The Learning Society*, Penguin, Harmondsworth.

ILEA (1967) *London Comprehensive Schools, 1966*, Inner London Education Authority, London.

JAMES, C. (n.d.) 'Introduction' to E. Mason (ed.), *New Roles for the Learner: Report of the 5th Pilot Course for Experienced Teachers*, The Goldsmiths' College Curriculum Laboratory, London.

JENKINS, D. (1961) *Equality and Excellence*, SCM Press, London.

JERSILD, A. T., THORNDIKE, R. L., GOLDMAN, B. and LOFTUS, J. J. (1939) 'An evaluation of aspects of the activity program in New York city public elementary schools', *Journal of Experimental Education*, vol. 8, pp. 166–207.

JESSOR, R., GRAVES, T. D., HANSON, R. C. and JESSOR, S. L. (1968) *Society, Personality, and Deviant Behavior*, Holt, Rinehart & Winston, New York.

KEATINGE, M. W. (1916) *Studies in Education*, A. & C. Black, London.

KIRCHENBAUM, H. and SIMON, S. B. (1974) 'Values and the Futures Movement in Education' in A. Tofler (ed.), *Learning for Tomorrow: The Role of the Future in Education*, Vintage Books, New York.

KOESTLER, A. (1964) *The Act of Creation*, Hutchinson, London. (Part I only (1970), Pan Books, London.)

KOHL, H. R. (1970) *The Open Classroom: A Practical Guide to a New Way of Teaching*, Methuen, London.

KOHLBERG, L. (1964) 'Development of Moral Character and Ideology' in M. L. Hoffman (ed.), *Review of Child Development Research*, vol. 1, Russell Sage, New York.

KOHLBERG, L. (1968a) 'Early education: a cognitive-developmental view', *Child Development*, vol. 39, no. 4, pp. 1013–62.

KOHLBERG, L. (1968b) 'Stage and Sequence' in D. Goslin (ed.), *Handbook of Socialization*, Rand McNally, Chicago.

LAWRENCE, D. H. (1933) *Fantasia of the Unconscious*, Heinemann, London.

LUMSDAINE, A. A. (1963) 'Instruments and Media of Instruction' in N. L. Gage (ed.), *Handbook of Research on Teaching: A Project of the American Educational Research Association*, Rand McNally, Chicago.

LUNN, J. B. (1970) *Streaming in the Primary School*, National Foundation for Educational Research in England and Wales, Slough.

LYNN, R. (1971) *An Introduction to the Study of Personality*, Macmillan, London.

McINTYRE, D. (1970) 'Assessment and Teaching' in D. Rubinstein and C. Stoneman (eds), *Education for Democracy*, Penguin, Harmondsworth.

MacKENZIE, N., JONES, H. and PAYNE, T. (1969) *Audio-Visual Resources in Sussex Schools*, Centre for Educational Technology, University of Sussex, Brighton.

MacMUNN, N. (1921) *The Child's Path to Freedom*, Bell, London.

MACMURRAY, J. (1935) *Reason and Emotion*, Faber & Faber, London.

McNEIL, J. and ROGERS, M. (eds) (1971) *The Multi-Racial School*, Penguin, Harmondsworth.

MADSEN, C. H., BECKER, W. C. and THOMAS, D. R. (1968) 'Rules, praise and ignoring: elements of elementary classroom control', *Journal of Applied Behavior Analysis*, vol. 1, pp. 139–50.

MALEWSKA, H. A. and MUSZYŃSKI, H. (1970) 'Children's Attitudes to Theft' in K. Danziger (ed.), *Readings in Child Socialization*, Pergamon, Oxford.

MARTIN, J. and NORMAN, A. R. D. (1970) *The Computerized Society*, Prentice-Hall, Englewood Cliffs, New Jersey.

MARTIN, J. P. (1971) 'The social consequences of conviction', *New Society*, vol. 18 (19 August), pp. 330–2.

MARTIN, R. D. (1970) 'Social stress', *New Society*, vol. 16 (17 December), pp. 1086–8.

Bibliography

MASON, E. (ed.) (n.d.) *New Roles for the Learner: Report of the 5th Pilot Course for Experienced Teachers*, The Goldsmiths' College Curriculum Laboratory, London.

MEDLEY, D. M. and MITZEL, H. E. (1963) 'Measuring Classroom Behavior by Systematic Observation' in N. L. Gage (ed.), *Handbook of Research on Teaching: A Project of the American Educational Research Association*, Rand McNally, Chicago.

MEGARGEE, E. I., LEVINE, R. V. and PARKER, Q. V. C. (1971) 'Relationship of familial and social factors to socialization in middle-class college students', *Journal of Abnormal Psychology*, vol. 77, no. 1, pp. 76–89.

MERLEAU-PONTY, M. (1962) *The Phenomenology of Perception,* Routledge & Kegan Paul, London.

METHODIST CONFERENCE (1970) *Christian Commitment in Education*, Report of the Methodist Conference Commission on Education, Epworth, London.

MICHIE, D. (1971) 'Artificial intelligence', *New Society*, vol. 18 (26 August), pp. 370–3.

MILLER, N. E. (1956) 'Liberalization of Basic S-R Concepts: Extension to Conflict Behavior, Motivation and Social Learning' in S. Koch (ed.), *Psychology, a Study of a Science: Vol. 2, General Systematic Formulations, Learning and Special Processes*, McGraw-Hill, New York.

MOCK, R. (1970) *Education and the Imagination*, Chatto & Windus, London.

MORRISON, A. and McINTYRE, D. (1969) *Teachers and Teaching,* Penguin, Harmondsworth.

MOUSTAKAS, C. E. (1956) *The Teacher and the Child: Personal Interaction in the Classroom*, McGraw-Hill, New York.

MOUSTAKAS, C. E. (1972) *Loneliness and Love*, Prentice-Hall, Englewood Cliffs, New Jersey.

MUSGROVE, F. (1971) *Power and Authority in English Education*, Methuen, London.

NIBLETT, W. R. (1954) *Education and the Modern Mind*, Faber & Faber, London.

NYE, F. I. (1958) *Family Relations and Delinquent Behavior*, Wiley, New York.

OAKESHOTT, M. (1962) *Rationalism in Politics*, Methuen, London.

OAKESHOTT, M. (1967) 'Learning and Teaching' in R. S. Peters (ed.), *The Concept of Education*, Routledge & Kegan Paul, London.

OPIE, I. and OPIE, P. (1959) *Lore and Language of Schoolchildren*, Clarendon Press, Oxford.

OPIE, I. and OPIE, P. (1969) *Children's Games in Street and Playground*, Clarendon Press, Oxford.

OVERY, P. (1971) 'The other press', *New Society*, vol. 17 (28 January), pp. 158–9.

PAGE, D. (1970) 'Against Higher Education for Some' in D. Rubinstein and C. Stoneman (eds), *Education for Democracy*, Penguin, Harmondsworth.

PATERSON, R. W. K. (1971) 'The Concept of Discussion: A Philosophical Approach' in T. Kelly (ed.), *Studies in Adult Education 2*, David & Charles, Newton Abbot, Devon.

PETERS, R. S. (1965) 'Education as Initiation' in R. D. Archambault (ed.), *Philosophical Analysis and Education*, Routledge & Kegan Paul, London.

PETERS, R. S. (1967) 'What is an Educational Process?' in R. S. Peters (ed.), *The Concept of Education*, Routledge & Kegan Paul, London.

PHENIX, P. H. (1964) *Realms of Meaning: A Philosophy of the Curriculum for General Education*, McGraw-Hill, New York.

PIAGET, J. (1932) *The Moral Judgement of the Child*, Routledge & Kegan Paul, London.
POWER, M. J., ALDERSON, M. R., PHILLIPSON, C. M., SCHOENBERG, E. and MORRIS, J. N. (1967) 'Delinquent schools?', *New Society*, vol. 10 (19 October), pp. 542–3.
PRESCOTT, D. A. (1938) *Emotion and the Educative Process*, The Committee on the Relation of Emotion to the Educative Process, The American Council on Education, Washington, DC.
PRINGLE, K., BUTLER, N. R. and DAVIE, R. (1966) *11,000 Seven-year-olds: National Child Development Study*, Longmans, London.
RANCE, P. (1971) *Record Keeping in the Progressive Primary School*, Ward Lock Educational, London.
RAZZELL, A. (1968) *Juniors: A Postscript to Plowden*, Penguin, Harmondsworth.
RHEES, R. (1969) *Without Answers*, Routledge & Kegan Paul, London.
RICHARDSON, E. (1967) *Group Study for Teachers*, Routledge & Kegan Paul, London.
RIESMAN, D. (1950) with N. Glazer and R. Denney, *The Lonely Crowd*, Yale University Press, New Haven, Conn.
ROSENTHAL, R. and JACOBSON, L. (1968) *Pygmalion in the Classroom*, Holt, Rinehart & Winston, New York.
RUBIN, I. (1969) 'Understanding Adolescence' in I. Rubin and L. A. Kirkendall (eds), *Sex in the Adolescent Years*, Collins/Fontana, London.
RUSSELL, B. (1916) *The Principles of Social Reconstruction*, Allen & Unwin, London.
SADLER, P. (1972) 'Leadership styles in flux', *New Society*, vol. 21 (21 September), pp. 546–8.
SCHOHAUS, W. (1932) *The Dark Places of Education*, Allen & Unwin, London.
SCHOOLS COUNCIL (1965) *Raising the School Leaving Age: A Co-operative Programme of Research and Development*, Working Paper no. 2, Schools Council/HMSO, London.
SCHOOLS COUNCIL (1968) *Enquiry I: Young School Leavers*, HMSO, London.
SCHOOLS COUNCIL (1971) *Choosing a Curriculum for the Young School Leaver*, Working Paper No. 33, Evans/Methuen Educational, London.
SCHWEBEL, A. I. and BERNSTEIN, A. J. (1970) 'The effects of impulsivity on the performance of lower-class children on four WISC subtests', *American Journal of Orthopsychiatry*, vol. 40, no. 4, pp. 629–36.
SCRE (1971) *A Study of Fifteen-Year Olds*, Scottish Council for Research in Education Publication no. 63, University of London Press.
SELYE, H. (1957) *The Stress of Life*, Longmans, London.
SIMON, B. (1970) 'Streaming and Unstreaming' in D. Rubinstein and C. Stoneman (eds), *Education for Democracy*, Penguin, Harmondsworth.
SMART, R. G. and JONES, D. (1970) 'Illicit LSD users: their personality and psychopathology', *Journal of Abnormal Psychology*, vol. 75, no. 3, pp. 286–92.
SMITHELLS, R. W. (1971) 'Better babies . . .', *University of Leeds Review*, vol. 14, no. 2, pp. 298–318.
SOLZHENITSYN, A. (1969) *Cancer Ward*, trans. N. Bethell and D. Burg, Bodley Head, London.
SPEER, A. (1970) *Inside the Third Reich: Memoirs*, Weidenfeld & Nicolson, London.
STENGEL, E. (1969) *Suicide and Attempted Suicide* (revised edition), Penguin, Harmondsworth.

185

Bibliography

STOTT, D. H. (1966) *Studies of Troublesome Children*, Tavistock Publications, London.

STROH, C. M. (1971) *Vigilance: The Problem of Sustained Attention*, Pergamon, Oxford.

SUGARMAN, B. N. (1967) 'Home and School' in J. Wilson, N. Williams and B. Sugarman, *Introduction to Moral Education*, Penguin, Harmondsworth.

SWIFT, D. F. (1965) 'Educational psychology, sociology and the environment', *British Journal of Sociology*, vol. 16, no. 4, pp. 334–50.

TANNER, J. M. (1961) *Education and Physical Growth: Implications of the Study of Children's Growth for Educational Theory and Practice*, University of London Press.

TAWNEY, R. H. (1931) *Equality*, Allen & Unwin, London.

TAYLOR, L. C. (1971) *Resources for Learning*, Penguin, Harmondsworth.

TAYLOR, W. (1969) *Society and the Education of Teachers*, Faber & Faber, London.

TILLICH, P. (1969) *Morality and Beyond*, Collins/Fontana, London.

TOWNSEND, H. E. R. (1970) *Immigrant Pupils in England: The LEA Response*, National Foundation for Educational Research in England and Wales, Slough.

TRANKELL, A. (1972) *Reliability of Evidence: Methods for Analyzing and Assessing Witness Statements*, Beckmans, Stockholm.

TRASLER, G. (1970) 'Delinquency' in H. J. Butcher and H. B. Pont (eds), *Educational Research in Britain 2*, University of London Press.

UNESCO (1972) *Learning to Be: The World of Education Today and Tomorrow*, Report of the International Commission on the Development of Education appointed by the Director-General of UNESCO, trans. P. C. Bowles, UNESCO /Harrap, London.

VANDERMEER, A. W. (1948) 'Professional Preparation of Junior High School Teachers' in *The Education of Teachers as Viewed by the Profession*, Official Group Reports of the Bowling Green Conference . . . National Education Association of the US, National Commission on Teacher Education and Professional Standards, Washington, DC.

VERNON, P. E. (1968) 'What is potential ability?', *Bulletin of the British Psychological Society*, vol. 21, no. 73, pp. 211–19.

VERNON, P. E. (1969) *Intelligence and Cultural Environment*, Methuen, London.

WALLEN, N. E. and TRAVERS, R. M. W. (1963) 'Analysis and Investigation of Teaching Methods' in N. L. Gage (ed.), *Handbook of Research on Teaching: A Project of the American Educational Research Association*, Rand McNally, Chicago.

WALSH, W. (1970) 'Introduction' to R. Mock, *Education and the Imagination*, Chatto & Windus, London.

WARNOCK, M. (1971) 'Seeking counsel', *New Society*, vol. 17 (28 January), pp. 157–8.

WARR, P. B. (1970) *Thought and Personality*, Penguin, Harmondsworth.

WARWICK, D. (1971) *Team Teaching*, University of London Press.

WEST RIDING (1971) 'Two cultures', *West Riding County Council Schools Bulletin* (July), pp. 1–2.

WHITE, R. K. and LIPPITT, R. (1960) *Autocracy and Democracy: An Experimental Inquiry*, Harper, New York.

WHITEHEAD, A. N. (1950) *The Aims of Education and Other Essays*, Benn, London.

WILLIAMS, J. A., BEAN, F. D. and CURTIS, R. L. (1971) 'The impact of parental constraints on the development of behavior disorders', *Social Forces*, vol. 49, no. 2, pp. 283–91.

WILLIAMS, N. (1967) 'What can the Experts tell us? What the Psychologist has to say' in J. Wilson, N. Williams and B. Sugarman, *Introduction to Moral Education*, Penguin, Harmondsworth.

WILSON, J. (1967a) 'What is Moral Education?' in J. Wilson, N. Williams and B. Sugarman, *Introduction to Moral Education*, Penguin, Harmondsworth.

WILSON, J. (1967b) 'What can we do about Moral Education?' in J. Wilson, N. Williams and B. Sugarman, *Introduction to Moral Education*, Penguin, Harmondsworth.

WILSON, J. (1968) *Education and the Concept of Mental Health*, Routledge & Kegan Paul, London.

WISEMAN, S. and PIDGEON, D. (1970) *Curriculum Evaluation*, National Foundation for Educational Research in England and Wales, Slough.

WITHALL, J. (1949) 'The development of a technique for the measurement of social-emotional climate in classrooms', *Journal of Experimental Education*, vol. 17, pp. 347–61.

WOODS, R. G. and BARROW, R. St C. (1975) *An Introduction to Philosophy of Education*, Methuen, London.

WRIGHT, D. (1971) *The Psychology of Moral Behaviour*, Penguin, Harmondsworth.

YARLOTT, G. (1972) *Education and Children's Emotions: An Introduction*, Weidenfeld & Nicolson, London.

YATES, A. (ed.) (1966) *Grouping in Education*, A Report sponsored by the UNESCO Institute for Education, Wiley for UNESCO, New York.

YOUNG, M. and ARMSTRONG, M. (1965) 'The flexible school, the next step for comprehensives', *Where?* Supplement no. 5, Advisory Centre for Education, Cambridge.

ZALKIND, S. S. and COSTELLO, T. W. (1962–3) 'Perception: some recent research and implications for administration', *Administrative Science Quarterly*, vol. 7, pp. 218–35.

187

Index

Abercrombie, M. L. J., 35, 119, 120, 121
Adolescence, 71–3, 74–5
. Allport, G. W., 83
Amidon, E. J., 94, 109
Anderson, H. H., 98, 99
Arblaster, A., 24
Armstrong, M., 15
Ashwell, V. C., 175
Attention (*see* Vigilance): control of, 52; reflective, 108
Authoritarianism, 133–4, 137, 176
Authority, 51, 167–8, 171; and discipline, 125; exercise of, 128–9; kinds of, 128; teacher's, 125–8

Bagley, C., 74
Baines, G., 9
Bannister, D., 140
Barbiana, School of, 29, 48, 60
Barnes, K. C., 96
Barnett, S. A., 121
Barrow, R. St C., 26
Beatty, W. H., 56, 58, 103
Belth, M., 25, 161
Bernstein, A. J., 124
Bills, R. E., 39
Bion, W. R., 26, 41
Birley, D., 29
Blishen, E., 139
Bolton, N., 111, 112
Brazier, D., 69
Brenner, M. W., 68
British Association, 22, 23
Broken homes, 66, 86

Bronfenbrenner, U., 40, 104
Brook, S. C., 167
Bruner, J. S., 175, 177
Buber, M., 23

Cannon, C., 88
Castle, E. B., 8, 19, 105, 130, 163
Chase, F. S., 172
Chester, R., 143
Children: alienation of, 28, 77–85, 140, 150; anxious to learn, 50–1; blameworthiness of, 147–8, 152, 155; blaming of, 157–8; clumsy, 68; contact with adults, 104; difficult, 49; early school leavers, 78–9; economically deprived, 69–70; educationally subnormal, 67–8; emotionally disturbed, 143–5; home background of, 6–8; immigrant, 32, 69, 71; indisciplined, 141–2, 169, 172; maladjusted, 69–70; moral development of, 19, 152–3; powers of, 108; respect for, 139; and responsibility, 147–9; self-concept of, 55–8, 66, 159; self-discipline in, 130–1, 132–3, 150
Classroom: arrangement of, 14; emotional climate in, 58, 61–2, 103, 138–43; social system of, 97
Clegg, A., 11, 69, 100, 105, 116
Cleugh, M. F., 100, 101, 103, 139, 165

Index

Coleridge, S. T., ix, 44
Collingwood, R. G., 166, 176
Competitiveness, 74, 104
Compulsion, 22
Connell, J. Z., 33
Controversy, 26
Cope, E., 161
Costello, T. W., 94
Culture: conflict, 49–50, 77–91; and learning, 114
Curriculum theory, 26

Dearden, R. F., 59
de Bono, E., 109
Delinquency, 85–91
Depression, 65–8
Dewey, J., 108
Discipline, 27, 78, 90, 140, 165, 178; and authority, 125; and freedom, 135–8; nature of, 129–30; and punishment, 146; purpose of, 132; self-imposed, 130–1, 132–3, 150
Disciplines, 26
Dodes, I. A., 107
Douglas, J. W. B., 8, 66, 77, 99, 105
Drug misuse, 81–2
Dufton, A., 29

Education: and computers, 45–6; cultural context of, 49; and emotional development, 42–4, 84; for leisure, 46; nature of, 23–6; product of, 21; and valuing, 46–7
Education Act 1944, 23, 29
Ellis, R. W. B., 151
Epstein, H. T., 97
Equality of opportunity, 29–30
Etzioni, A., 128, 140
Evan-Wong, L., 74
Examinations, 11, 26, 28, 32–5
Existential vacuum, 164

Failure: and alienation, 78; not

blameworthy, 162–3; damage caused by, 33; and meaning, 164–5; unavoidable, 141, 168
Fear, 64–5
Festinger, L., 140
Field, F., 69
Flanders, N. A., 94, 99
Frank, A., 51, 72
Frankau, P., 99
Frankl, V. E., 164
Fransella, F., 140
Freedom: 135–8; and punishment, 149
Freire, P., 28
Fromme, A., 123
Frye, N., 27
Frymier, J. R., 84

Galton, F., 38
Gattegno, C., 108
Getzels, J. W., 97, 98
Goldberg, M. L., 51
Goodlet, G. R., 100, 101
Goodman, P., 91, 156
Gordon, I. J., 14, 37, 48, 55, 109, 110, 118, 119, 169
Gould, R., 17
Green, T. E., 114, 115
Guilford, J. P., 38, 110
Guilt, 159
Gurrey, P., 24, 122, 123, 166

Hannam, C., 3, 167, 176
Hare, W., 148, 152
Hayek, F. A., 177
Headteacher, 11, 12
Hebb, D. O., 37
Henry, J., 114, 176
Hilsum, S., 115
Himmelweit, H. T., 31
Hirst, P. H., 24, 26, 126, 148, 175
Holt, J., 96, 123
Homans, G. C., 102
Hudson, L., 38, 40, 109
Hunt, A., 54
Hutchins, R. M., 23, 77

190

Imagination, 9, 44–5
Indoctrination, 54
Integrated day, 117–19
Intelligence, 5, 36–7; not an absolute, 36; education of, 36–41; and experience, 37; tests, 36, 38–40

Jackson, P. W., 98
Jacobson, L., 105, 172
James, C., 21
Jenkins, D., 30, 78
Jessor, R., 87
Jones, D., 82

Kirchenbaum, H., 47
Koestler, A., 178
Kohl, H. R., 14, 137, 138, 166, 168
Kohlberg, L., 19
Kounin, J., 144

Lawrence, D. H., 24
Laziness, 65, 68, 105
Leisure, 27–8, 46
Lippitt, R., 98
Love, 83–5
Lumsdaine, A. A., 95
Lunn, J. B., 105
Lynn, R., 10

McIntyre, D., 35, 175
MacMunn, N., 146
Macmurray, J., 36, 41, 42, 43
McNeil, J., 105
Madsen, C. H., 100
Malewska, H. E., 86
Martin, J., 40, 45
Martin, J. P., 75
Martin, R. D., 73
Mason, C., 110
Mason, E., 107
Meaning, will to, 164
Medley, D. M., 96
Megargee, E. I., 143

Megson, B., 11, 69, 100, 105, 117
Merleau-Ponty, M., 111, 112
Methodist Conference, 22
Michie, D., 36
Miller, N. E., 98
Mills, I. H., 66
Mitzel, H. E., 96
Mock, R., 44, 96, 136, 137
Moral development, 19, 152–3
Morale, 13–14, 138–43
Moral education, 132, 133, 147
Morrison, A., 175
Moustakas, C. E., 98, 105
Murdoch, I., 63
Musgrove, F., 78, 126, 127, 135, 140, 171, 172, 178
Muszyński, H., 86

Newsom Report, 74
Niblett, W. R., 148
Norman, A. R. D., 40, 45
Nye, F. I., 86, 87

Oakeshott, M., 24, 121
Observing, 1, 4, 6, 12, 92, 96, 98, 167; use of analytic schemata, 94–6
Opie, I. and P., 59
Over-achievers, 37
Overy, P., 81

Page, D., 32
Paterson, R. W. K., 121, 122
Peters, R. S., 23, 24, 115, 121, 126, 148, 175
Phenix, P. H., 26, 27, 29, 115, 116
Piaget, J., 152
Pidgeon, D., 21, 28
Play, 59–60
Plowden Report, 31
Power, M. J., 88
Prescott, D. A., 55
Primary schooling, lasting influence of, 105

Index

Pringle, K., 67
Psychological conditioning, 48
Punishment, 129, 146–60; and blaming, 157–8; of delinquents, 156-7; educational function of, 149, 153–4; effects of, 152, 159; and freedom, 149–52, 158; imposition of, 152; inappropriate, 155–6; and shame, 155; timing of, 158–9

Questioning, art of, 122–4

Rance, P., 169
Razzell, A., 9, 118
Reason and emotion, 41–3
Records and reports, 119, 169
Rhees, R., 177
Richardson, E., 174
Riesman, D., 80, 103, 120
Rogers, M., 105
Roosenburg, A.-M., 143, 144
Rosenthal, R., 105, 172
Rubin, I., 136
Russell, B., 168

Sadler, P., 102
Schohaus, W., 131, 132, 149
School: accidents in, 9; alienation from, 22, 63–4, 79; allocation of resources in, 18; building, 8; careers guidance in, 16–17; catchment area of, 6–8; council, 13; and delinquency, 87–8; educational aims of, 21–5; mealtimes, 11, 18; and parents, 15; pastoral organization of, 14–15; quality of life in, 9–15; recreational facilities of, 17; rules, 18–20; social agencies and, 16; staff meetings, 13
Schwebel, A. I., 124
Self-assessment, 35
Selye, H., 73, 74

Sheehen, J., 18
Simon, B., 30
Simon, S. B., 47
Skinheads, 82–3
Smart, R. G., 82
Smithells, R. W., 74
Smyth, P., 3, 167, 176
Social conditioning, 101
Social evolution, 42
Solzhenitsyn, A., 4
Speer, A., 79
Stengel, E., 66, 75
Stephenson, N., 3, 167, 176
Stott, D. H., 74
Streaming, 30–1
Streather, J., 143
Stress, 73–6, 80
Stroh, C. M., 93, 94
Students: and children, 3–4; on teaching practice, 2–3, 161–78
Stupidity, 53, 63–5, 173–4
Sugarman, B. N., 108
Suicide, 66
Swift, D. F., 51 .

Tanner, J. M., 52
Tawney, R. H., 29, 30
Taylor, L. C., 15, 54, 107, 115
Taylor, W., 21, 94
Teacher: education of, 1; as learner, 48; loneliness of, 174; need for maturity in, 163, 165; relationships with pupils, 50–3, 55, 56–8, 66, 73, 89, 98–100, 102, 172–7
Teaching: activities of, 113, 114–15, 117; child-centred, 108; class teaching, 107, 115–16; discussion in, 120–2; an ethical activity, 178; failure in, 162–3, 164–5; group teaching, 119–20; humour in, 178; and learning, 113; method in, ix; methods of, 107; practice, 161–2, 167; not a science, 177; team

teaching, 118–19; uneducative, 22
Text books, 116–17
Thelen, H. A., 97
Thinking: convergent, 33, 110; divergent, 33, 109–10; and language, 109; psychology of, 111–12
Tillich, P., 178
Tips for teachers, 2
Tostig, 86, 135
Trankell, A., 1
Trasler, G., 85, 86, 87, 88, 154
Travers, R. M. W., 95
Tutor, 1, 162, 172

Vaizey, J., 18
VanderMeer, A. W., 144, 167
Vernon, P. E., 38
Vigilance, 94

Wallen, N. E., 95
Warnock, M., 77
Warr, P. B., 111
Warwick, D., 118
White, R. K., 98
Whitehead, A. N., 24, 113
Williams, J. A., 143
Williams, N., 132, 142, 176
Wilson, J., 19, 22, 126, 132, 147, 154, 166, 176
Wiseman, S., 21, 28
Woods, R. G., 26
Wright, D., 86, 87, 88, 142, 156, 157, 158, 159

Yarlott, G., 175
Yates, A., 30, 38
Young, M., 15
Youth culture, 79–83

Zalkind, S. S., 94